DIVINATION, POLITICS, AND
ANCIENT NEAR EASTERN EMPIRES

Society of Biblical Literature

Ancient Near East Monographs

Number 7
DIVINATION, POLITICS, AND
ANCIENT NEAR EASTERN EMPIRES

DIVINATION, POLITICS, AND
ANCIENT NEAR EASTERN EMPIRES

Edited by
Alan Lenzi
Jonathan Stökl

Society of Biblical Literature
Atlanta

The Ancient Near East Monographs/Monografias Sobre El Antiguo Cercano Oriente series is published jointly by the Society of Biblical Literature and the Universidad Católica Argentina Facultad de Ciencias Sociales, Políticas y de la Comunicación, Centro de Estudios de Historia del Antiguo Oriente.

For further information, see:
http://www.sbl-site.org/publications/Books_ANEmonographs.aspx
http://www.uca.edu.ar/cehao

Library of Congress Cataloging-in-Publication Data

Divination, politics, and ancient Near Eastern empires / edited by Alan Lenzi and Jonathan Stokl.
   pages cm. — (Society of Biblical Literature ancient Near East monographs ; Volume 7)
  Includes index.
  ISBN 978-1-58983-996-0 (paper binding : alk. paper) — ISBN 978-1-58983-998-4 (electronic format) — ISBN 978-1-58983-997-7 (hardcover binding : alk. paper)
  1. Divination—Middle East—History To 1500. 2. Mythology , Middle Eastern—History—To 1500. 3. Occultism—Religious aspects—Judaism. 4. Middle East—Religion. 5. Religion and politics—Middle East—History—To 1500. 6. Assyro-Babylonian religion. I. Lenzi, Alan, editor of compilation.
  BL613.D59 2014
  133.309394—dc23

              2014010036

Table of Contents

List of Abbreviations

AB	Anchor Bible Commentary Series
AB	Assyriologische Bibliothek
ABD	*Anchor Bible Dictionary*, 6 vols.
AbrNSup	Abr-Nahrain: Supplement Series
AfO	*Archiv für Orientforschung*
AfOB	Archiv für Orientforschung Beiheft
AJEC	Ancient Judaism and Early Christianity
AJSR	*Association for Jewish Studies Review*
ANET	Pritchard, *Ancient Near Eastern Texts Relating to the Old Testament*
AOAT	Alter Orient und Altes Testament
AOS	American Oriental Series
ARM	Archives Royales de Mari
ATD	Das Alte Testament Deutsch
BAK	Hunger, *Babylonische und assyrische Kolophone*
BBR	Zimmern, *Beiträge zur Kenntinis der babylonischen Religion*
BCSMS	*Bulletin of the Canadian Society for Mesopotamian Studies*
BEATAJ	Beiträge zur Erforschung des Alten Testaments und des antiken Judentum
BET	Beiträge zur biblischen Exegese und Theologie
BETL	Bibliotheca Ephemeridum Theologicarum Lovaniensium
Bib	*Biblica*
BibIntSup	Biblical Interpretation Supplement
BibOr	Biblica et Orientalia
BiOr	*Bibliotheca Orientalis*
BIOSCS	*Bulletin of the International Organization for Septuagint Studies*
BKAT	Biblischer Kommentar, Altes Testament
BMes	Bibliotheca mesopotamica
BNP	*Brill's New Pauly*
BPO 3	Reiner and Pingree, *Babylonian Planetary Omens*, part three
BZAW	Beihefte zur Zeitschrift für die alttestamentliche Wissenschaft
CAD	*Chicago Assyrian Dictionary*
CBET	Contributions to Biblical Exegesis and Theology
CBQ	*Catholic Biblical Quarterly*
CBQMS	Catholic Biblical Quarterly Monograph Series
CDA	Black, George, and Postgate, *A Concise Dictionary of Akkadian*
CDLJ	Cuneiform Digital Library Journal
CDOG	Colloquium der Deutschen Orient-Gesellschaft
CHANE	Culture and History of the Ancient Near East

CM	Cuneiform Monographs
ConBOT	Coniectanea Biblica Old Testament Series
COP	Cambridge Oriental Publications
COS	Hallo and Younger, *The Context of Scripture*, 3 vols.
CRRAI	Compte Rendu, Rencontre Assyriologique Internationale
CT	*Cuneiform Texts from Babylonian Tablets in the British Museum*, 54 Vols.
CTH	Laroche, *Catalogue des textes hittites*
DDD	van der Toorn *et al*, *Dictionary of Deities and Demons in the Bible*
DJD	Discoveries in the Judaean Desert
DNP	*Der neue Pauly: Enzyclopädie der Antike*
DSD	*Dead Sea Discoveries*
EE	*Enūma Eliš*
ESHM	European Seminar on Historical Methodology
ET	English Translation/Text
FAT	Forschungen zum Alten Testament
FLP	Tablet from The Free Library, Philadelphia
FM	Florilegium marianum
FOTL	Forms of Old Testament Literature
FRLANT	Forschungen zur Religion und Literatur des Alten und Neuen Testaments
GMTR	Guides to the Mesopotamian Textual Record
HANES	History of the Ancient Near East Studies
HSM	Harvard Semitic Monographs
HTR	*Harvard Theological Review*
IAH	Bremer, *Iurisprudentiae Antehadrianae*, 2 vols.
IAR[6]	Huschke, *Iuriprudentiae Anteiustianae Reliquiae*, 6th ed., 2 vols.
ICC	International Critical Commentary Series
IEJ	Israel Exploration Journal
JANER	*Journal of Ancient Near Eastern Religion*
JANER	*Journal of Ancient Near Eastern Religion*
JAOS	*Journal of the American Oriental Society*
JBL	*Journal of Biblical Literature*
JCS	*Journal of Cuneiform Studies*
JHebS	*Journal of Hebrew Scriptures*
JJS	*Journal of Jewish Studies*
JNES	*Journal of Near Eastern Studies*
JSJ	*Journal for the Study of Judaism in the Persian, Hellenistic, and Roman Periods*
JSJSup	Supplements to the Journal for the Study of Judaism
JSNT	*Journal for the Study of the New Testament*
JSOT	*Journal for the Study of the Old Testament*

JSOTSup	Journal for the Study of the Old Testament Supplement Series
JSS	*Journal of Semitic Studies*
KAT	Kommentar zum Alten Testament
KTU	Dietrich, Loretz, and Sanmartín, *Die Keilalphabetischen Texte aus Ugarit*
LAPO	Littératures anciennes du Proche-Orient
LHBOTS	Library of Hebrew Bible / Old Testament Studies
LSTS	Library of Second Temple Studies
LXX	Septuagint
MARI	*Mari: Annales de recherches interdisciplinaires*
MC	Mesopotamian Civilisations
MT	Masoretic Text
N.A.B.U.	*Nouvelle assyriologique brèves et Utilitaires*
NCBC	New Century Bible Commentary
ND	Tablets from Nimrud
NICOT	New International Commentary on the Old Testament
NovT	*Novum Testamentum*
NRSV	New Revised Standard Version
OBO	Orbis biblicus et orientalis
OIP	Oriental Institute Publications
OIS	Oriental Institute Seminars
Or	*Orientalia*, new series
OTL	Old Testament Library
PAPS	Proceedings of the American Philosophical Society
PIHANS	Publications de l'Institut historique-archéologique néerlandais de Stamboul
PTSDSSP	Princeton Theological Seminary, Dead Sea Scrolls Project
RA	*Revue d'assyriologie et d'archéologie orientale*
REB	Revised English Bible
RevQ	*Revue Qumran*
RINAP 4	Royal Inscriptions of the Neo-Assyrian Period, Leichty, *Esarhaddon*
RMA	Campbell-Thompson, *Reports of the Magicians and Astrologers*
SAA	State Archives of Assyria
SAA 2	Parpola and Watanabe, *Neo-Assyrian Treaties and Loyalty Oaths*
SAA 3	Livingstone, *Court Poetry and Literary Miscellanea*
SAA 4	Starr, *Queries to the Sun God*
SAA 8	Hunger, *Astrological Reports to Assyrian Kings*
SAA 9	Parpola, *Assyrian Prophecies*
SAA 10	Parpola, *Letters from Assyrian and Babylonian Scholars*
SAA 12	Kataja and Whiting, *Grants, Decrees and Gifts of the Neo-Assyrian Period*
SAA 13	Cole and Machinist, *Letters from Priests*
SAA 16	Luukko and van Buylaere, *Political Correspondence of Esarhaddon*

SAAB	*State Archives of Assyria Bulletin*
SAACT	State Archives of Assyria Cuneiform Texts
SAAS	State Archives of Assyria Studies
SAAS	State Archives of Assyria Studies
SBLMS	Society of Biblical Literature Monograph Series
SBLSCS	Society of Biblical Literature Septuagint and Cognate Studies
SBLSymS	Society of Biblical Literature Symposium Series
SBLWAW	Society of Biblical Literature Writings from the Ancient World
SSN	Studia Semitica Neerlandica
STDJ	Studies on the Texts of the Desert of Judah
TBN	Themes in Biblical Narrative
TCL	Textes Cunéiformes du Louvre
TCS	Texts from Cuneiform Sources
TDOT	*Theological Dictionary of the Old Testament*
TSAJ	Texte und Studien zum antiken Judentum
VAS 10	Vorderasiatische Schriftdenkmäler 10
VT	*Vetus Testamentum*
VTSup	Vetus Testamentum Supplements
WMANT	Wissenschaftliche Monographien zum Alten und Neuen Testament
WO	*Welt des Orients*
WUNT	Wissenschaftliche Untersuchungen zum Neuen Testament
ZA	*Zeitschrift für Assyriologie*
ZAW	*Zeitschrift für die alttestamentliche Wissenschaft*

Introduction

Jonathan Stökl and Alan Lenzi

This volume is the result of a session of the Prophetic Texts in their Ancient Contexts seminar at the 2011 national meeting of the Society of Biblical Literature in San Francisco. The session was entitled "Divination, Propaganda, and Empire." The aim of the session was to clarify the context of prophecy and other forms of divination within their respective political and/or theological empires. The essays by Jeffrey Cooley, Beate Pongratz-Leisten, Göran Eidevall, Joseph Blenkinsopp, and Ehud Ben Zvi in the present volume are revised versions of the original presentations in that session. To cover a wider spectrum of cases we invited Casey Strine and Alex Jassen to contribute to the volume, and we both added contributions of our own to the mix.

The question of how biblical and other ancient Near Eastern texts were shaped by their political setting(s) within a number of political and theological empires is extremely relevant in the current intellectual climate. Post-colonial theorists have carried out very valuable work on this and related questions, which is mostly related to the way that texts were used by empire builders to justify their actions and how those texts are read today in post-colonial settings.[1]

Similar questions are also being asked in more historically oriented research on the empires of the ancient Near East, the territories which were ruled by them, and the literatures produced therein. This volume is part of this larger enterprise. The contributors examine divinatory texts of technical and intuitive origin to un-

---

[1] See among many others Homi K. Bhabha *The Location of Culture* (London: Routledge, 1994) and idem (ed.), *Nation and Narration* (London: Routledge, 1990). The field of postcolonial reading of biblical texts is burgeoning. For a good introduction to the field see R. S. Sugirtharaja, (ed.), *The Postcolonial Biblical Reader* (Malden, MA / Oxford: Blackwell, 2006).

derstand how they interact with the ancient imperial settings in which they were conceived and read and in which they were used to construct meaning and to understand the surrounding reality.

The first essay by Jeffrey Cooley ("Propaganda, Prognostication, and Planets") starts with an introduction to propaganda studies, serving simultaneously as a theoretical introduction to the entire volume. He reviews the recent literature on the topic and notes the important distinction between *integrative* and *agitative* aspects of propaganda. Following Ellul, Cooley suggests *integrative propaganda* aims to unify and stabilize the audience of the propaganda, while the purpose of *agitative propaganda* aims to change their behavior.[2] He goes on to look carefully at attestations of unusual interpretations of celestial omens by otherwise competent diviners in Neo-Assyrian texts. Adducing royal inscriptions which also include such unusual interpretations, Cooley shows that the diviners were likely influenced by their royal overlords.

The second essay by Beate Pongratz-Leisten ("The King at the Crossroads between Divination and Cosmology") investigates the royal appropriation of divination as part of the mytho-political worldview of the ancient Near East, particularly in the so-called "historical omens." After a review of the evidence for the historical omens, Pongratz-Leisten focuses on Assurbanipal and his demand to be entered into the tradition of historical omens. She argues that this represents Assurbanipal's sidestepping of the traditional control of divine information through diviners, and that the claim represents Assurbanipal's attempt to become the "epitome of the ideal king."

Jonathan Stökl's essay, "Divination as Warfare," presents a study of the way in which information from the divine sphere—mostly but not exclusively gained through prophecy—was alluded to in diplomatic correspondence between Old Babylonian Mari and Aleppo as well as in 2 Kings 23 // 2 Chronicles 35 and 2 Kings 18–19 // Isaiah 37–39. The way in which a foreign god claims authority over a territory in some of these texts is interpreted as a necessary pre-condition and/or a byproduct of universalistic theologies. The study compares the structure of the ancient Near Eastern and biblical diplomatic communication, specifically with regard to their use of divine information and the agency of gods in them, to the Roman rite *evocation*, in which the Romans claimed the support of the gods of a besieged city for themselves.

In his contribution ("Revisiting Biblical Prophecy, Revealed Knowledge Pertaining to Ritual, and Secrecy in Light of Ancient Mesopotamian Prophetic Texts") Alan Lenzi returns to his monograph on *Secrecy and the Gods* to refine the explanation for the open communication of prophecy and divinely revealed knowledge

---

[2] Jacques Ellul, *Propaganda: The Formation of Men's Attitudes* (New York: Knopf, 1965).

pertaining to ritual by prophets in the Hebrew Bible.[3] In his monograph, Lenzi followed Holladay's idea that prophets in Israel/Judah began to communicate directly and openly to the people rather than the king due to the influence of the way in which Neo-Assyrian imperial messengers communicated with subdued populations.[4] In the present essay Lenzi suggests that most ancient Mesopotamian prophetic oracles were in fact semi-public (with the possible exception of ARM 26 206); thus, they are similar to the open proclamations of prophetic oracles to the people as depicted in the Bible. Lenzi looks for a new explanation to explain the open communication of revealed knowledge pertaining to ritual in the Hebrew Bible in the potentially destabilizing nature of ancient Mesopotamian prophecy and in Seth Sanders' ideas of the "shift in horizons" in the writing of biblical history, law, and especially prophecy under the Western imperial pressures from the eighth century BCE on.[5]

Casey Strine ("*Chaoskampf* against Empire") offers a reading of the Gog of Magog pericope (Ezekiel 38–39), building on the work in which he and C. L. Crouch find allusions to the *Chaoskampf* tradition in this text and elsewhere in Ezekiel.[6] He rejects recent attempts to date the pericope to the Hellenistic age and instead dates it to the sixth century and thus a Neo-Babylonian imperial context. Basing himself on the work of James C. Scott, Strine understands the references to the *Chaoskampf* as *hidden transcripts* of the Judean exiles against the Neo-Babylonian empire, thereby adding this important category to the debate about how prophetic and other divinatory texts react to and deal with the imperial situation in which they were conceived.

Göran Eidevall ("Propagandistic Constructions of Empires in the Book of Isaiah") asks how the book of Isaiah interacts with empire—whether it undermines or upholds it. Eidevall follows the initial Neo-Assyrian setting in which we find—as may be expected—signs of both mimicry and mockery, which is part of the ambiguity of colonial literature as identified by Bhaba. However, Eidevall identifies a third stage in this literature which moves away from ambiguity to a more single-minded propagandistic nature of the text criticizing Assyria. After an "Egyptian Interlude," the reader will find themselves in the setting of the Babylonian Empire,

---

[3] Alan Lenzi, *Secrecy and the Gods: Secret Knowledge in Ancient Mesopotamia and Biblical Israel* (SAAS 19; Helsinki: The Neo-Assyrian Text Corpus Project, 2008).

[4] John S. Holladay, Jr., "Assyrian Statecraft and the Prophets of Israel," *HTR* 63 (1970): 29–51.

[5] Seth Sanders, *The Invention of Hebrew* (Urbana/Chicago: University of Illinois Press, 2009).

[6] See C. L. Crouch, "Ezekiel's Oracles against the Nations in Light of a Royal Ideology of Warfare," *JBL* 130 (2011): 473–92 and C. L. Crouch and Casey A. Strine, "YHWH's Battle against Chaos in Ezekiel: The Transformation of Judahite Mythology for a New Situation," *JBL* 132 (2013): 883–903.

which is depicted with antipathy and ambivalence. Eidevall then looks into how the book reacts to the Persian Empire, concluding with an examination of the imperial enterprise in which YHWH is the overlord.

In his contribution on the book of Isaiah ("The Theological Politics of Deutero-Isaiah"), Joseph Blenkinsopp focuses on the figure of Cyrus as a Davidic figure, who replaces the "native" Judean kings as the divinely chosen leader. As Blenkinsopp shows, Isaiah 40–66 is the only mention of David in Isa 55:1–5. The reference to a "nation you do not know and a nation that does not know you will come in haste" (Isa 55:5) is explained as a reference to Cyrus (see, e.g., Isa 41:25; 42:6; 45:3, 4).

Ehud Ben Zvi approaches the prophetic corpus ("The Yehudite Collection of Prophetic Books") as it would have been read by *literati* in the late Persian and early Hellenistic periods. After a short review of some recent studies on ancient empires, Ben Zvi turns to an introduction to social memory and the way that Persian period Yehudian (Judean) *literati* (re-)read their traditions, added to them, and constructed authors, authority, and their (hybrid) world. Ben Zvi asks why there is not more criticism of the Persian Empire in texts of the early Hellenistic period, since by then the necessity to express such criticism through *hidden transcripts* (*a la* Scott) would have ceased.[7] Ben Zvi argues that the absence of a negative indictment on the Persian rulers and Cyrus in particular should be regarded as significant. Ben Zvi and Blenkinsopp follow similar lines of argumentation here, with the proviso that according to Ben Zvi Cyrus is only "*partially* Davidize[d]." Indeed, Ben Zvi sees Isa 55:5 as an "example of appropriation and reshaping of imperial memories." However, Ben Zvi then goes on to ask why there is so little about Cyrus in the prophetic corpus, if he is understood as a new Davidide. Ben Zvi looks to the (partly pseudo-)historical setting of prophetic books in the pre-Persian period and more importantly to the trend to understand world history as moving toward a new empire to come, namely, YHWH's empire. According to Ben Zvi this represents fairly standard "under-dog dreams of empire," in which the rhetoric of the human political empire has been internalized. Against the historical "Arameanization" of Yehud stands the theological "'Israelization' of the entire world."

The last essay in this volume ("Power, Politics, and Prophecy in the Dead Sea Scrolls and Second Temple Judaism") by Alex Jassen moves the discussion yet further in time to the late Second Temple period. Jassen understands the various groups behind the Dead Sea Scrolls as generally being in a politically weaker position than other groups, such as the Hasmoneans and the Jerusalem priesthood.

---

[7] This is particularly surprising as the royal historiographical tradition and criticism of certain rulers is very much part of the Hellenistic tradition in cuneiform. In Mesopotamia, the criticism takes the form of a *hidden transcript*. For an example see Caroline Waerzeggers, "The 'Nabonidus Debate' in Babylonia, c. 200 BCE," in *Jewish Cultural Encounters in the Ancient Mediterranean and Near Eastern World Debate* (ed. M. Popovič; Leiden/Boston: Brill), forthcoming.

Significantly, the dynamics described by Jassen are similar in nature to those described for the late Persian and early Hellenistic period with their emphasis on eschatological retribution within a divine empire; what appears to be relatively new or at least given much more emphasis is the describing of prophets whose messages are not aligned with that of the author of the particular manuscript as "false prophets."

The essays collected in this volume cover a wide scope: from diplomatic correspondence in second millennium BCE Mari to the eschatological hopes expressed in the Dead Sea Scrolls. The common goal is to understand how "empire" influenced prophetic and divinatory communication between the divine and human realms and how this was put to use as and influenced by propaganda from those in power.

We would like to thank de Gruyter for allowing us to print Beate Pongratz-Leisten's essay on divination and cosmology, which forms part of chapter nine of her *Religion and Ideology in Assyria* (Berlin: de Gruyter, 2014), as well as Eerdman's Publishing for permitting us to print the essay by Joseph Blenkinsopp, which is nearly equivalent to chapter four of his *David Remembered: Kingship and National Identity in Ancient Israel* (Grand Rapids: Eerdmans, 2013), 54–70.

Finally, we would like to thank Ehud Ben Zvi, Roxana Flammini, and Martti Nissinen for accepting the volume into the *Ancient Near Eastern Monograph* series of the Society of Biblical Literature. We hope that publishing the studies through this venue will make them available to a wide readership.

February 2014

1

Propaganda, Prognostication, and Planets[1]

Jeffrey L. Cooley

INTRODUCTION: ON "PROPAGANDA" AND ANCIENT NEAR EASTERN STUDIES

The issue of whether or not the term "propaganda" can be appropriately applied to ancient Iraq was highlighted in the well-known article on the subject by A. Leo Oppenheim, who treated particularly the Neo-Assyrian and Neo-Babylonian Periods. Despite the fact that this article was a contribution to an anthology assembled by pioneering propaganda scholar Harold Lasswell, Oppenheim did not employ the term "propaganda" a single time.[2] For Oppenheim, the royal inscriptions were primarily "ceremonial" in nature, though they had the added effect of lionizing the monarch and enlightening members of his court.[3] In the same volume, Finkelstein presented the primary objection to applying the concept to material from Mesopotamian antiquity, namely, that propaganda "presumes a situation or context where a number of competing ideologies or sources of authority seek the allegiance or loyalty of large masses of persons."[4] In light of this, though he, in

---

[1] I would like to thank the editors, Alan Lenzi and Jonathan Stökl, for their insightful comments and invitation to participate in this volume. Additionally, I am grateful for the editorial help of Benjamin Miyamoto. An earlier version of a section of this paper benefitted from the critical comments of Gary Beckman and anonymous reviewers for which I am quite thankful.

[2] A. Leo Oppenheim, "Neo-Assyrian and Neo-Babylonian Empires," in *Propaganda and Communication in World History* (ed. Harold Lasswell; 3 vols.; Honolulu: University Press of Hawaii, 1979), 1: 111–44.

[3] Oppenheim, "Neo-Assyrian and Neo-Babylonian Empires," 116, 118.

[4] J. J. Finkelstein, "Early Mesopotamia, 2500–1000 B.C." in *Propaganda and Communication in World History*, 50–110, 53. Certainly, some modern evaluations of propaganda in the twentieth century follow the mass-oriented model, e.g., Jacques Ellul, *Propaganda: The Formation of*

contrast to Oppenheim, did use the term "propaganda" in his discussion, Finkelstein maintained that a better characterization of the ancient Near Eastern sources
might be simply "polemic."[5]

In spite of Oppenheim's reluctance, the term "propaganda" has often been
used in discussions of the literature of the ancient Near East, often quite effectively, but sometimes with little reflection on the term's use in contemporary studies
of propaganda. In its least effective employ, the word seems simply to indicate the
often manipulated portrayal of the king, his administration, and his enemies to a
public.[6] On the other hand, several scholars of the ancient Near East use the term
with considerable sophistication. The application of propaganda studies to the
Neo-Assyrian period in particular has offered rich returns: the work of such scholars as Reade, Winter, Liverani, Tadmor and Nevling Porter are outstanding examples of how propaganda, properly understood, can allow for sensitive and powerful
readings of political self-representation in ancient Iraq.[7] Though some scholars of

---

Men's Attitudes (New York: Knopf, 1965). But this does not mean their insights, properly modified, cannot be applied to ancient contexts.

   [5] Finkelstein, "Early Mesopotamia," 54 and 64. In this vein, see Hayim Tadmor, who
states, "I believe that we are fully justified in using the term in the context of outright political polemic" ("Propaganda, Literature, and Historiography," in *Assyria 1995: Proceedings of the
10th Anniversary Symposium of the Neo-Assyrian Text Corpus Project* [ed. Simo Parpola and Robert
M. Whiting; Helsinki: Neo-Assyrian Text Corpus Project, 1997], 325–38, 333). In spite of Tadmor's significant contribution to the topic at hand, it must be noted that propaganda is more
than mere argument; rather, in any definition of the term, the end goal of gaining group
support through action must always remain highlighted.

   [6] Similarly, Göran Eidevall, in his *Prophecy and Propaganda: Images of Enemies in the Book of
Isaiah* (ConBOT 56; Winona Lake: Eisenbrauns, 2009), never defines the term, but seems to use
it to describe the expression of an ideology, with little attention given to the specific behaviors it seeks to elicit. Though not denying an active element, a similar focus on ideological
consent can be found in Eric Seibert, *Subversive Scribes and the Solomonic Narrative: A Rereading
of 1 Kings 1–11* (LHBOTS 436; London: T & T Clark, 2006), 13. See also Aarnoud van der Deijl,
*Protest or Propaganda: War in the Old Testament Book of Kings and in Contemporaneous Ancient Near
Eastern Texts* (SSN 51; Leiden: Brill, 2008), which focuses specifically on the justification of
war in the Hebrew Bible. While van der Deijl is well engaged with studies of propaganda in
the ancient Near East, it must be noted that the *ex post facto* dissemination of one's *casus belli*
is not necessarily propaganda, as modern propaganda theorists would understand it. Though
he neither attempts to define what he means by the term "propaganda," nor does he engage
with important modern theorist such as Ellul or Lasswell, he at least does draw on important
ancient Near Eastern studies scholars who have.

   [7] Julian Reade, "Ideology and Propaganda in Assyrian Art," in *Power and Propaganda: A
Symposium on Ancient Empires* (ed. M. T. Larsen; Copenhagen: Akademisk Forlag, 1979), 329–43;
Irene, J. Winter, "Royal Rhetoric and the Development of Historical Narrative in Neo-
Assyrian Reliefs," *Studies in Visual Communication* 7 (1981): 2–38; Mario Liverani, "The Ideology of the Neo-Assyrian Empire," in *Power and Propaganda*, 297–317; Barbara Nevling Porter,
Images, Power, Politics: Figurative Aspects of Esarhaddon's Babylonian Policy (Philadelphia: American Philosophical Society, 1993), and "Assyrian Propaganda for the West: Esarhaddon's Stelae for Til Barsip and Sam'al," in *Essays on Syria in the Iron Age* (AbrNSup 7; Louvain: Peeters,
2000), 143–76. It should be noted that Winter focuses not on the propagandistic, but rather
on the purely ideological thrust of the NA palace reliefs; however, she does understand the

ancient Israel and Judah have occasionally been reluctant to apply the term to the Hebrew Bible,[8] there have been many important contributions especially in the last couple of decades of the last century.[9] One of these contributions was also the first monograph solely dedicated to the subject of propaganda in the Hebrew Bible as a whole, namely, Rex Mason's *Propaganda and Subversion in the Old Testament*.[10] This focused work itself has spawned a number of other studies, such as those by Seibert and van der Deijl.[11]

Current definitions of propaganda are by no means completely unified.[12] Nonetheless, there are certain salient commonalities, as a couple of examples will suffice to demonstrate. Communication scholars Garth S. Jowett and Victoria O'Donnell offer this definition in their popular text on the subject: "Propaganda is the deliberate, systematic attempt to shape perceptions, manipulate cognitions, and direct behavior *to achieve a response that furthers the desired intent of the propagandist*."[13] Philip Taylor, in his study of the role of propaganda in armed conflict throughout history, defines the term in this way:

> By propaganda, then, I mean the deliberate attempt to persuade people to think and behave in a desired way. Although I recognize that much propaganda is accidental or unconscious here I am discussing the conscious, methodical and planned decisions to employ techniques of persuasion designed to achieve specific goals that are intended to benefit those organizing the process.[14]

In sum, what is shared by most modern studies of the term, including the definitions offered here is that propaganda is deliberate persuasive communication,

---

ultimately agitative goals of propaganda, and is reluctant to separate propaganda from the plain dissemination of ideology (Winter, "Royal Rhetoric," 23).

[8] This is in no doubt due to the theological assumptions of many biblical scholars regarding the Hebrew Bible, on the one hand, and to the common characterization of propaganda as a necessarily misleading rhetoric, on the other. See, e.g., John Walton, *Ancient Israelite Literature in its Cultural Context: A Survey of Parallels between Biblical and Ancient Near Eastern Texts* (Grand Rapids: Zondervan, 1989), 115.

[9] For an outstanding, though brief, survey, see Seibert, *Subversive Scribes*, 14–17, to which my own overview here is indebted.

[10] Rex Mason, *Propaganda and Subversion in the Old Testament* (London: SPCK, 1997).

[11] Seibert, *Subversive Scribes*; van der Deijl, *Protest or Propaganda*. Liverani, following his Marxist understanding of propaganda, understands the entire biblical text as a propagandistic work composed to consolidate power (Mario Liverani, "Propaganda," *ABD* 5: 474–77).

[12] For a survey of categorized definitions, see Randal Marlin, *Propaganda and the Ethics of Persuasion* (Peterborough: Broadview Press, 2002), 16–21. Marlin offers his own definition of the term: "the organized attempt to affect belief or action or inculcate attitudes in a large audience in ways that circumvent or suppress an individual's adequately informed, rational, reflective judgment" (*Propaganda and the Ethics of Persuasion*, 22).

[13] Garth S. Jowett and Victoria O'Donnell, *Propaganda and Persuasion* (3rd ed.; London: Sage Publications, 1999), 6 (italics mine).

[14] Philip M. Taylor, *Munitions of the Mind: A History of Propaganda from the Ancient World to the Present Day* (3rd ed.; Manchester: Manchester University Press, 2003), 6.

the goal of which is to convince people to think specific things and perform certain acts that further the objectives of the originator of the communication.[15] In the academic study of propaganda these desired patterns of thought and behavior are often referred to as *action*. The kind of *action* that the propaganda desires to elicit determines the kind of propaganda employed. The *action* and the propaganda that leads to it can thus be divided into two categories: *integration* and *integrative propaganda*, and *agitation* and *agitative propaganda*.[16] The first primarily connotes the desired effect of making an audience passively accepting of the propagandists' direction and leadership.[17] As Ellul characterizes it, *integration* stabilizes and unifies the audience and is a long-term undertaking.[18] Though *integration* is often a goal unto itself, it can also effectively create a fertile and reliable field in which the second kind of *action*, *agitation*, can grow. *Agitation* refers primarily to the desired behaviors that the propagandist seeks to provoke.[19] It must be emphasized that the desired behaviors, the *actions* of *integration* and *agitation*—and not merely thought processes that lead to them—are really the end goals of propaganda as it is currently understood.[20]

Note also what is *not* included in these contemporary definitions of the term offered by scholars who approach the phenomenon from the perspective of communications: a definition of just who the audience is.[21] One of the reasons for Oppenheim's rejection of the word "propaganda" I believe, revolved around the assumption that by definition the intended audience for propaganda must be the general public.[22] Certainly, modern propaganda campaigns, as seen in many coun-

---

[15] Propaganda differs from mere persuasive rhetoric in that the latter is "interactive and attempts to satisfy the needs of both persuader and persuaded" (Jowett and O'Donnell, *Propaganda*, 1).

[16] Jowett and O'Donnell, *Propaganda*, 11–12. In line with the rest of his study, Ellul maintains that *integration* can only occur in modern societies (*Propaganda*, 74–75). Though these useful analytical labels are often employed by scholars working with more contemporary materials (as recently as Marlin, *Propaganda and the Ethics of Persuasion*, 36–39), they are rarely employed by those who use the heuristic to approach ancient Near Eastern cultures. I believe them to be useful and appropriate labels and will use them throughout this work.

[17] Jowett and O'Donnell, *Propaganda*, 12.

[18] Ellul, *Propaganda*, 75.

[19] Jowett and O'Donnell, *Propaganda*, 11–12.

[20] Mario Liverani hints at this understanding ("The Ideology of the Neo-Assyrian Empire," in *Power and Propaganda: A Symposium on Ancient Empires* [Copenhagen Studies in Assyriology 7; ed. M. T. Larsen; Copenhagen: Akademisk Forlag, 1979], 299). For a full appreciation of the contemporary understanding, see, in particular, Nevling Porter, who states, "By proposing that Esarhaddon's three stelae should be included in the discussion of Assyrian propaganda, I mean to suggest that the visual and verbal imagery of the stelae was designed less to inform than to persuade, and that the stelae appear to have been designed at least in part to influence the political attitudes and behaviour of audiences in the cities where the stelae were erected" ("Assyrian Propaganda for the West," 144).

[21] Perhaps an outlier here is Marlin who in his definition highlights "a large audience" (*Propaganda and Persuasion*, 22).

[22] Finkelstein goes on to note that "propaganda" in ancient Near Eastern texts was targeted at the "segment of the population that was a real or potential threat to the political

tries in the last century, were and are often directed to the public at large. These campaigns assume both access to the media sources by which the propaganda is propagated as well as a high level of literacy. Newspapers, leaflets, posters, film, radio, television, and most recently, the internet and social media are widely distributed or accessible, and they are universally comprehensible in a literate society. This is in stark contrast to the ancient Near East in general: images were largely concentrated in areas of restricted access, such as the palace and temple, and textual media, often featured side-by-side with the images, could only be appreciated by relatively tiny segments of the population. Nonetheless, one of the observations noted in the modern study of contemporary propaganda is that it is not solely directed at the general public.[23] Indeed, since specific groups of people have different political connections and skill sets, it follows that in order to elicit specific behaviors from such groups propaganda can be used to target them. Thus, any audience, not just the general public, can be the target of a propaganda campaign.

Previous studies on the use of texts and visual communication in the Neo-Assyrian period have concluded that the Assyrian crown indeed targeted specific groups with carefully focused propaganda. For example, Reade's study of the Neo-Assyrian palace reliefs argues that these images were strategically situated to address specific audiences (e.g., courtiers and foreign visitors).[24] Winter convincingly argued that that the standard inscriptions and their accompanying reliefs seem to carry the same message, but were directed at literate and non-literate groups respectively.[25] Similarly, Nevling Porter's study of Esarhaddon's stelae from Til Barsip and Sam'al demonstrates that the creators of Esarhaddon's Til Barsip and Sam'al stelas understood the local history of reception of Assyrian hegemony and fit their images and texts to suit.[26]

Modern history has shown that possible targeted audiences do not only include uneducated masses, of course, but also the educated, privileged elite. Indeed, the more important the targeted group is to the individual goals of the propagandist, the more propagandistic attention and effort that group will receive. While it might be popularly assumed that the uneducated masses are the most susceptible to the often misleading rhetoric of the propagandist, the fact is that those groups who have the most invested in culturally formulated symbolic systems are quite vulnerable as well. *We* might expect them to be more skeptical. (They are "scholars" like us, are they not?) But they are a fertile target for propaganda. This is be-

---

authority at any given moment" which was never the public at large ("Early Mesopotamia," 53).

[23] "The traditional propaganda audience is a mass audience, but that is not always the case with modern propaganda. To be sure, mass communication in some form will be used but it may be used in conjunction with other audience forms such as small groups, interest groups, a group of the politically or culturally elite, a special segment of the population, opinion leaders, and individuals" (Jowett and O'Donnell, *Propaganda*, 286–87).

[24] Reade, "Ideology and Propaganda," 338–39.

[25] Winter, "Royal Rhetoric," 19–21.

[26] Nevling Porter, "Assyrian Propaganda for the West." See also Tadmor, "Propaganda, Literature, and Historiography;" and Porter, *Images, Power, Politics*, 105–17 (especially 116).

cause, as Ellul notes, "one of propaganda's most important devices [is] . . . the manipulation of symbols."[27]

Oppenheim astutely noted that the kings of ancient Iraq exercised their political authority by skillful manipulation of two systems, namely, the bureaucratic and the symbolic.[28] While all members of Mesopotamian society from king to slave participated to some degree in both systems, the latter system was most fully appreciated by the literate elite. After all, they were the only ones who had the skills required to appreciate and grasp the full panoply of symbols—visual, ritual, and *textual*—that the monarchs controlled in order attain their political goals. We can reasonably assume that the implied audience of the Neo-Assyrian royal inscriptions, in particular, or at least in part, was the literate intelligentsia.[29] The literate elite of Babylonia and Assyria would have been an ideal target for a propaganda campaign in the Neo-Assyrian period. As noted, previous studies have argued that certain royal inscriptions were targeted at specific audiences. Only those with some access to the mechanisms of the state could have been exposed to the spectrum of media expected in a propaganda campaign. The literate elites are the ones who saw the palace reliefs with their own eyes; they are the ones who proximately observed the spectacle of the state cultus; they are the ones who had access to the officially composed royal inscriptions; and ultimately, they are the ones who had the ability to compose and read them. Furthermore, the greatest internal threat to the Assyrian king was not a dissatisfied general public who might take up arms in open rebellion, but rather those closest to him who comprised the administrative apparatus of the state—family, officials, etc.[30] These are the king's primary audience, those whom he needed to convince so that they might be loyal and motivated to implement his policies.

---

[27] Ellul, *Propaganda*, 111.

[28] Oppenheim, "The Neo-Assyrian and Neo-Babylonian Empires," 111–13.

[29] Tadmor, "Propaganda, Literature, and Historiography," 332; cf. J. A. Brinkman, "Through a Glass Darkly: Esarhaddon's Retrospects on the Downfall of Babylon," *JAOS* 103 (1983): 35–42 (41); Nevling Porter, *Images, Power, Politics*, 116; and F. M. Fales and G. B. Lanfranchi, "The Impact of Oracular Material on the Political Utterances and Political Action in the Royal Inscriptions of the Sargonid Dynasty," in *Oracles et prophéties dans l'antiquité: Actes du colloque de Strasborgh, 15-17 juin 1995* (ed. J.-G. Heintz; Travaux du Centre de recherche sur le Proche-Orient et la Grèce antiques 15; Strasbourg: de Bocard, 1997), 99–114 (113).

Oppenheim maintained that some version of the contents of the royal inscriptions must have been disseminated orally to the general public, even if only unofficially (Oppenheim, "The City of Assur in 714 B.C." *JNES* 19 [1960]: 133–47). Tadmor's caveat, that there is no actual evidence for an official mechanism for a public dissemination, needs to be taken seriously (Tadmor, "Propaganda, Literature, and Historiography," 332). Nonetheless, the fact that information from the royal inscriptions somehow spread despite their cuneiformity can be maintained on the grounds that specific tropes typical of that genre seem to have been used and polemically abused by Judahite prophet-scribes. See Peter Machinist, "Assyria and Its Image in the First Isaiah," *JAOS* 103 (1983): 719–37; Shawn Zelig Aster, "The Image of Assyria in Isaiah 2:5–22: The Campaign Motif Reversed," *JAOS* 127 (2007): 249–78.

[30] It is undoubtedly the case, however, that the support of the general populace could be a real concern. See Finkelstein, "Early Mesopotamia," 54–58.

The goal of this study, then, is to begin the analysis of the handful of references to celestial divination found in the Assyrian royal inscriptions from the perspective of propaganda studies by approaching one text in particular, Esarhaddon's Assur A inscription. Doing so, I believe, will help us solve some of the outstanding problems in regards to the celestial phenomena recorded in these inscriptions and their mantic implications.

CELESTIAL DIVINATION IN THE NEO-ASSYRIAN ROYAL INSCRIPTIONS: ESARHADDON'S ASSUR A

The relative density of references to divination in the inscriptions of the Sargonids is a well-known phenomenon.[31] But specific references to celestial divination in these texts are few and far between.[32] While Sargon II mentioned the positive results of celestial divination in his famous Letter to Assur,[33] and Sennacherib seems to have labeled several gates after celestial features, the first clear reference in the royal inscriptions *per se* to that mantic practice occur during the reign of Esarhaddon.

The first of these occurs in the beginning of Assur A, Esarhaddon's description of his renovation of the temple Ešarra in Assur, and is the focus of my discussion. The text is known from at least nine exemplars: seven clay prisms, one stone tab-

---

[31] For an overview of prophecy in particular, see Martti Nissinen, *References to Prophecy in Neo-Assyrian Sources* (SAAS 7; Helsinki: Neo-Assyrian Text Corpus Project, 1998). For a discussion of the quasi-use of celestial divination in the Neo-Babylonian inscriptions of Nabonidus, see Paul-Richard Berger, "Imaginäre Astrologie in spätbabylonischer Propaganda," in *Die Rolle der Astronomie in den Kulturen Mesopotamiens Morgenlandischen Symposion (23.-27. September 1991)* (ed. H. D. Galter; Graz: RM Druck & Verlagsgesellschaft, 1993), 275–89.

[32] For overviews, see Ulla Koch-Westenholz, *Mesopotamian Astrology: An Introduction to Babylonian and Assyrian Celestial Divination* (CNI Publications 19; Copenhagen: Museum Tusculum Press, 1995), 152–61 and Beate Pongratz-Leisten, *Herrschaftswissen in Mesopotamien: Formen der Kommunikation zwischen Gott und König im 2. und 1. Jahrtausausend v. Chr.* (SAAS 10; Helsinki: Neo-Assyrian Text Corpus Project, 1999), 38–46.

[33] François Thureau-Dangin, *Une relation de la huitième campagne de Sargon (714 av. J.-C.)* (TCL 3; Paris: Geuthner, 1912). For discussion, see A. Leo Oppenheim, "The City of Assur," 133–47; and F. M. Fales, "Narrative and Ideological Variations in the Account of Sargon's Eighth Campaign," in *Ah, Assyria . . . : Studies in Assyrian History and Ancient Near Eastern Historiography Presented to Hayim Tadmor* (ed. M. Cogan and I. Eph'al; Jerusalem: Magnes, 1991), 129–47. While the text is quite similar to the royal inscriptions in style, content, etc., I am not including it in my discussion here, since its implied audience is rather uncertain (Oppenheim, "The City of Assur," 138; Koch-Westenholz, *Mesopotamian Astrology*, 153–54; Pongratz-Leisten, *Herrschaftswissen*, 30–39; David Brown, *Mesopotamian Planetary Astronomy-Astrology* [CM 18; Groningen: Styx, 2000], 14 n.31). Oppenheim, for example, maintained that the letter was to be read publically for the citizens of Assur itself ("The City of Assur," 143). The celestial phenomena described and their mantic interpretation present several problems similar to those of Assur A

let, and one clay tablet.[34] As is typical of such royal inscriptions, all of the copies were found deliberately buried in the foundations of various structures in Assur, minus the clay tablet whose exact provenance is unknown. If Esarhaddon had intended the message of Assur A to be relayed to a general audience, clearly there would have been more effective means of doing so than burying the text in the ground. Perhaps we must assume that dissemination of the text, and its agenda, was to be accomplished first in its repeated manufacture and then by word of mouth among individuals who could comprehend the text's specific significance.

In any case, Assur A has several mantic references all of which confirm the legitimacy of Esarhaddon's activity, not just those which concern celestial divination.[35] The references to hepatoscopy, lecanomancy, or prophecy merely highlight in broad terms the positive or reliable nature of the oracles generated through these methods. In marked contrast, those deriving from celestial divination are manifestly more sophisticated and include rather precise details regarding specific omens. Indeed, the celestial divination references are so specific that we are able to situate them within the contemporaneous practice. Against this background, Esarhaddon's mantic assertions in terms of this specific tradition are revealed to be highly unorthodox and problematic.

Yet, in spite of the difficulties presented by the inscription's celestial oracles, its technical sophistication is an important indicator of its implied audience and assumes that its audience had a knowledgeable background in the practice of celestial divination, perhaps even technical training. Winter noted a similar kind of specificity in her study of the development of the narrative program of Neo-Assyrian palace reliefs, that

> the ability to receive the message contained in the program . . . is a direct function of the effectiveness and clarity of the presentation of the message, the packaging . . . , and of the cognitive competence of the audience: the stored knowledge brought to the situation, ability to understand signs and signals, and skill in decoding. . . .[36]

That is to say, the creator of such an ideologically loaded message (in Winter's case, the designer of the reliefs in Assurnaṣirpal II's palace, in contrast to that of reliefs from later in the period) must understand his audience, and employ an audience-appropriate symbolic system.

Esarhaddon begins to describe his mantically-delivered divine approval, at the beginning of the text proper, shortly after his own titulary:

3′ ᵈ[30 u ᵈ]UTU DINGIR.MEŠ maš-šu-te	In [order] to give the land and the
4′ áš-[šú] de-en kit-te	people verdicts of truth and jus-

---

[34] For these and the following archaeological data, see the summary chart in RINAP 4: 119–20.

[35] RINAP 4 57 ii 12–13, 14–26, iii 42–iv 6.

[36] Winter, "Royal Rhetoric," 29.

5′ ù mi-šá-ri	tice, the gods [Sîn and] Šamaš, the
6′ a-na KUR u UN.MEŠ šá-ra-ku	twin gods, took the road of truth
7′ ITI-šam-ma ḫar-ra-an kit-te	and justice monthly. They made
8′ ù mi-šá-ri ṣab-tu-ma	(their simultaneous) appearance
9′ UD.[1].KAM UD.14.KAM	regularly on the [1st][37] and 14th
10′ ú-sa-di-ru ta-mar-tú	days.[38]

Koch-Westenholz describes this statement as a "general reference to the auspicious omens of opposition and, probably, conjunction of the sun and the moon on the proper dates. This is a literary phrase like 'may Sin and Shamash bless him without cease.'"[39] Though her characterization has gained some acceptance,[40] there are nonetheless problems with it. While the statement in Assur A is a generalization, it is an intentional generalization of a very specific set of astronomical phenomena and presumes their specific divinatory applications: both of these astronomical events are considered auspicious. For example, SAA 8 409, a report from the celestial diviner Rašili, notes an omen associated with the auspicious beginning of a month:

1	DIŠ ina UD.1.[KÁM IGI KA] GI.NA	If (the moon) [becomes visible] on
2	ŠÀ KUR DÙG -a	the 1st day: reliable [speech]; the
3	UD.[1].KÁM DINGIR KI DINGIR	land will become happy.
	in-nam-mar	On the [1st][41] day the god will be
4	MÌ.SIG₅ šá LUGAL be-lí-ia	seen with the other: good for the
		king my lord.[42]

Rašili here seems to equate a month which has begun on the first, i.e., in an ideal manner, with the gods (undoubtedly the sun and moon) being seen with each oth-

---

[37] The reconstruction of "1" in the brackets is offered by Francis Rue Steele without explanation ("The University Museum Esarhaddon Prism," *JAOS* 71 [1954]: 1–12, 4); he is followed by Koch-Westenholz (*Mesopotamian Astrology*, 155) and Pongratz-Leisten (*Herrschaftswissen*, 41). This reconstruction appears likely for two reasons. First, the missing sign would have been located in a rather slim space between two fragments (UM 32-33-5 and Ass 12260 + VAT 8411), and it seems unlikely that there is space for anything larger than a single vertical wedge, particularly since the beginning of the following KÁM sign needs to fit in the gap as well. Second, there is specific positive mantic significance placed on both the 1st and 14th, when the "gods appear together" (i.e., the sun and moon are either in opposition or conjunction), as evidenced by the omina cited below. In contrast, Leichty offers no reconstruction of the obscurity (RINAP 4 57 i 9′), while Borger suggested "13(?)," though this was clearly a guess (Borger, *Ash* 2 § 2 i 37).

[38] RINAP 4 57 i 3′–10′.

[39] Koch-Westenholz, *Mesopotamia Astrology*, 155.

[40] E.g., Pongratz-Leisten, *Herrschaftswissen*, 41.

[41] Campbell-Thompson was also unclear as to the reading here, transliterating *ana* UD ..
... DINGIR *in-nam-mar* (RMA 46a). The photo reveals that the tablet is rather difficult to read (available through the CDLI: http://www.cdli.ucla.edu/dl/photo/P237931.jpg). Nonetheless, the fact that the omen is being read in conjunction with an omen regarding the first of the month seems to indicate that this must be the meaning.

[42] SAA 8 409:1–4.

er. The apodoses are appropriately positive. Likewise, SAA 8 15 reports a solar-lunar opposition on the 14th:

6	1 UD.14.KÁM 30 u 20 KI a-ḫa-meš	If on the 14th day the moon and
	IGI.MEŠ	sun are seen together: reliable
7	KA GI.NA ŠÀ-bi KUR DÙG-ab	speech, the land will become hap-
8	DINGIR.MEŠ ᵏᵘʳURI.KI	py. The gods will remember Akkad
9	a-na da-mì-iq-ti	favorably; joy among the troops;
10	i-ḫa-sa-su	the king will become happy; the
r. 1	ḫu-ud ŠÀ-bi ERIM-ni	cattle of Akkad will lie in the
2	ŠÀ-bi LUGAL DÙG-ab	steppe undisturbed.[43]
3	MÀŠ.ANŠE ᵏᵘʳURI.KI	
4	ina EDIN par-ga-niš NÁ-iṣ	

The variant apodoses offered by the diviner (lines 8–rev. 4) who wrote this report, the chief scribe Issar-šumu-ereš, are all overwhelmingly positive and cover multiple facets of the land, including the status of the religious climate, the army, the monarchy, and livestock.

Returning to Assur A, Esarhaddon would have us believe that the sun and moon appeared in happy conjunction on the first of the month and in blissful opposition on the 14th on a monthly basis (araḫšamma, line 7′). But this was not and could not have been the case. The appearance of the sun and moon in relation to each other are not this regular, and Esarhaddon certainly had to deal with the negative apodoses of such inauspicious phenomena on many occasions. For example, lunar-solar oppositions occur frequently on dates other than the 14th, and reports and letters which mention this phenomenon are so common that these texts are difficult to date with precision.[44] Nonetheless, because the oppositions are common, there is little doubt that they occurred with relative frequency during Esarhaddon's eleven-year reign. For example, the chief scribe Issar-šumu-ereš, who served both Esarhaddon and his son Assurbanipal, writes of a lunar-solar opposition on the 15th:

1	DIŠ UD.15.[KÁM] ᵈ30 [u ᵈUTU]	If on the 15th day the mo[on and
2	it-ti a-ḫa-mì-iš IGI.LAL	sun] are seen together: a strong
3	ˡᵘKÚR dan-nu ᵍⁱˢTUKUL.MEŠ-šú	enemy will raise his weapons
4	a-na KUR i-na-šá-a	against the land; the enemy will
5	KÁ.GAL.MEŠ ˡᵘKÚR i-na-qar	tear down the city gates. If the
6	DIŠ ᵈ30 u ᵈUTU la ú-qí-ma ir-bi	moon or the sun does not wait
7	na-an-dur UR.MAḪ u UR.BAR.RA	(for the other), but sets: raging
		of lion and wolf.[45]

Esarhaddon's fronted summary of the celestial omens of his reign in Assur A contrasts with the mantic crises with which he had to deal, it seems, rather regularly

---

[43] SAA 8 15:6–10, rev. 1–4.
[44] E.g., SAA 8 23, 91, 92, 134, 136, 173, 202–203, 306; SAA 10 94, 105, 125, 135.
[45] SAA 8 24:1–7.

as attested in the reports and particularly the letters. Nonetheless, his assertion does not serve a polemical purpose. Unlike the public quarrel the later Nabonidus had with his Neo-Babylonian court diviners, there is no obvious argument in Esarhaddon's inscription, no engagement with a counter-claim or an apology for otherwise unusual interpretations.[46] On the contrary, the Assyrian monarch's announcement serves as a programmatic declaration. The text dates to within the first couple of years of his reign; thus, the statements regarding the consistently positive phenomena cannot be based on a long history of real observations, even if we assume that they were falsely portrayed as universally positive.[47] By stating that the sun and moon always fit into their ideal, auspicious schemes, Esarhaddon is actively denying that he has ever—or will ever—have to initiate the appropriate *namburbî* to alter an otherwise negative oracular fate. In propagandistic terms, there is no doubt that it serves an *integrative* purpose (which seems to be Koch-Westenholz's characterization), assuring the implied audience that Esarhaddon has the gods' approval.[48] But, as a statement clearly directed at literate diviners it is also *agitative* in nature. The gods, he stresses, *always* give the king positive signs. It thus sets a mantic agenda for all diviners who would serve the king: interpret omens positively!

Esarhaddon follows his mantic summary with two other specific celestial omina (i 11'–ii 13). The first specific omen revolves around a set of circumstances involving the planet Dilbat/ Venus:

11' ^{mul}dil-bat na-baṭ MUL.MEŠ	Venus, the brightest of the stars,
12' *ina* ^{im}MAR.TU	was seen in the west, [in the
ii 1 [*ina* KASKAL *šu*]-*ut* ^{d}*é-a*	Path] of Ea. Concerning the se-
2 *in-na-mir šá kun-nu*	curing of the land (and) the rec-
3 *ma-a-te* [*šá*] *su-lum*	onciliation of its gods, it (Venus)
4 DINGIR.MEŠ-*šá ni-ṣir-tú*	reached (its) secret (place) and
5 *ik-šu-ud-ma it-bal*	then disappeared.[49]

In this case, Esarhaddon is not inventing a celestial situation out of whole cloth as he is in his previous statement regarding the regular ideal appearances of the sun and moon; rather, the observed celestial phenomenon here described is in fact accurate according to astronomical reconstructions of the night sky as it appeared in 680 BCE.[50] This particular omen entails three different astronomical events: 1) Venus rising in the west, in a certain section of the sky known as the Path of

---

[46] For Nabonidus' public argument with his diviners, see Peter Machinist and Hayim Tadmor, "Heavenly Wisdom," in *The Tablet and the Scroll: Near Eastern Studies in Honor of William Hallo* (ed. M. E. Cohen, D. C. Snell, and D. B. Weisberg; Bethesda: CDL Press, 1993), 146–51.

[47] Two of the copies of the inscription are dated to 679 BCE (RINAP 4 57).

[48] Koch-Westenholz, *Mesopotamian Astrology*, 155.

[49] RINAP 4: 57 i 11'–12', ii 1–6.

[50] Hermann Hunger and David Pingree, *MUL.APIN: An Astronomical Compendium in Cuneiform* (AfOB 24; Horn: Berger, 1989), 146–47.

Ea;[51] 2) Venus reaching something called its "secret"; and 3) Venus setting. All of these ominous events are attested in the celestial divination omen collections where they occur in multiple, interconnected and, it seems, developing forms.[52] In regard to Esarhaddon's interpretation of these celestial phenomena in Assur A, it would be fruitful to delineate that development by examining two of the tablets that contain various Venus omens. The first of these that offers a form of the omen applied by Esarhaddon, is K.7936, and lists Venus's potential appearance in the various celestial Paths of Ea, Anu, and Enlil:

7	DIŠ ^{mul}dil-bat ina KASKAL šu-ut ^dé-a IGI-ir LUGAL MAR.TU ^{ki} GABA.RI NU.TUK-ši	If Venus becomes visible in the Path of Ea: the king of Amurru will have no rival.
8	DIŠ ^{mul}dil-bat ina KASKAL šu-ut ^da-nim IGI-ir LUGAL NIM^{ki} GABA.RI NU.TUK-ši	If Venus becomes visible in the Path of Anu: the king of Elam will have no rival.
9	DIŠ ^{mul}dil-bat ina KASKAL šu-ut ^den-líl IGI-ir LUGAL URI^{ki} GABA.RI NU.TUK-ši	If Venus becomes visible in the Path of Enlil: the king of Akkad will have no rival.[53]

Notable in K.7936 for our purposes here are the associations made between sections of the sky and geographic regions on earth, a feature which is common in celestial divination literature: the Path of Ea with Amurru, the Path of Anu with Elam, and the Path of Enlil with Akkad.[54] Venus's appearance (innamir) in a specific path indicates prosperity for that path's mundane association.

The direct significance of K.7936 in relation to Esarhaddon's Assur A comes from line 7: šumma Dilbat ina ḫarrān šūt Ea innamir šar Amurri šānina ul īši, "If Venus becomes visible in the Path of Ea: the king of Amurru will have no rival." In Assur A, Esarhaddon states that Dilbat nabāṭ kakkabī ina Amurri ina ḫarrān šūt Ea innamir, "Venus, the brightest of the stars, was seen in the west, [in the Path] of Ea" (i 11′–ii 2). Thus, though it is not stated explicitly in Assur A, Venus's appearance in the Path of Ea bodes well for Amurru.

These omens as preserved in K.7936 are clearly somehow related to those in another tablet from Kuyunjik, DT 47. This latter tablet adds an important element to understanding Esarhaddon's reference to Venus's celestial activity, namely, the mantic significance assigned to the planet's niṣirtu. This concept in celestial divina-

---

[51] For the Paths of Ea, Anu, and Enlil, see the brief discussion in Erica Reiner and David Pingree, Enūma Anu Enlil Tablets 50–51: Babylonian Planetary Omens 2 (BMes 2/2; Malibu: Undena Publications, 1981), 17–18.

[52] The exact nature of the relationships between omen collections, such as those discussed here, is often difficult to ascertain, to be sure, and it is quite conceivable that all these examples cited are merely contemporary variations of the same list of omens. For a discussion of these and other related tablets, see Erica Reiner and David Pingree, Babylonian Planetary Omens Part 3 (CM 11; Groningen: Styx, 1998) (henceforth BPO 3), 1–2, 199–208.

[53] K.7936:7–9 (BPO 3, 210–11; cf. K.3601+:7–9; BPO 3 213–14).

[54] For such associations, see Koch-Westenholz, Mesopotamian Astrology, 98.

tion is first attested, as far as we can determine, on the Assur A inscription itself.[55] Apparently sometime around or after the beginning of the 7ᵗʰ Century, BCE, when Esarhaddon's Assur A was composed and copied, a celestial diviner created omens that included specific reference to the planet's *ašar niṣirti* (literally "secret place," often translated as "hypsoma") and these, too, were included on DT 47:[56]

27′	[DIŠ ᵐᵘ]ᴵ*dil-bat* KI *ni-ṣir-ti* KUR-*ud* SIG₅ *ana* ᵐᵘ¹UR.GU.LA KUR-*ma* : 1 2/3 KASKAL GÍS *i*[-*šaq-qam-ma*]	[If] Venus reaches (her) secret place: favorable – she reaches the Lion, variant: [she climbs] 1 2/3 *bēru*.
28′	[DIŠ ᵐᵘ]ᴵ*dil-bat* KI *ni-ṣir-ti la* KUR-*ud-ma it-bal* KUR *ur-ta*[*ḫ-ḫas*]	[If] Venus does not reach the secret place and disappears: the land will suf[fer].
29′	[DIŠ ᵐᵘ]ᴵ*dil-bat ina* ⁱᵐMAR.TU ITI-*ma* KI *ni-ṣir-ti* KUR-*ma u i*[*t-bal*]	[If] Venus becomes visible in the West, reaches the secret place and di[sappears]:
30′	DINGIR.MEŠ KI ᵏᵘʳMARᵏⁱ SILIM.MA T[UK.MEŠ]	the gods [will be] reconciled with Amurru.
31′	[DIŠ ᵐᵘ]ᴵ*dil-bat ina* ⁱᵐMAR.TU IGI-*ma* KI *ni-ṣir-ti* <*la*> KUR-*ma u* [*it-bal*]	[If] Venus becomes visible in the west, does <not> reach the secret place and [disappears]:
32′	DINGIR.MEŠ KI ᵏᵘʳMARᵏⁱ *i-šab-b*[*u-su*]	the gods will be ang[ry] with Amurru.[57]

Clearly, Venus reaching its *ašar niṣirti* is generally auspicious, particularly if the planet sets when in that celestial location. If the planet does so in the western sky, the positive nature of the phenomenon is aptly applied to the west, i.e., Amurru. Of course, Venus's appearance in its secret place in the west is precisely the astronomical situation described in Assur A: *Dilbat nabāṭ kakkabī ina Amurri* [*ina ḫarrān*] *šūt Ea innamir . . . niṣirtu ikšudma itbal*, "Venus, the brightest of the stars, was seen in the west [in the Path] of Ea . . . it reached (its) secret (place) and then disappeared" (i 11′–ii 2, 5–6). Here as well, though it is not stated plainly by Esarhaddon, the mantic significance of Venus's movements is especially auspicious for Amurru.

To summarize, the activity of Venus in Esarhaddon's Assur A draws on an assemblage of omens related to the planet's appearance in the Path of Ea in the west, its reaching its secret place, and then its disappearance. All of these elements are attested in the omen literature cited above, and all of them bode well for Amurru.

The third mantically significant celestial activity observed and reported in Assur A, concerns the planet Mars:

---

[55] The role of Esarhaddon or his celestial diviners in innovating the term itself is unclear. See Koch-Westenholz, *Mesopotamian Astrology*, 52 n.3, and Klaus Koch, "Neues von den babylonischen Planeten-Hypsomata," *WO* 31 (2000/2001): 46–71 (46).

[56] Most recently, Koch has rejected the label *hypsoma*, since the use of the term does not correspond to the classical definition (Koch, "Neues von den babylonischen Planeten-Hypsomata," 46–71).

[57] DT 47: 27′–32′ (*BPO* 3, 232–33).

6	^{mul}ṣal-bat-a-nu pa-ri-is	Mars, the giver of decisions of
7	pur-se-e ^{kur}MAR.TU.KI	the land Amurru, shone brightly
8	ina KASKAL šu-ut ^dé-a	in the Path of the Ea (and) it
9	ib-il ṣi-in-da-šú	revealed its sign concerning the
10	šá da-na-an mal-ki u KUR-šú	strengthening of the ruler and
11	ú-kal-lim gis-kim-bu-uš	his land. [58]

I am unfamiliar with an omen describing the appearance of Mars in the Path of Ea from either the published omen compendia or from the reports and letters. A bright Mars (ba'ālu) is, however, normally a bad thing. For example, Bulluṭu summarizes the planet's ill quite succinctly:

r. 3	DIŠ ^dṣal-bat-a-nu ú-ta-na-at-ma SIG₅ ib-il-ma a-ḫi-tú	If Mars becomes faint, it is good; if it becomes bright, misfortune. [59]

The planet's general malice extends to its mundane associations; Mars is malevolent, and it is associated with countries that are malevolent to the diviner and his royal clients. In the Great Star List, a celestial divination compendium whose composition is usually dated to the Sargonid Period, the planet is associated with one of the traditional enemies of the Land:

236	^{ul}MAN-ma ^{mul}a-ḫu-ú ^{ul}na-ka-ru	The Sinister, The Strange, The Hostile,
237	^{ul}sar₆-ru ^{ul}ḪUL ^{ul}KA₅.A ^{ul}NIM.MA^{ki}	The Liar, The Evil, The Fox, The Star of Elam.
238	^{ul}ṣal-bat-a-nu	Mars.
239	7 zik-ru-šu	7 are its names. [60]

In the tradition of the Great Star List, then, Mars is to be mundanely associated with Elam. As is the case with many such divinatory associations, however, there are multiple traditions. Thus, the diviner Rašili understands the planet as referring to either of the traditional eastern or western foreign enemies of the Land, and writes the king:

r. 5	^{mul}ṣal-bat-a-nu MUL ^{kur}MAR.TU^{ki}	Mars is the star of Amurru. [61]

In Assur A, Esarhaddon states in no uncertain terms (in contrast to his description of relevant Venus phenomena) that Mars's mundane association is Amurru: ṣal-batānu pāris pursê Amurri, "Mars, the giver of decisions of the land Amurru" (ii 6–7).

In light of the omens cited above, Esarhaddon appears to make a mantically powerful case for the divinely ordained legitimacy of his reign. The stars are right.

---

[58] RINAP 4 57 ii 6–11.
[59] SAA 8 114: rev. 3.
[60] Koch-Westenholz, *Mesopotamian Astrology*, 198–201, lines 236–40.
[61] SAA 8 383: rev. 5.

Nonetheless, the obvious problem with the celestial phenomena observed and reported in Assur A is that they are not, in fact, propitious for Assyria, which is normally identified as Subartu in the mantic tradition; they are, rather, an *eu-angelion* for Syria and the West (i.e., Amurru)! Thus, we are left with two questions. First, why does the king choose to report these particular celestial phenomena and to comment upon them? Certainly there was other notable astronomical activity that could have been featured as the focus of divinatory attention. Second, why does he choose to cite these particular omens to interpret those phenomena? Any celestial diviner—indeed anybody—worth his salt would have noted that Amurru is *not* Assyria. The answer is based, I believe, in this text's propagandistic, *agitative* function, as it was in regard to the positive framing of solar-lunar oppositions (in i 3'–10').

The apodoses of Venus omens feature a range of concerns. Nonetheless, there is an unsurprising focus on agricultural (and occasionally sexual) fecundity. For example, of the seventy-two apodoses found in the so-called "Venus Tablets of Ammiṣaduqa," forty-three deal explicitly with the status of crops or rainfall.[62] Thus the auspicious appearance of the planet at the beginning of the reign of the king is to be taken as a sign that, with his rise to the throne, the land's gods will be reconciled (*sulum ilāniša*) with it, and as a result the goddess plans on rewarding it with ample and secure agricultural produce. This blessing is to be taken, thenceforth, as a mantic given. Subsequent ominous events should be based on the "fact" that the goddess has already visibly shown her approval of Esarhaddon's kingship.

As for the appearance of the red planet in Assur A, a prominent Mars, as stated above, is normally trouble. But Mars' mantic malice is by no means random; rather, it is normally presented in terms of violence (such as the initiation of conflict, particularly with foreign enemies) and as bringing about the destruction of livestock, presumably via disease. In either case, his bright appearance should not be understood in good terms. Nonetheless, Esarhaddon would have his audience believe that the planet's exceptional luminosity at the initiation of his reign is, in fact, a positive omen. The decision/oracle (*purussû*) of even that god has been appropriated by the king. If even Mars is on the king's side, how can anyone be against him? Diviners should take note: the red planet's pervasive pestilence has been purged!

But this inscription's most stunning mantic claim is that, with relation to both the Venus and the Mars omens, Assyria is to be identified with Amurru. No modern commentator to my knowledge has dealt with this identification, and almost every later known mantic association militates against it. Certainly, it is conceivable that

---

[62] Erica Reiner and David Pingree, *Babylonian Planetary Omens Part 1: Enūma Anu Enlil: Tablet 63, the Venus Tablet of Ammiṣaduqa* (BMes 2/1; Malibu: Undena Publications, 1975), 13–14. Crop production and rainfall = apodosis types 1–5, 9, 13, 16, 17, 23–27 (type 1 = omens #2, 6, 12, 15, 30b, 31a, 32ab, 41, 52–55; type 2 = #23b, 27a, 28b, 31b; type 3 = #21; 30a; type 4 = #7, 51; type 5 = #34; type 9 = #1, 57; type 13 = #26b, 28a, 29b, 36, 39; type 16 = #59; type 17 = #8, 9, 17, 18, 46, 47, 50, 60; type 23 = #26a; type 24 = #19; type 25 = #45; type 26 = #5; type 27 = #40). Further examples may be found in *BPO 3*.

lying behind this association is the possible Aramean descent of the Sargonid line, or at the least Esarhaddon's predilection for Harran.[63] Nonetheless, Assyria's consistent divinatory identification in contemporary texts is Subartu, not Amurru. As the Assyrian diviner Nabu-aḫḫe-eriba explains to the king, in what must have been an excruciatingly obvious exegetical moment: anīnu Subartu, "We are Subartu."[64] The diviners are normally not that boorish, however; they typically assume that the king understands the association. As for the normal identification of Amurru, the Babylon-based Assyrian diviner Mar-Issar explains to Esarhaddon:

19	i-su-ri ᴵᵘum-ma-ni ina UGU ᵏᵘʳMAR.TU	Perhaps the scholars can tell
20	me-me-e-ni a-na MAN EN-ía i-qa-bi-i-u	something about the (concept)
21	ᵏᵘʳa-mur-ru-u ᵏᵘʳḫa-at-tu-u	"Amurru" to the king, my lord.
22	ù ᵏᵘʳsu-tu-u šá-niš	Amurru means the Hittite coun-
23	ᵏᵘʳkal-di	try (Syria) and the nomad land
		or, according to another tradi-
		tion, Chaldea.[65]

How, then, should we explain this problem in Assur A? The omen in Esarhaddon's inscription is deliberate and specific. It is not merely a general assertion that the gods favor the king. Since the real knowledge of celestial divination otherwise shown in the inscription is too good, it would be silly to say simply that the king (or his agent composing the inscription) does not know what he is talking about. On the contrary, the king knows precisely what he is doing. In terms of propaganda, the text is to be considered both *integrative* and *agitative*. By establishing that the gods have mantically shown their support for Esarhaddon's reign, the king is presenting himself as the uncontested, divinely approved monarch. This comforting assertion establishes the king's authority and legitimacy and thus serves an *integrative* function. But the specific divinatory claims also *agitate*. The Venus and Mars circumstances serve as examples of how the king expects his diviners to approach ominous phenomena throughout his reign. By appropriating the Amurru association for Assyria, Esarhaddon is stating that all omina, if they are positive, should be considered for application to the king and Assyria regardless of the hermeneutical gymnastics required. And while there would have been skeptics among the diviners regarding the applicability of these omens to the king, Esarhaddon could, in this paradigmatic instance, point to the fact that his reading of the phenomena, however outlandish it might have seemed, played out in reality. To paraphrase the omen: *malku u mātīšu idninū*, "The ruler and his land grew stronger."

---

[63] For a brief discussion of the idea of the Sargonid's Aramean extraction, see Earl Leichty, "Esarhaddon's Exile: Some Speculative History," in *Studies Presented to Robert D. Biggs, June 4, 2004* (ed. Martha T. Roth et al; Chicago: Oriental Institute), 189–91. For Sargonid patronage of Harran, see Steven W. Holloway, *Aššur is King! Aššur is King!: Religion in the Exercise of Power in the Neo-Assyrian Empire* (CHANE 10; Boston/Leiden: Brill, 2001), 388–425.

[64] SAA 8 60:4

[65] SAA 10 351:19–23.

Indeed, Esarhaddon secured his throne and restored the temple to the god Assur. After all, the fulfillment of an oracular fate is the truest test of a prognostication.

THE EFFECTS OF ESARHADDON'S PROPAGANDA: *AGITATIVE ACTION*

Since propaganda's ultimate goal is to motivate groups to undertake specific action that favors the circumstances of the propagandist, it is important to ask if there is any evidence that the community of celestial diviners received Esarhaddon's programmatic assertions and incorporated them into their thought and acted on them. Ideally, I would like to present a detailed statistical analysis of the omens cited for application in the reports to Esarhaddon, with a breakdown including the percentage of positive/negative apodoses correlated with particular celestial diviners and the diviners' respective physical loci. That is, however, outside the scope of this modest study. What I can point to in this limited foray are examples of diviners blatantly breaking the rules of mantic hermeneutics. While these methods of exegesis are admittedly rather flexible, there are, nonetheless, certain rules that tended to be applied nearly ubiquitously, and the diviners themselves were undoubtedly conscious of them.[66] So, when a particular diviner bends or breaks these rules, it is sometimes obvious. And I suggest that in such cases unorthodox mantic practice might be best understood as the diviners' response to royal propaganda.

The diviners in the king's employ were charged to observe and report anything that could be mantically significant, and this often included phenomena that were inauspicious. As the Babylonian diviner Zakir writes:

1	DIŠ 30 TÙR NIGIN-*ma* ^{mul}GÍR.TAB	If the moon is surrounded by a
2	*ina* ŠÀ-*šú* GUB NIN.DINGIR.RA.ME	halo, and the Scorpion stands in
3	*uš-taḫ-ḫa-a* NITA.ME	it: *entu*-priestesses will be made
4	: UR.MAḪ.ME ÚŠ.ME-*ma*	pregnant; men, variant: lions will
5	A.RÁ TAR.ME	rage and cut off traffic.[67]

The omen is clearly negative, and the diviner assumes that his client, the king, will recognize it as such. But Zakir cannot simply push the target of the omen off to a hostile neighboring state (which is another method for diverting an omen's target, as we will see below); while lions/men harassing traffic is a misfortune that could befall any nation, other nations do not have *entu*-priestesses. Nonetheless, the diviner writes that it should cause the king no concern:

6	*it-tum ul ta-lap-pat*	The sign does not affect (us).
r. 1	*áš-šú ma-aṣ-ṣar-tum šá* LUGAL	Because of the king's watch I
2	*ana* LUGAL EN-*ía áš-pu-ra*	wrote to the king my lord.[68]

---

[66] Brown, *Mesopotamian Planetary Astronomy-Astrology*, 157.
[67] SAA 8 307:1–5.
[68] SAA 8 307:6, rev. 1–2.

He does not say just how he arrives at this conclusion, but it is clear that he has casually dismissed the portent as irrelevant. He does note, however, that the sole reason he is reporting it is because it is his responsibility to do so.[69]

Occasionally the unorthodox nature of an oracle is so egregious that even the diviner himself feels the need to explain his interpretive logic. In the much-discussed SAA 10 112, for example, we see the Babylonian celestial diviner Bel-ušezib deliberately adjust the traditional method of interpreting an omen so that it would result in Esarhaddon's favor during a campaign against the Manneans.[70] The diviner discusses the possible oracular significance of the benchmark lunar appearances: the crescent moon at the beginning of the month, and the full moon on the 15th or 16th of the month. The king should be concerned according to the normal rules of omen interpretation:

21	DIŠ 30 NU IGI.LAL-*ma us-ka-ru* IGI-*ir* *nu-kúr*-ME *ina* KUR GÁL.MEŠ	If the moon is not seen but the crescent is seen, there will be hostilities in the land.[71]

As noted in Esarhaddon's mantic program introduced in Assur A (above), the appearance of the full moon on the 15th, rather than the 14th, is not welcome news:

---

[69] See Koch-Westenholz, *Mesopotamian Astrology*, 66. Another Babylonian diviner, Munnabitu, also reflects on his responsibilities to Esarhaddon in SAA 8 316: rev. 12–14:

LUGAL *ṭè-e-mu il-tak-na-an-ni* um-ma EN.NUN-a *ú-ṣur u mim-ma šá ti-du-ú qí-ba-a en-na mim-ma šá ina pa-ni-ía ba-nu-ú ù šá-lam* KUR *ina* UGU LUGAL *be-lí-ía ṭa-a-bu a-na* LUGAL *al-tap-ra*	The king gave an order to me: "Keep watch for me, and whatever you know tell me." Now I have written to the king whatever appears auspicious to me, and the well-being of the land is good, in respect to the king my lord.

While the epistolary context makes Munnabitu's comments admittedly somewhat telegraphic, on the face of it the diviner seems to understand his obligation to the king as reporting strictly propitious omens (see discussion in A. Leo Oppenheim, "Divination and Celestial Observation in the Late Assyrian Empire," *Centaurus* 14 [1969]: 97–135 (114–15); and Koch-Westenholz, *Mesopotamian Astrology*, 65–66). Nonetheless, a brief scan of this diviner's other reports (SAA 8 316–322) shows that he has no qualms about reporting negative omens to the king, even going so far at one point to suggest the performance of a *namburbî* to obviate the oracular fate portended by a lunar eclipse. I am tempted to postulate that, were the order in which these reports were written apparent, we might see a development in regard to how Munnabitu appreciates his role in counseling the king (i.e., towards a more jingoistic character), but this is entirely speculative.

[70] This summary is based on the lengthy discussion in Giovanni B. Lanfranchi, "Scholars and Scholarly Tradition in Neo-Assyrian Times: A Case Study," *SAAB* 3 (1989): 99–114. See also Brown, *Mesopotamian Planetary Astronomy-Astrology*, 157–58; and Koch-Westenholz, *Mesopotamian Astrology*, 148–49.

[71] SAA 10 112:21.

| 23 | UD.15.KÁM 30 u 20 KI a-ḫa-meš IGI.MEŠ | (If) the moon and the sun are seen together on the 15th day: a strong enemy will raise his wea- |
| 24 | KÚR dan-nu ᵍⁱˢTUKUL.ME-šú ana KUR ÍL-a KÁ URU-ka KÚR ina-qar | pons against the land; the enemy will tear down your city gates.[72] |

Now, according to the normal rules of exegesis, the mātu/KUR should refer to Esar-haddon's land (i.e., Assyria; or at the very least, Akkad/Babylonia, which by exten-sion is Esarhaddon's land). The enemy, nakru/ˡᵘKÚR, should refer to foreign enemies of the mātu. Earlier in the letter, however, Bel-ušezib has turned this exegetical principle on its head, indicating to his master in no uncertain terms how the omens to follow should be understood:

4	... ki-i us-ka-ru	Whether it was a crescent, or
5	šu-ú ki-i UD.15.KÁM in-na-mar ù ki-i UD.16.KÁM	whether it appears on the 15th, or whether they (the moon and
6	in-nam-ma-ru lum-nu-um šu-ú ina UGU ᵏᵘʳman-na-a-a	sun) appear on the 16th day, it is an evil portent, and it concerns
7	šu-ú a-šar ˡᵘKÚR ina UGU KUR i-te-eb-bu-ú	the Manneans. Wherever an enemy attacks a country, the
8	KUR ḪUL-nu an-na-a i-zab-bil ...	country will carry this evil por-tent.[73]

Any of the possible lunar phenomena, Bel-ušezib concedes, are negative omina. But the diviner maintains that the king has nothing to worry about, because in such situations the mātu/KUR does not a priori refer to Assyria/Babylonia, but ra-ther, the mātu/KUR is the land that is being attacked, whatever region that happens to be; and that land is to bear the negative consequences of the observed omen. That is to say, in this particular situation Esarhaddon, as the aggressor, is in fact the nakru/ˡᵘKÚR, while the defending nation, Mannea, is the mātu/KUR! This is a dramatic reorientation of the normal hermeneutical conventions. As noted, nor-mally the Land (mātu/KUR) refers to the country of the Mesopotamian monarch, while the foreigner/enemy (nakru/ˡᵘKÚR) is just that; and certainly the original author of the omen intended it this way. Bel-ušezib, however, has twisted the omen rather dramatically. His reading is not a slender alteration of hermeneutics resulting in a subtle alteration of meaning. On the contrary, the diviner completely reverses the application of the omen!

How do we evaluate Bel-ušezib's novelty in interpretation? Lanfranchi main-tains that the diviner was engaging in normal, if pioneering, scholarship.[74] Alterna-tively, Koch-Westenholz suggests the man a "crackpot."[75] While not dismissing these possibilities entirely, I suggest that the diviner was properly responding to Esarhaddon's propaganda campaign. He was finding a way, in spite of the pressure

---

[72] SAA 10 112:23–24.
[73] SAA 10 112:4–7.
[74] Lanfranchi, "Scholars and Scholarly Tradition," 111–14.
[75] Mesopotamian Astrology, 149.

of the interpretive tradition that he inherited, to apply otherwise negative omina to the king's benefit. This does not exclude blatant sycophancy, incompetence, or methodological innovation on Bel-ušezib's part. On the contrary, it contextualizes it.

Another possible example of the effects of Esarhaddon's propaganda can be seen in one of the diviners' reports interpreting the celestial events that took place around the 16ᵗʰ of Adar, 669 BCE, about a decade into Esarhaddon's reign.[76] Both Saturn and a bright Mars, it seems, were observed in a lunar halo. The Babylonian diviner Rašili sees this as good news for the king:

1	DIŠ 30 TÙR NÍGIN-*ma* [2 MUL.MEŠ *ina* TÙR KI 30 GUB.MEŠ]	If the moon is surrounded by a halo, and [two stars stand in the
2	BALA UD.MEŠ [GÍD.DA.MEŠ]	halo with the moon]: a reign of
3	DIŠ 20 *ina* TÙR [30 GUB *ina* KUR *kit-tú* GÁL]	[long] days. If the sun [stands] in the halo [of
4	DUMU *it-*[*ti* AD-*šú kit-tú i-ta-mi*]	the moon: there will be truth in
5	*sa-lam* [*kiš-šá-ti*]	the land], the son [will speak the
6	30 TÙR NÍGIN-*ma* [ᵐᵘˡUDU.IDIM.SAG UŠ *ina* ŠÀ-*šú* GUB-*ma*]	truth with his father; universal] peace.
		The moon was surrounded by a halo [and Saturn stood in it].[77]

First, Rašili deals with the conjunction of Saturn and Mars in the lunar halo, citing an omen that describes two unspecified stars appearing in such a configuration with the moon. The lack of specificity in the omen allows for its application here. Then the diviner cites another omen, whose protasis describes the appearance of the *sun* within a lunar halo, a seemingly impossible event. In a manner typical of the exegesis of the celestial diviners, one celestial feature can be equated with a certain set of other features. This method broadens the possible phenomena to which any particular omen can apply. In this particular case, Rašili has equated the sun with Saturn, a common connection.[78]

The diviner goes on to deal with the other star that was observed in the celestial halo:

7	DIŠ 30 TÙR NÍGIN-*ma* ᵐᵘˡ[*ṣal-bat-a-nu ina* ŠÀ-*šú* GUB]	If the moon is surrounded by a halo, and [Mars stands in it]: loss
8	ZÁḪ *bu-lim ina* [KUR DÙ.A].BI *me-re-*[*šú*]	of cattle; in [the who]le [land] cultiva[ted fields] and dates will
9	*u* ZÚ.LUM.MA NU SI.SÁ	not prosper; Amurru will dimin-
10	ᵏᵘʳMAR.TUᵏⁱ TUR-[*ir*]	ish.
r. 1	DIŠ 30 TÙR <NÍGIN-*ma*> ᵐᵘˡŠUDUN *ina* ŠÀ-*šú* GUB-*iz*	If the moon <is surrounded> by a halo, and the Yoke star stands in

---

[76] For a discussion and summary of the reports related to this, see Koch-Westenholz, *Mesopotamian Astrology*, 140–51, 180–85.

[77] SAA 8 383:1–6.

[78] See the discussion of the logic behind this association in Brown, *Mesopotamian Planetary Astronomy-Astrology*, 69–70.

2	LUGAL ÚŠ-ma KUR-su TUR-ir	it: the king will die, and his land
3	LUGAL NIM.MA^ki ÚŠ	will diminish; the king of Elam
4	^mulŠUDUN ^mulṣal-bat-a-nu	will die.
		— The Yoke star means Mars.[79]

It is the red planet that was seen there, and this might not be good. Rašili cites two omens he believes apply in this situation. In both cases, possible apodoses are quite negative and could cause concern for the king. In the first case, two possible apodoses indicate the loss of livestock and agricultural produce for the whole land. This is not a problem, however, because Rašili ties the possible apodoses to a third that directs these disasters to the west, to Amurru. The second omen describes the appearance of the Yoke star (^{mul}ŠUDUN/nīru, normally equated with Boötes) in a lunar halo, another apparent astronomical impossibility.[80] Again, the first apodosis is terrible: "the king will die, and his land will diminish." But the diviner makes it clear that it is not *the* king and *his* land, i.e., Esarhaddon and Assyria, that will suffer; rather, it is the king of Elam and his land that will. In case it was not obvious by this point, Rašili then states what should have been evident: the Yoke star in this omen is to be identified as Mars.[81]

Rašili then summarizes the results of his reading of the celestial phenomena:

r. 5	^mulṣal-bat-a-nu MUL ^kurMAR.TU^ki	Mars is the star of Amurru; evil
6	ḪUL šá ^kurMAR.TU^ki u NIM.MA[^ki]	for Amurru and Elam. Saturn is
7	^mulUDU.IDIM.SAG.UŠ MUL	the star of Akkad. It is good for
	^kurURI[^ki]	the king [my] lord.[82]
8	SIG₅ šá LUGAL be-lí-[ia]	

As in Assur A, Mars is associated with Amurru—however, in line with orthodox hermeneutics, Amurru is not to be taken as code for Assyria.[83] Rather, the land of Esarhaddon is Akkad, here not to be equated with Assyria *per se* but with Babylonia, over which the Assyrian monarch rules. While Rašili's reading does not overtly respond to the details of Esahaddon's propaganda in Assur A, nonetheless, his desire to interpret celestial phenomena plausibly understood as ominous in an auspicious manner should not merely be taken as soulless toadying. I suggest, rather, that it is the result of the king's multi-faceted propaganda campaign, of which Assur A is but an example, to orient prognostications positively to the monarch's benefit.

If Rašili's hermeneutics, though skewed toward the king, are nevertheless within the spectrum of acceptable mantic practice, the prognostication offered by

---

[79] SAA 8 383:7–10, rev. 1–4.

[80] Cf. MUL.APIN I iv 31–39, i.e., the list of stars in the moon's path does not include this constellation.

[81] This equation also found in the Great Star List (Koch-Westenholz, *Mesopotamian Astrology*, 190–91:102).

[82] SAA 8 383: rev. 5–8.

[83] RINAP 4 57 ii 6–11.

another Babylonian diviner, Šapiku, is exegetically egregious. The diviner begins his reading by noting the full moon on the 16th of the month:

1	DIŠ UD.16.KÁM 30 *u* 20 KI *a-ḫa-meš* IGI.MEŠ	If on the 16th day the moon and sun are seen together: one king
2	LUGAL *ana* LUGAL ḪUL-*tim* KIN-*ár* LUGAL *ina* É.GAL-*šú*	will send (messages of) evil to another; the king will be shut up
3	*a-na* ŠID.MEŠ ITI *ú-ta-sar*	in his palace for the length of a
4	GÌR KÚR *ana* KUR-*šú* GAR-*an* KÚR *šal-ṭa-niš* DU.MEŠ	month; the step of the enemy will be set towards his land; the enemy will march around victoriously.[84]

At first glance, Šapiku seems to be offering the king a negative understanding of this phenomenon. In light of Bel-ušezib's prognostication above (SAA 10 112), I suggest that Šapiku, too, assumes that the *nakru* here should be understood as Assyria, while the *mātu* has to be its enemies, particularly since a full moon on the 16th is a positive omen consistently applied to Subartu/Assyria.[85] The fact that the diviner ends his reading on an overwhelmingly positive note supports this understanding.

Šapiku then applies some of the same omens Rašili applied above, namely, Mars in a lunar halo and the sun in a lunar halo (notably, he does not equate the Yoke/^{mul}ŠUDUN/*nīru* with Mars, as Rašili did).[86] Thus far, the diviner has applied his omens more or less responsibly. But the way in which he concludes his reading is surprising. Šapiku explains to the king, in direct contrast to Rašili's orthodox associations, that Mars stands for Assyria, while Saturn is for Amurru:

7	^d*ṣal-bat-a-[nu* MUL *šá]* ^{kur}SU.BIR₄.KI *ba-'i-il*	Mar[s, the star of] Subartu, is bright and carries radiance; this
8	*ù šá-ru-ru na-ši* SIG₅ *šá* ^{kur}SU.BIR₄.KI *šu-ú*	is good for Subartu. And Saturn, the star of Amurru, is faint, and
9	*ù* ^{mul}UDU.IDIM.SAG.UŠ MUL *šá* ^{kur}MAR.TU	its radiance is fallen; this is bad for Amurru; an attack of an en-
10	*un-nu-ut ù šá-ru-ru-šú ma-aq-tu*	emy will occur against Amurru.[87]
11	ḪUL *šá* ^{kur}MAR.TU^{ki} *ti-ib* <<KUR>> KÚR	
12	*a-na* ^{kur}MAR.TU^{ki} *ib-ba-áš-ši*	

As stated, this is in conflict with the typical associations applied by his colleagues. It is, I would argue, at least a partial response to the propaganda vision of celestial divination presented in Esarhaddon's Assur A. There, Esarhaddon maintained that Mars was the star of Amurru, and that Amurru meant Assyria. After at least a dec-

---

[84] SAA 8 491:1–4.

[85] Cf., SAA 8 82, 102, 111, 177.

[86] SAA 8 491:5–9.

[87] SAA 8 491: rev. 7–12.

ade of identifying Subartu rather than Amurru as Assyria, Šapiku has no desire to make this claim. However, Esarhaddon's other programmatic assertion—that a bright Mars (*ṣalbatānu . . . ib'il*)[88] bodes well for Assyria—is adopted by the diviner and is applied to the astronomical situation in order to create an auspicious reading. This can be understood as a result of effective *agitative* propaganda on Esarhaddon's part.

CONCLUSION: CELESTIAL DIVINATION IN ASSUR A AS PROPAGANDA

If we categorize the Neo-Assyrian royal inscriptions as true propaganda directed toward the literate intelligentsia, we have to identify the desired outcome, the *action* which the particular presentation of celestial divination of the propaganda campaign was intended to provoke in its audience. The most obvious is simply *integration*. The king is presented as the pious recipient of the gods' mantic guidance. The fact that he receives accurate guidance, as evidenced by the successful outcomes of his application of that counsel, indicates that the gods support him. Furthermore, if the gods support him, so should the audience.

I suggest, moreover, that the presentation of celestial divination in the royal inscriptions, such as Esarhaddon's Assur A, was also meant to be *agitative*, that is to elicit specific behavior in his audience. By framing the mantic counsel provided by the gods as always auspicious, it was meant to color future interpretations of mantic phenomena in the king's favor. The cheery prognostications offered Esarhaddon by Zakir, Rašili and Šapiku are, in a sense, rather typical, even if their hermeneutics are sometimes acrobatic. As Koch-Westenholz notes, the celestial diviners of the Neo-Assyrian period demonstrate a certain "tendency to see things from the bright side," framing their readings in a positive light whenever possible.[89] I do not argue with this assessment. I contend, however, that this penchant for optimism is not merely the reflex of an opportunistic or competitive initiative. Rather, the diviners are responding to the propaganda of the crown. Esarhaddon (or his propagandist, i.e., the scholar who composed the inscription) deliberately and systematically calibrated his own image in the royal inscriptions to elicit the specific mantic tone in which he wished the diviners to frame their forecasts. This is a far cry from von Soden's evaluation of Esarhaddon, in which the monarch is a superstitious pawn of manipulative "astrologers."[90] But it is also a modification of Parpola's more cautious appraisal, that Esarhaddon's diviners were primarily guided by their own professional ethics.[91] I propose instead that the diviners were following the lead of their monarch, so that their activity would, perhaps, bring additional

---

[88] RINAP 4 57 ii 6–11.

[89] Koch-Westenholz, *Mesopotamian Astrology*, 144.

[90] Wolfram von Soden, *Herrscher im Alten Orient* (Berlin: Springer, 1954), 125.

[91] Simo Parpola, *Letters from Assyrian Scholars to the Kings Esarhaddon and Assurbanipal, Part II: Commentaries and Appendices* (AOAT 5/2; Neukirchen-Vluyn: Neukirchener Verlag, 1983), XVII–XX.

royal favor. This belief was founded on the king's stated designs, as expressed in such texts as Assur A.

There is more than this, however. In conforming to the agenda set by the king, in acting on his propaganda, the diviners themselves were transformed. As Ellul notes,

> For action makes propaganda's effect irreversible. He who acts in obedience to propaganda can never go back. He is now obliged to *believe* in that propaganda because of his past action. He is obliged to receive from it his justification and authority, without which his action will seem to him absurd or unjust, which would be intolerable. He is obliged to continue to advance in the direction indicated by propaganda, for action demands more action.[92]

Though Ellul's words are rather dramatic, they nonetheless ring true. At first the diviners were not the initiators, but were, rather, the targets of the propagandist; however, when they began to offer readings that mantically confirmed the gods' support for the crown, they too became satellite propaganda agents.[93] They became locally-based, living witnesses of the image the king wished to project.

My evaluation leads to a further issue. I have argued that Esarhaddon could manipulate the mantic system to his benefit, but it is still unclear whether he was a true believer in celestial divination. In Koch-Westenholz's evaluation:

> It has been suggested that ominous events, cleverly manipulated, were cited merely to allay the fears of the rank-and-file soldiers on a campaign, or to justify what the king wished to do anyway. This is most unlikely. Propitious omens may indeed have been put to effective use in royal propaganda; but all available evidence suggests that the kings themselves believed in divination just as sincerely as everyone else.[94]

What I have maintained here is that, more than simply using the academic results of divination for propagandistic purposes, the Assyrian monarch sought to manipulate the results of the mantic process for his own benefit. Can this be reconciled with the idea that Esarhaddon seemed to genuinely believe in the validity of the practice as a method which could reveal the will of the gods?

Though we should always remember that the inner thoughts of any ancient personage are only accessible to us through our reconstructions of their words and deeds, I would answer this question in the affirmative, even in light of this study. As Koch-Westenholz has noted, certain of Esarhaddon's diviners—Balasî and Nabû-aḫḫe-eriba, for example—had no misgivings about offering him negative readings.[95] A large number of letters sent to the Assyrian monarchs originating with *Assyrian* scholars suggest the performance of or offer advice on a *namburbî*. This is witness to the fact that Esarhaddon did not trust all of his diviners equally. Levels

---

[92] Ellul, *Propaganda*, 29.
[93] Similarly, see Liverani, "The Ideology of the Neo-Assyrian Empire," 302.
[94] Koch-Westenholz, *Mesopotamian Astrology*, 161.
[95] Koch-Westenholz, *Mesopotamian Astrology*, 144–45.

of trust were not solely linked to loyalty and scribal competence. The model I present here supposes that Esarhaddon treated his diviners based on the particular ways in which he thought them useful. This fact was recognized previously by Oppenheim; it seems some scholars, for example, were solely responsible for celestial observation *sans* interpretation.[96] Those he was closest to were the ones he took seriously when it came to mantic and ritual matters that were of substance to the well-being of the state. They gave him honest divinatory counsel to which he responded ritually (in terms of performing appropriate *namburbîs*, etc.) and/or in terms of policy, and he compensated them appropriately.[97] Other diviners in the king's employ served as alternative observers of astronomical phenomena and, ultimately, as targets of and eventually agents of the king's propaganda. This is similar to Oppenheim's conclusion, that it was really only the diviners at the central Assyrian court that had influence on the king's policy decisions.[98] But it adds another dimension. While the crown benefited from the data they collected, the interpretations they offered, and any new techniques they developed, the scribes were, as the product of the king's propaganda, the scholarly manifestation of the gods' patronage of Esarhaddon. Their presence in the traditional intellectual centers across the land, such as Babylon, Borsippa, Uruk, Nippur, and Kutha, meant that they had a robust potential as agents of Assyrian propaganda within important administrative circles. This is related to the idea, fully developed by Nevling Porter, that Esarhaddon capitalized on the Babylonian model of ideal kingship for the purpose of maintaining his hegemony in the south.[99] I maintain, however, that this was done more aggressively than via simple patronage of ancient Babylonian institutions, and that the king did not just passively project an image in stone relief and clay tablets. In asserting this desired image in his own inscriptions Esarhaddon actively and systematically encouraged diviners to find mantic justification for his authority.[100]

---

[96] Oppenheim, "Divination and Celestial Observation," 118.

[97] On the matter of compensation, see the brief discussion by Oppenheim, "Divination and Celestial Observation," 115–17 and Brown, *Mesopotamian Planetary Astronomy-Astrology*, 45. As for the *namburbî*, the ritual is only mentioned five times in the reports, three times by Assyrian diviners (SAA 8 71, 82, 206) and twice by Babylonians (288 and 320). The vast majority of references to performing a *namburbî* come, of course, from the letters of the Assyrian scholars (see the index in SAA 10, 349 for references).

[98] Oppenheim, "Divination and Celestial Observation," 120–21.

[99] Porter, *Image, Power, Politics*, especially 77–117.

[100] In a sense, this aspect of the royal inscriptions functions opposite to material such as the *Kuthean Legend of Naram-Sin*, a cautionary tale composed by religious professionals that warned kings to respect the will of the gods as related by diviners so that they would be victorious in warfare (for the text, see Joan Goodnick Westenholz, *Legends of the Kings of Akkade: The Texts* [MC 7; Winona Lake: Eisenbrauns, 1997], 263–368). In contrast, the royal inscriptions caution the diviners that the gods have shown their approval of the king by virtue of his victory on the field of combat. Thus, they should respect the king's divinely mandated authority and interpret the omens "correctly."

2
The King at the Crossroads between
Divination and Cosmology

Beate Pongratz-Leisten

INTRODUCTION

In the last decades, Assyriology has gone to great lengths to divest divination of its magical overtone and redefine it as a form of early science. Jean Bottéro, in his 1974 article "Symptômes, signes, écritures," was one of the first ancient Near Eastern scholars to stress the central position of divination in Mesopotamian intellectual life, and scholars concerned with divinatory texts followed in this vein.[1] The diviners produced treatises of their craft, which in their vocabulary, technical nomenclature, the same procedure and strict order of the analysis, investigation, and explanation showed great uniformity with treatises of other disciplines,[2]

---

[1] This article contains sections from Chapter Nine of my book *Religion and Ideology in Assyria*, in preparation.

[2] Jean Bottéro, "Symtômes, signes, écritures," in *Divination et Rationalité* (ed. J.-P. Vernant et al.; Paris: Éditions du Seuil, 1974), 70–193, 81. See more recently also the contributions by Francesca Rochberg now available in her volume of collected essays, *In the Path of the Moon. Babylonian Celestial Divination and its Legacy* (Leiden and Boston: Brill, 2010 ; see further Niek Veldhuis, "The Theory of Knowledge and the Practice of Celestial Divination," in *Divination and Interpretation of Signs in the Ancient World* (ed. Amar Annus; Oriental Institute Seminars 8; Chicago: The Oriental Institute of the University of Chicago, 2010), 77–91; Eckart Frahm, "Reading the Tablet, the Exta, and the Body: The Hermeneutics of Cuneiform Signs in Babylonian and Assyrian Text Commentaries and Divinatory Texts," in *Divination and Interpretation of Signs in the Ancient World*, 93–141; his *Babylonian and Assyrian Text Commentaries* (Guides to the Mesopotamian Textual Record 5; Münster: Ugarit-Verlag, 2011); and Abraham Winitzer, "Writing and Mesopotamian Divination: The Case of Alternative Interpretation," *JCS* 63 (2011): 77–94.

demonstrating that it was the same universal logic that lay behind all scientific treatises, whether these were on the subject of legislation, medicine, mathematics, musicology, or divination. While such a new modern approach to divination was crucial to our understanding of the ancient theory of knowledge, the categorization of divination as science simultaneously distorted our modern perspective insofar as it separated divination, at least on the surface, from what we categorize as religion, creating an artificial divide between science and religion.[3] Religion is, however, in itself a category that misrepresents ancient cultures by insinuating a divide between the sacred and the profane. By tracing their theory of knowledge back to divine origins, the ancients themselves reveal their framework of thought, namely, that divination originated with the gods and thus was part of the cosmic order.

The cosmic order was conceived as cosmic stability (*kittu*) decreed by the gods and civic order or "straightness" (*mīšaru*) enacted by the king as a means of rendering judgments (*dīna dânu, purussâ parāsu*). The very purpose of the oracles was to gain foreknowledge of and to align any human plans with divine intentionality as it was inscribed into the cosmic scheme. The function of the human legal system was to readjust and restore the civil order as part of the cosmic order.[4] Yet the ultimate judicial authority again lay with the gods who could be appealed to by means of oaths and the ordeal.

The ancient Sumero-Babylonian system of thought conceived of cultural texts such as omen compendia and myth equally as products of divine creation. The *Catalogue of Texts and Authors*[5] and the *Enmeduranki Legend*,[6] both dating to the first millennium BCE, trace the origin of divination back to the gods thus illustrating that line of thought best. However, notwithstanding the message of the colophons affirming that the scribe did not alter the text, there was no notion of a closed canon. Rather, the ancients considered their cultural texts as part of the cosmic truth and stability (*kittu*) determined by divine decree in the mythical past. Such reasoning entails a different notion of the sacredness of the text, as the notion of inalterability applies to the content rather than to the process of textualization of the individual text. The fact that the *Catalogue of Texts and Authors* assigned the knowledge of the exorcist together with the most important omen compendia including *Enūma Anu Enlil* and two major poems dealing with Ninurta's deeds to the god Ea, therefore, is of utmost importance for our understanding of the meaning of

---

[3] Francesca Rochberg, "The Two Cultures and the Historical Perspective on Science as a Culture," *Forum for Public Policy* 2006, which is freely available online at the following URL: http://www.forumonpublicpolicy.com/archive07/rochberg.pdf.

[4] Sophie Démare-Lafont, "Judicial Decision-Making: Judges and Arbitrators," in *The Oxford Handbook of Cuneiform Culture* (ed. K. Radner and E. Robson; Oxford: Oxford University Press), 335–57.

[5] W. G. Lambert, "A Catalogue of Texts and Authors," *JCS* 26 (1962): 59–77.

[6] W. G. Lambert, "The Qualifications of Babylonian Diviners," in *Festschrift für Rykle Borger zu seinem 65. Geburtstag: tikip santakki mala bašmu* (CM 10; ed. S. M. Maul; Groningen: Styx: 1998), 141–58.

the institution of kingship, its interaction with diviners, and ancient historiography. Ninurta in his role as a warrior defending the cosmic order against chaos
epitomized the mission of kingship. Foreknowledge of the will of the gods was crucial to royal performance, as it had to be aligned with the original cosmic scheme.
Coupling divination and the Ninurta mythology in the ancient *Catalogue* inscribed
the mandate of kingship into the cosmic scheme as designed by the gods. This
combination of combat myths and omen compendia further highlights the paradigmatic function of both genres for the cultural debate revolving around the
kings as historical figures. Both genres formed the paradigm for the ancient historiography as represented by the annals, which in a tropological way reiterated the
same great story of the king having contributed to establishing the cosmic order
and thus having met the expectations brought to the office of kingship.[7] In contrast to the modern endeavor to write an event history, historical details represented just additional variations to the plotline as told in the original combat myth.
Myth as a referential system thus formed the matrix of the historical account,[8] and
the omen compendia as an intellectual reflection on rulership per se provided the
paradigmatic framework. It is with that notion of the cultural texts at the interface
between the dynamics of a continuous process of textual production and the authoritative cosmological framework that I will pursue my inquiry into the royal
appropriation of divination.

The Sources

In the ancient Near East, divination probably predated the origin of writing.[9]
Among the various divinatory techniques of extispicy, i.e., examining the entrails
in general, more specifically hepatoscopy, i.e., the examination of the liver, was
the most prominent one, and, according to Oppenheim likely the first to come into
existence. While no omen reports have been transmitted from the early periods,
Early Dynastic profession lists and numerous administrative tablets from Ebla[10]
point to the practice of extispicy performed during the third millennium BCE. The
administrative documents from Ebla listing sheep for the purpose of extispicy not
only reveal that it was practiced on a large scale on behalf of the court, but also
point to the king's sponsorship and patronage of the craft. The close relationship

---

[7] On the notion of tropological narrative see Hayden White, *Figural Realism: Studies in the Mimesis Effect* (Baltimore: Johns Hopkins University Press, 1999).

[8] For this kind of understanding of myth see Hans Blumenberg, *Work on Myth* (Cambridge: MIT Press, 1985) and the excellent essay by Markus May, "Von Blumenberg zu Bloom (und retour): Intertextualität als quasimythologische Struktur," in *Komparatistik als Arbeit am Mythos* (ed. M. Schmitz-Emans and U. Lindemann; Heidelberg: Synchron, 2004), 139–51.

[9] A. Leo Oppenheim, *Ancient Mesopotamia: Portrait of a Dead Civilization* (rev. ed.; completed by E. Reiner; Chicago / London: University of Chicago Press, 1977), 216.

[10] Alfonso Archi, "Divination at Ebla," in *Festschrift Gernot Wilhelm anlässlich seines 65. Geburtstages am 28. Januar 2010* (ed. J. Fincke; Dresden: Islet-Verlag, 2009), 45-56.

between the king and the diviners as royal advisors in cultic, political, diplomatic, and administrative affairs, as illustrated by letters from the Old Babylonian period onward, finds support in the seals of the diviners positioning themselves in direct relation to the king, as illustrated by the seal of Asqudum, diviner to king Zimri-Lim of Mari. For instance: "Zimri-Lim, appointed by the god Dagan; Asqudum, the diviner."[11]

After the mention of divination in the administrative texts from Ebla, several hundred years had to pass before the divinatory practice itself was transmitted in writing, and by the early second millennium BCE three major genres emerged in a short sequence:

1) the liver models from Mari, dating to the early second millennium BCE, known as the so-called *šakkanakku* period, which partially overlapped the end of the Ur III period and survived its collapse for several more decades.

More than half of these omens sound like reports; however, as their verbal forms are in the preterite, they seem to have had a different purpose, which so far has been recognized as didactic but which could equally be paradigmatic, as illustrated by the following examples:

Rutten, *RA* 35, No. 3:

a-mu-ut Na-ra-am-^d*Sîn*	Omen of Naram-Sîn
sá A-pí-sá-al	who conquered Apišal.
il-qá-é	

Rutten, *RA* 35, No. 6:

a-mu-ut	Omen
ṣú-hu-ra-im	of diminishment
si[12] *I-bí-*^d*Sîn*	of Ibbi-Sîn
ba-taq(?) ma-ti-šu i-ba-al-ki-li-šu	against whom a fraction of his country made a revolt.[13]

Support for the suggestion of reading these omens mentioning the kings of the Akkad and Ur III period as exemplary with regard to the office of kingship comes from Hazor where several liver models have been found.[14] The editors of one of these liver models state:

---

[11] Dominique Charpin, "Patron and Client: Zimri-Lim and Asqudum the Diviner," in *The Oxford Handbook of Cuneiform Culture*, 248-69.

[12] Read here as *ší*, the relative pronoun in the genitive.

[13] See Marguerite Rutten, "Trente-deux modèles de foies en argile inscrits provenant de Tell-Hariri (Mari)," *RA* 35 (1938): 36-70.

[14] Benno Landsberger and Hayim Tadmor, "Fragments of Clay Liver Models from Hazor," *IEJ* 14 (1964): 201-218; Wayne Horowitz, Takayoshi Oshima, and Abraham Winitzer, "Hazor 17: Another Clay Liver Model," *IEJ* 60 (2010): 133-45. The text on the Hazor liver model runs as follows:

What is striking about this model with its accompanying text is its similarity not only to the liver model tradition but, more importantly, to the Old Babylonian omen collections from Mesopotamia proper. This is made clear by a review of some of the points already discussed, including: 1) the standard interpretation of the double *manzāzum*/*naplastum*; 2) the explanation of the cleft as a forecast of rebellion on the basis of the set of associations KAK-shape → KAK → sign → *kakku* (weapon) → *bartum* (rebellion); 3) the relation of predictions of darkness/obscurity (< *eṭû*) with the *padānu*; and 4) an example of the "temporal interpretive theme". More-over, in its wording and subject matter, the text follows standard conventions for the Mesopotamian divination tradition (*bārûtu*). Thus, Hazor 17 belongs to the mainstream of the extispicy divination tradition of Mesopotamia.[15]

Hazor 17 shows similarity with the omen collection of the extispicy series (*bārûtu*) attested from Middle Assyrian Assur and other Neo-Assyrian capitals. Further liver models have been found at Ugarit and Ekalte.[16]

The other two genres that originated somewhat later during the Old Babylonian period, i.e., the first half of the second millennium BCE, consist of:

2) omen reports containing either fortunate or unfortunate omens for a particular inquiry and

3) omen compendia, among them the extispicy series (*iškar bārûti*) as the most important one.

Other series were added either already during the Old Babylonian period or later, among them the astrological series *Enūma Anu Enlil*, the series *Šumma izbu* (dedicated to malformed birth),[17] *Šumma ālu* (If a city [is set on high]),[18] and the physiognomic series (*Alamdimmû*)[19] to mention only the most important ones.

During the first millennium ancient scholarship adduced commentaries of all kinds, such as excerpt series, factual commentaries (*mukallimtu*), linguistic commentaries (*ṣâtu*), and explanatory series.[20] Only during the first millennium, an-

---

a) . . .

b) In the afternoon, it will become dark, the enemy I will kill.

c) In the evening, it will become dark, the enemy I will kill.

d) Like the start (opening) of a rebellion.

e) A man will reach the realm of wisdom.

f) A god received the prayer of a man.

[15] Horowitz, Oshima, and Winitzer, "Hazor 17: Another Clay Liver Model," 142.

[16] Jan-Waalke Meyer, *Untersuchungen zu den Tonlebermodellen aus dem Alten Orient* (AOAT 39; Neukirchen-Vluyn: Neukirchner Verlag; Kevelaer: Butzon & Bercker, 1987).

[17] Erle Leichty, *The Omen Series Šumma izbu* (TCS 4; Locust Valley: J. J. Augustin, 1970).

[18] Sally M. Freedman, *If a City is Set on a Height: The Akkadian Omen Series Šumma ālu ina mêlê šakin* (2 vols.; Occasional Publications of the Samuel Noah Kramer Fund 17, 19; Philadelphia: Samuel Noah Kramer Fund, 1998-2006).

[19] Barbara Böck, *Die Babylonisch-assyrische Morphoskopie* (AfOB 27; Wien: Selbstverlag des Instituts für Orientalistik der Universität Wien, 2000).

[20] Such as the excerpt series *Šumma Sîn ina tāmartīšu*, see Niek Veldhuis, "The Theory of Knowledge and the Practice of Celestial Divination," in *Divination and Interpretation of Signs in*

other extispicy series was created known as the *tamītu* oracles addressed to the sun god Šamaš and the storm god Adad.[21] These *tamītu* oracles, while dealing primarily with affairs of private individuals, also contain some historical omens referring to Hammurapi and Samsu-ditana. Unrelated to divinatory practice they were of a purely textual nature and are attested only in copies from first millennium BCE Nimrud and Nineveh.

Since its appearance in writing, divination formed a major part of the scholarly and royal libraries and the temple libraries, with the divination tablets in Assurbanipal's library making up more than a quarter of the holdings thus showing its importance in the ancient world view.[22] A recent and significant advance in Assyriological scholarship has been the distinguishing between omen reports as related to the practice of divination and the definition of omen compendia, by contrast, as purely textual rather than observation-based creations.[23]

For the purpose of my argument this distinction is crucial. The rulers of the ancient Near East, as I will demonstrate, not only made extensive use of divinatory practice for ad-hoc decision-making in daily affairs but also appropriated divination as a system of thought for their ideological self-representation. It is the latter aspect that I will now investigate in more depth with particular attention to divination texts in addition to the royal inscriptions, which have been a subject of inquiry in that regard in my book on knowledge of rulership.[24]

For a better understanding of the royal interest in usurping divination for ideological purposes, two aspects need to be addressed first: 1) the positioning of kingship in the ancient worldview and 2) the meaning of the historical omens.

---

the Ancient World, 77–91, 81–87. For the commentary texts, see Frahm, *Babylonian and Assyrian Text Commentaries: Origins of Interpretation*. For the explanatory texts, see Alasdair Livingstone, *Mystical and Mythological Explanatory Texts of Assyrian and Babylonian Scholars* (Oxford: Clarendon, 1986; repr. Winona Lake: Eisenbrauns, 2007).

[21] W. G. Lambert, *The Babylonian Oracle Questions* (MC 13; Winona Lake: Eisenbrauns, 2007).

[22] Ulla S. Koch, "Sheep and Sky: Systems of Divinatory Interpretation," in *The Oxford Handbook of Cuneiform Culture*, 447–69.

[23] Seth F. C. Richardson, "gir₃-gin-na and Šulgi's 'Library': Liver Omen Texts in the Third Millennium (I)," *CDLJ* 2006/3; online: http://cdli.ucla.edu/pubs/cdlj/2006/cdlj2006_003.html; Seth F. C. Richardson, "On Seeing and Believing: Liver Divination and the Era of Warring States (II)," in *Divination and Interpretation of Signs in the Ancient World*, 225–66; Abraham Winitzer, "Writing and Mesopotamian Divination: The Case of Alternative Interpretation," *JCS* 63 (2011): 77–94.

[24] Beate Pongratz-Leisten, *Herrschaftswissen in Mesopotamien: Formen der Kommunikation zwischen Gott und König im 2. und 1. Jahrtausend v. Chr.* (SAAS 10; Helsinki: The Neo-Assyrian Text Corpus Project, 1999); see also recently Karen Radner, "Royal Decision-Making: Kings, Magnates, and Scholars," in *The Oxford Handbook of Cuneiform Culture*, 358–79.

The Position of Kingship in the Ancient Worldview and Religion

As stated at the beginning of this article, in MesopotamIa, gods and men were equally subject to the cosmic order. Everything and everyone, human or divine, had an assigned place and function.[25] The gods were considered to control the forces of nature and manifest themselves in natural phenomena, and thus contribute to the operation of the cosmic order. The institution of kingship was mandated to uphold the social order through enforcing justice and correct human social behavior so that the cosmic order went undisturbed. Kingship was thus the hub between the social and the cosmic order, and the ideal king was charged with implementing the requirements of civil society as well as securing the cult of and communication with the gods. Natural phenomena—celestial, atmospheric and seismic events such as eclipses, earthquakes, floods, and storms, as well as terrestrial ominous events happening in town and country[26]—were regarded as forms of expression exploited by deities to manifest their intentionality.[27] In that system of thought, in particular contexts and under particular circumstances, the gods could turn all things—animate or inanimate—into conduits for expressing decisions made in relation to human life, which then had to be decoded by divinatory experts.[28] Thus, in astrology and extispicy the constellations and the liver were considered as carriers of divine writing, conveying information regarding human life and cosmic truth (*kittu*). Scholars' references to the celestial phenomena as "heavenly writing" (*šiṭir šamê*) or "writing of the firmament" (*šiṭir burūmê*), and the categorization of the liver as the "tablet of the gods" (*ṭuppi ša ilī*), are indicative of this perspective. Any important action intended by the king, whether of political, administrative, or cultic nature, had to be analyzed for its repercussions for the cosmic order, and, therefore, had to be submitted to divine judgment by means of the diviner's inquiry into the omens inscribed on the liver. The diviner while presenting the inquiry to Šamaš used judicial terminology,[29] asking the sun god Šamaš "to judge the case" (*dīna diānu*) and "put truth" (*kitta šakānu*) into the entrails of the sheep.[30]

---

[25] This notion is reflected best in the Sumerian composition *Enki and the World Order*. Jerrold S. Cooper is preparing a new edition.

[26] A. Leo Oppenheim "Divination and Celestial Observation in the Last Assyrian Empire," *Centaurus* 14 (1969): 97–135.

[27] Anne Marie Kitz, "Prophecy as Divination," *CBQ* 65 (2003): 22–42.

[28] On the cognitive process that discerns between the anatomical or pathological features, their cultural encoding as signs, and interpretation as oracles in extispicy for instance, see Jean-Jacques Glassner, "La fabrique des presages en Mésopotamie: la sémiologie des devins," in *La raison des signes: Présages, rites, destin dans les sociétés de la Méditerranée ancienne* (ed. S. Georgoudi et al.; Religion in the Graeco-Roman World 174; Leiden: Brill, 2012), 29–53.

[29] Bottéro, "Symptômes, signes, écritures," 139–42.

[30] See HSM 7494: 11-12 in Ivan Starr, *The Rituals of the Diviner* (BMes 12; Malibu: Undena Publications, 1983), 30.

In view of the king's pivotal position between divination and legislation it comes as no surprise that we might find historical omens referring to particular kings interspersed between other omina in the omen compendia.

THE MEANING OF THE HISTORICAL OMENS

Historical omens, i.e., allusions to historical persons, are as old as the first recording of omen reports on liver models from Mari dating to the 19th century BCE.[31] As soon as they were discovered, Assyriology began intensely debating the question of their value for historical reconstruction.[32] In 1980, Jerrold Cooper settled the question decisively, arguing that they had no value for reconstructing third millennium history.[33] In Assyriology the liver models from Mari were deemed of didactic purpose in the context of the professional training of the diviners. The fact that they include historical omens referring to the kings of Akkade and the Ur III dynasty as well as to the legendary kings Gilgameš and Etana, however, in my view, links them with the textual production of omen compendia rather than the reports and gives them a paradigmatic purpose. This is further supported by the fact that among the historical omens there are several omens formulated in the past tense rather than the durative, which points to the future:

If there is a 'well being' groove [on the sheep's liver] that is like the squatting of a young bull, it is the omen of Gilgameš, who had no rival.

If the gall bladder is shaped like a lizard, it is the mark of Sargon.

If the heart is like a testicle, it is the omen of Rimush, whom his servants killed with their cylinder seals.

If the fetus is like a lion, it is an omen of Naram-Sîn, who subdued the world.

If the fetus is compact, it is an omen of Ibbi-Sîn: disaster.[34]

---

[31] Rutten, "Trente-Deux modèles de foies," *RA* 35 (1936): 36–52 and pls. 1-18.

[32] J. J. Finkelstein ("Mesopotamian Historiography," *PAPS* 107 [1963]: 461-472, 463) and A. Kirk Grayson, ("Divination and the Babylonian Chronicles: A Study of the Rôle Which Divination Plays in Ancient Mesopotamian Chronography," in *La divination en Mésopotamie ancienne et dans les regions voisines* [CRRAI 14; Paris: Presses universitaires de France, 1960], 69–76) argued for a historical value of these entries. Voices against this approach include Hans G. Güterbock, "Die historische Tradition und ihre literarische Gestaltung bei Babyloniern und Hethitern bis 1200," *ZA* 42 (1934): 47-91 and Erica Reiner, "New Light on Some Historical Omens," in *Anatolian Studies Presented to H. G. Güterbock* (ed. B. Kurt et al.; PIHANS 35; Istanbul: Nederlands Historisch-Archaeologisch Instituut in het Nabije Oosten, 1974), 257–61.

[33] Jerrold S. Cooper, "Apodotic Death and the Historicity of Historical Omens," in *Death in Mesopotamia: Papers Read at the XXVIe Rencontre assyriologique internationale* (ed. B. Alster; Mesopotamia 8; Copenhagen: Akademisk Forlag, 1980), 99–105.

[34] Quoted after Piotr Michalowski, "Commemoration, Writing, and Genre in Ancient Mesopotamia," in *The Limits of Historiography: Genre and Narrative in Ancient Historical Texts* (ed.

These so-called historical omens, attested for the first time in the liver models from Mari and then carried on into the first omen series created during the Old Babylonian period, were transmitted into the first millennium omen compendia. They include references to Sargon and Naram-Sîn, both kings of Akkad, and Ibbi-Sîn, king of Ur, and legendary kings such as Gilgameš and Etana as well as Gušur, first king of Kiš, and Kubaba, founder of the third dynasty of Kiš.[35] The number of the historical omens is minimal compared to the thousands of omens collected in the various omen series. More than fifty percent of the omen entries contained apodoses that were primarily concerned with political and military matters, i.e., the king's involvement with court intrigues, domestic traitors, usurpers, border garrisons, the success of the army in the field, and the loyalty of his populace, officials, vassal kings, and members of the royal family.[36] These omen entries referring to royal action in their entirety provide a rich repertoire of possible constellations and interactions in which a king might find himself involved, and thus can be read as paradigmatic in nature.[37] Numerous apodoses of this kind, with regard to the verbal forms, instead of using the third person to refer to the king, are cast in the first or second person thus invoking the notion of divinatory practice. Yet, rather than interpreting these omen entries as being copied from former oracle reports I would like to argue that the references to kingship in the liver models and in the omen compendia served a purpose entirely different from observational practice, namely, to inscribe royal performance in the authoritative tradition of the mythical past.

The fact that the scholars derived their material for the apodoses not only from historical kings but also from literary sources such as the *Gilgameš Epic* or the *Etana Myth* reiterates the paradigmatic nature of these historical omens.[38] What is more, these historical omens were always interspersed among other apodoses, and until the first millennium they never formed a group of their own. The sparse evidence of the historical omens led Piotr Michalowski to consider them as "vignettes of the past," as "anecdotes lost in a vast ominous landscape."[39] He writes:

C. Kraus; Mnemosyne, bibliotheca classica Batava. Supplementum 191; Leiden / Boston: Brill, 1999), 69–90, 76.

[35] I am grateful to Jean-Jacques Glassner for the discussion of these figures in the omen tradition in his paper "The Diviner as Historian" delivered at our workshop *Ancient and Modern Perspectives on Historiography in the Ancient Near East*, held at ISAW, April 12th, 2013.

[36] Richardson, "On Seeing and Believing," 247.

[37] Similarly Mogens Trolle Larsen ("The Mesopotamian Lukewarm Mind: Reflections on Science, Divination and Literacy," in *Language, History, and Literature: Philological and Historical Studies Presented to Erica Reiner* [AOS 67; ed. F. Rochberg-Halton; New Haven: The American Oriental Society, 1987], 203-25, 212-13), who described them as prescribing legitimate behavior in present and future circumstances.

[38] Ivan Starr, "The Place of Historical Omens in the System of Apodoses," *BiOr* 43 (1986): 628–42, 631.

[39] Michalowski, "Commemoration, Writing, and Genre," 76.

> Of the thousands of such omens known to us today, slightly over 60 are "historical," and these acquire a special status only when they are decontextualized and seriated into modern collections of historiographic data. Omens were an extremely important part of the culture, but they were hardly the privileged repositories of historical knowledge.[40]

Nonetheless Michalowski admits to the importance of Finkelstein's essay[41] in that

> it was the first major attempt to analyze historiography "from the native point of view," rather than as a reflex of modern intuitive concepts. Finkelstein was searching for a sense of the past; he was not interested in whether something actually happened, in the colloquial sense, but rather in the way in which earlier events, real or imaginary, were portrayed. In this way he almost succeeded in separating himself from earlier studies on history writing, which always seemed to return to the point of origin, searching for the original kernel of truth that simply "must" lie hidden behind the textual distortions of history.[42]

Although in the end Finkelstein was also searching for a genre that had a "privileged connection with historical reality," his qualification of the omen texts—and here we should include all the omens referring to royal action—as lying at the root of Mesopotamian historiography has been so far unique and is invaluable for our modern understanding of how the ancients viewed their past.

The Interface between the Historical Omens and Pseudo-Chronicles

The intertextual relationship between the omen compendia containing historical omens and two chronicles, the *Chronicle of Early Kings*, which covers kings from Sargon of Akkad (c. 2334-2279 BCE) until the reign of Agum III (c. 1450 BCE), and the *Weidner Chronicle*, which starts with kings from as early as the Early Dynastic period through the reign of Šulgi (2094-2047 BCE),[43] confirms that the historical omens like any other omens concerned with the king's action were paradigmatic in nature. Both chronicles were composed during the first millennium BCE, and the latter is primarily concerned with the king's incorrect behavior towards Marduk's temple in Babylon. Both chronicles can be considered pseudo-chronicles as they do not provide any valuable information regarding the history of events. Rather, their concern is with potential violations of the cult committed by the kings, which on occasion touch upon the bizarre, as do various historical omens as well.[44]

The exemplary value attached to the early kings of Akkade in the omen compendia and the chronicles further applies to the historical legends, all three of

---

[40] Michalowski, "Commemoration, Writing, and Genre," 76.

[41] See note 32 above.

[42] Michalowski, "Commemoration, Writing, and Genre," 76–77, n. 29.

[43] A. Kirk Grayson, *Assyrian and Babylonian Chronicles* (TCS 5; Locust Valley: J. J. Augustin, 1975), 47.

[44] Reiner, "New Light on Some Historical Omens."

them coalescing around these paradigmatic royal figures who had constructed the "first empire"[45] in history and, therefore had gained universal significance in the cultural memory. Yet it is important to state that in the omen series Sargon and Naram-Sîn mostly appear as fortunate rulers, while legendary tradition created a divide between the two, turning Sargon into the paradigmatic fortunate ruler while the tradition regarding Naram-Sîn was mixed.[46] Overall, the intertextuality between omen compendia, pseudo-chronicles, and literature supports the idea of an entirely text-based—rather than observation-based—composition process with regard to the omen compendia.

With the omen compendia, including their numerous anonymous references to kings and princes and the few interspersed historical omens, as well as the pseudo-chronicles and historical legends the ancient scholars had created a corpus of cultural authoritative texts that inscribed the royal office and royal performance in all its facets in the cosmic order as foreseen by the gods. The world view and the paradigmatic nature of the liver models together with the omen compendia as cultural metaphors for royal performance explain why, under particular historical circumstances, kings should express an interest in appropriating either the practice or the learned textual production of divination for their ideological self-representation. The latter case is exemplified by King Assurbanipal, who not only assembled a vast corpus of omen compendia in his library but also showed a particular interest in the historical omens revolving around the kings of Akkad.

ASSURBANIPAL'S USURPATION OF THE OMEN COMPENDIA

One of the many tablets from Assurbanipal's library at Nineveh contains a compilation of exclusively "historical omens" concerned with the kings Sargon and Naram-Sîn of Akkad. I quote from the first lines of this text:

1. If the gall-bladder completely surrounds the liver, it is the omen of Sargon who by this omen
2. marched on the land of Elam, defeated the Elamites,
3. imposed on them . . . (and) cut off their food supplies.[7]
4. If the gall-bladder completely surrounds the liver and [its[7] to]p[7] falls upon it; the gall bladder hangs down
5. it is the omen of Sargon, who marched on the land of Amurru,
6. defeated the land of Amurru, and conquered the entire world.
7. If the right side of the liver is four times as thick as its left side[7], and the caudate lobe lies on top of it,
8. it is the omen of Sargon who by this omen . . . dominion over Babylon.
9. He removed soil from the . . . gate and . . . named it Babylon.

---

[45] See Mario Liverani (ed.), *Akkad: The First World Empire: Structure, Ideology, Traditions* (HANES 5; Padova: Sargon, 1993).

[46] Joan Goodnick Westenholz, *Legends of the Kings of Akkade: The Texts* (MC 7; Winona Lake: Eisenbrauns, 1997).

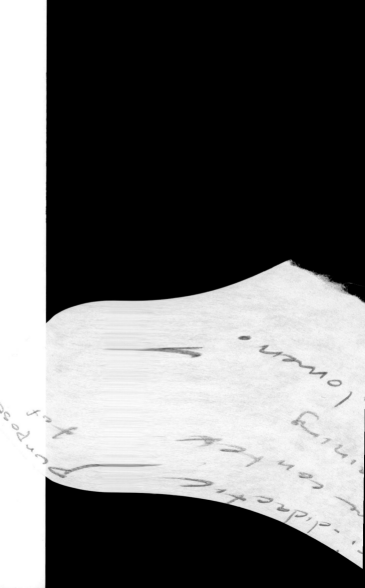

10. [In front of[7]] Akkad he built (another) city, and named it [Babylon].
11. [. . .] he settled [therein[7]].[47]

Assurbanipal is not only famous for presenting himself as an intellectual conversant in divination in his colophons.[48] This tablet with an assemblage of historical omens concerned with the kings Sargon and Naram-Sîn of Akkad demonstrates the cultural significance Assurbanipal associated with these kings who had entered the historiographic tradition as epitomes of imperial politics from the Old Babylonian period onward and whose legends circulated at the courts of the Sargonid kings. In addition to this omen collection two other texts from Assurbanipal's reign reveal the king's interest in the historical kings mentioned in the omen compendia: one is a letter which lists historical omens concerned with Assurbanipal and Šamaš-šum-ukīn (Rm 2, 455) to be discussed below, and the other is an omen text (Rm 2, 134), written in Neo-Babylonian script, which refers to the kings Assurbanipal, Hammurapi and Itti-Marduk-balāṭu and also dates to the reign of Assurbanipal.[49]

The letter (Rm 2, 455) written to the king in the aftermath of his war against Tammarītu II of Elam was sent by a diviner who asks the king in which form he should enter the apodosis referring to Assurbanipal's victory over the Elamite king. It represents a unique testimony to the king's aspiration of not only being accepted in the ranks of scholarship but to obtain his place as paradigmatic king in ancient historiography as well. Unfortunately, the obverse is very badly preserved, and so I will confine myself to rendering a translation of the preserved section on the reverse:

Rev.
1. [Omen for Assurbani]pal, mighty king, reverent prince, of whom (it is said) Ištar (walks) at the side of his a[rmy]
2. cut off [the head of Teumman, king of Ela]m in the midst of battle and the son of Bēl-iqīsha
3. . . . . -tuk of the Elamite they hung around his neck, and Assurbanipal
4. [went to Nineve]h, his royal residence. They were exulting joyfully and performed music,
5. the messenger[7] of Ummanigash, king of Elam, he killed in front of Assurbanipal, king of the universe,
6. and he sat on his throne. Assurbanipal, king of the universe, at the command of
7. [. . .] Tammarītu, king of Elam, together with his magnates
8. rolled before him [in?] Nineveh, his royal residence.

---

9. [whom Assur and] Ištar love and lead with their full content, and Tammarītu

---

[47] K.2130:1–11, see Starr, "The Place of Historical Omens," 635.

[48] Hermann Hunger, Babylonische und assyrische Kolophone (AOAT 2; Kevelaer: Butzon & Bercker; Neukirchen/Vluyn: Neukirchener Verlag des Erziehungsvereins, 1968), nos. 100 and 101.

[49] Starr, "The Place of Historical Omens," 630.

10. who had plotted for help of Šamaš-šum-ukīn, he himself, the diviner and his magnates
11. went and kissed his feet, Tammarītu and the diviner accused each other in front of him.

---

12. [If . . . the right and left side of the station are . . . it is the omen of Assurbanipal, king of the universe, (of whom it is said) that Šamaš and Ištar walk at the side of his army and
13. killed (his enemies) in the midst of battle and effected their defeat.

---

14. [If . . .] in the lift of the head of the right lung there is a sign/omen (predicting) the annihilation of the army, it is an omen of Šamaš-šum-ukīn,
15. [the treacherous brother, who] fought against the army of Assurbanipal, the beloved of the great gods, (but) was defeated.
16. . . . they seized in the midst of battle and . . . in front of Assurbanipal, king of the universe.
17. [omen of?] Šamaš-šum-ukīn, unfavorable.

---

18. [I have sent] to the king my lord, [the omens from the *bārû*]*tu* series, which I have previously excerpted from the series.
19. The king my lord may see the earlier ones, these are the omens of the king, my lord.
20. [Whatever is] acceptable to the king, my lord, we will enter into the series . . . of Tammarītu
21. [who] plots for help of Šamaš-šum-ukīn.
Edge
22. . . . we have written for the omens of Tammarītu.
23. May . . . of your gods . . . [50]

With his demand to be entered into the omen series, king Assurbanipal revived the tradition of historical omens, which is last known to have been applied to King Itti-Marduk-balāţu (1139-1132 BCE), a king of the Second Dynasty of Isin, in a text that likewise dates to Assurbanipal's reign, i.e., the seventh century BCE.[51] The crucial aspect of Assurbanipal's demand reflected in the letter of the diviner is that he knew about the tradition of historical omens, i.e., entering kings' individual names into the apodoses, and that he deemed it important to be included in the line of exemplary kings known as imperial figures in the omen compendia including Sargon and Naram-Sîn of Akkad as well as Gilgameš and others. The letter of the diviner is unique in various ways: it is the latest example of an historical omen to be entered into the omen series of extispicy (*iškar bārûti*); it confirms that although there existed a notion of a standardized corpus of the established extispicy

---

[50] Theo Bauer, *Das Inschriftenwerk Assurbanipals* (AB nf 1-2; 2 vols.; Leizpig: Hinrichs, 1933), 85–87.

[51] An extispicy text written in Neo-Babylonian script (Rm 2, 134) mentions the names of Assurbanipal, Hammurapi, and Itti-Maduk-balāţu, see Ivan Starr, "Historical Omens Concerning Aššurbanipal's War Against Elam," *AfO* 32 (1985): 60–67.

series together with various commentaries,[52] the compilation process remained dynamic and subject to change; it also provides direct insight into the significance Assurbanipal in particular assigned to the omen series, and conveys intriguing information about his aspirations to rank among the paradigmatic kings of Mesopotamian history.

This usurpation of the omen compendia differed fundamentally in its function from the practice of taking omens, as it did not serve the immediate goal of promulgating the message that the individual king's reign or intended actions had found divine approval, and that the king, consequently, had met the expectations linked with the ideal type of kingship. Rather, by inscribing himself into the authoritative and paradigmatic corpus of the omen compendia, Assurbanipal had stepped outside the system of communication with the gods as controlled by the diviners and turned himself into the epitome of the ideal king acting in compliance with the cosmic order (kittu).

Such development was fostered by the scholars of Nineveh who had also undertaken some editing of the bārûtu series with regard to "creating pairs of omens so that 'right' / 'left' in the protases correspond to 'the king' / 'the enemy' in the apodoses,"[53] thus combining their competent copying from Babylonian predecessors with the creation of a new composition that put the king at center stage. What is more, the version of the bārûtu series that dates to the reign of Assurbanipal contains two omens "which state that 1) Sargon defeated Elam and 2) Sargon enlarged his palace,"[54] considered in reality to be deeds of Assurbanipal rather than Sargon II and reveals commonalities with the tablets 14–16 of the series "interpretation" (Multābiltu), which again contains omens referring to Assurbanipal.[55]

All this evidence and the hitherto unattested "orientation tablet" assigning to each subsection of the liver and the lung the designation "right" and "left" which bears Assurbanipal's colophon claiming that he wrote the tablet in the assembly of the scholars,[56] and the fact that commentaries and excerpts from commentaries might contain illustrations of the kakku and padānu features of the liver or parts of

---

[52] Francesca Rochberg, "Continuity and Change in Omen Literature," in Munuscula Mesopotamica: Festschrift für Johannes Renger (ed. B. Böck et al.; AOAT 267; Münster: Ugarit-Verlag, 1999), 415–27; Frahm, Babylonian and Assyrian Text Commentaries; Veldhuis, "The Theory of Knowledge and the Practice of Celestial Divination."

[53] Ulla Jeyes, "Assurbanipal's bārûtu," in Assyrien im Wandel der Zeiten: XXXIXe Rencontre Assyriologique Internationale Heidelberg 6.-10. Juli 1992 (ed. H. Waetzoldt and H. Hauptmann; Heidelberger Studien zum Alten Orient 6; Heidelberg: Heidelberger Orientverlag, 1997), 61–65, 63.

[54] Jeyes, "Assurbanipal's bārûtu," 63, who notes "[o]men 1 of K.2130 (obv. 1-3) refers to the defeat of Elam and omen 8 (obv. 27-29) refers to the enlargement of the palace."

[55] Jeyes, "Assurbanipal's bārûtu," 64 with reference to Jean Nougayrol, "Note sur Barûtu, Chapitre X Tablette 15" Iraq 31 (1969): 59-63, 59.

[56] Jean Nougayrol, "Le foie 'd'orientation' BM 50494," RA 62 (1968): 31-50, 34-36; for the most complete one see CT 31 1-5. For the colophon see Hunger, Babylonische und assyrische Kolophone, no. 318 (Asb. type b).

the lung—obviously meant to facilitate the king's reading[57]—are further tokens of Assurbanipal's direct involvement in the re-creation of the scholarly divinatory texts belonging to the stream of tradition.

CONCLUSIONS

My discussion of the king's appropriation of the scholarly take on divination as expressed in the omen compendia has been dominated by the fact that divination and myth—combat myth in particular—as the two strategies of ancient interpretation appear side by side in the first millennium text of the *Catalogue of Texts and Authors* as the creations of the god Ea. The god Enki/Ea, as is well-known from a variety of myths, played a crucial role in guaranteeing the communication between the divine and human worlds and in supporting the divine hero and warrior (Ninurta, Marduk) in situations of crisis with his magic knowledge. In my view the association of divinatory and magic knowledge as well as combat myth forms part of a larger ancient framework of thought on the mechanisms that fueled the office of kingship. It also reveals the responsibilities of the individual king, and, simultaneously, determines the range and constraints of interpretation modern scholarship can bring to Assurbanipal's appropriation of the omen compendia, as much more than self-aggrandizing or propaganda was at stake. Assurbanipal was not the first Sargonid king to refer to divination as the overall scheme framing his royal actions. When planning the restoration of Marduk's temple in Babylon and the refurbishing of the statues of the Babylonian gods whom Sennacherib had taken to Assyria after his destruction of Babylon, King Esarhaddon evoked the regular course of the stars as the system of reference to assure the world of his rightful action:

> In order to triumph (and) to show overpowering strength, he (the god Marduk) revealed to me good omen(s) concerning the (re)-entering of Esagil. The stars of heaven stood in their positions and took the correct path (*harrān kitti*) (and) left the incorrect path (*harrān lā kitti*). Every month, the gods Sîn and Šamaš together, at their appearance, answered me with a firm "yes" concerning the renewing of the gods, the completion of the shrines of the cult centers, the lasting stability of my reign, (and) the securing of the throne of my priestly office. (RINAP 4 48: 57b-61a)

With this statement the Assyrian king anchors his actions in the cosmic regularity of the heavens (*harrān kitti*). It not only reveals once more Esarhaddon's deep involvement with the practices of astrology and astronomy as already known from

---

[57] Jeyes, "Assurbanipal's *bārûtu*," 63; for illustrated *padānu* commentaries see CT 20 23, 25, 26, 28, 29, CT 20 27-28 (K.4069) + CT 20 21 (81-2-4, 397); Ki 1904-10-9, 100. Illustrated *hašû* commentaries are: CT 31 38-40; K.3967*, 81-2-4, 443*.

his correspondence with the astrologers but equally reflects a world view that considered kingship as an integral constituent of the cosmic order.

Royal appropriation of omen practice to make their individual reign successful, on the one hand, and royal appropriation of the textual stream of tradition as represented in the omen compendia to turn themselves into paradigmatic models of kingship, on the other, thus stand out as cultural key strategies used by these two kings to reflect a notion of cosmic order in which divine intentionality and human (i.e., royal) agency were inextricably intertwined.

3
Divination as Warfare:
The Use of Divination across Borders*

Jonathan Stökl

INTRODUCTION

Astrology, hepatoscopy and prophecy were commonly used by ancient Near Eastern rulers in order to acquire access to information from the divine spheres so that they could improve their own decisions.[1] Divination is, thus, an enterprise that saw most of its activity within the borders of a state. Indeed, few diviners and few practitioners of ecstatic religion seem to be overly concerned with foreign events unless they directly impact on local events, whether the diviners are central or marginal.[2] Simplifying I. M. Lewis' distinction between central and margin-

* The research for this paper was carried out while I was a post-doctoral researcher at the ERC project Babylon at Leiden University, under the aegis of Dr. Caroline Waerzeggers. I would like to thank Dr. Waerzeggers for her support while writing this paper. I would also like to thank Alan Lenzi and the anonymous reviewer for their comments to an earlier draft.

[1] Beate Pongratz-Leisten, *Herrschaftswissen in Mesopotamien: Formen der Kommunikation zwischen Gott und König im 2. und 1. Jahrtausend v. Chr* (SAAS 10; Helsinki: The Neo-Assyrian Text Corpus Project, 1999) .

[2] For the terminology of central and marginal diviners see I. M. Lewis, *Ecstatic Religion: An Anthropological Study of Spirit Possession and Shamanism* (Pelican Anthropology Library; Harmondsworth: Penguin, 1971 [more easily available in the second {Routledge, 1989} and third {Routledge, 2003} editions]). Where Lewis uses the term "prophet" I prefer "diviner," see the discussion in Jonathan Stökl, *Prophecy in the Ancient Near East: A Philological and Sociological Comparison* (CHANE 56; Leiden: Brill, 2012), 7–14; Martti Nissinen, "Prophecy and Omen Divination: Two Sides of the Same Coin," in *Divination and Interpretation of Signs in the Ancient World* (ed. Amar Annus; OIS 6; Chicago: Chicago University Press, 2010), 341–51.

al diviners, one might say that central diviners speak in favor of the political system and marginal prophets challenge that system.

Lewis may, however have been too quick in positing this difference, inasmuch as so-called "marginal" diviners challenge the political system of the state—they do not tend to challenge the political power of the group to which they belong. In other words, marginal diviners can be understood as supporting an alternative centrality, and in terms of that alternative centrality, they operate like central diviners. In effect, their predictions and announcements against the state can be understood as attacking not so much the central governing group of "their" state, but the outside group which they want to challenge and overcome.

While this may be the case in general, this paper will be looking at what may be construed as the opposite case: central (i.e. state) diviners of one country who address the ruler of another. As we shall see, their messages usually are worded in the same way that the deity would address the king or elite of the country in which their main sanctuary was located. This implies that they regarded their authority as including the other king's sphere of influence: elements of foreign policy can thereby be understood to be turned into a form of domestic policy of the deity speaking—and with it, the domestic policy of the king in whose realm housed the deity's main sanctuary.[3] Thus, we will see that Addu of Kallassu, a form of Adad whose main sanctuary was in the neighboring state of Yamḫad, centered on Aleppo, makes demands of Zimri-Lim, king of Mari.[4] A case in point is the famous letter FM 7 39, in which Addu of Kallassu addresses Zimri-Lim as if the latter were answerable to him in the same way as King Ḫammurapi of Yamḫad. Another example of this kind of behavior can occasionally be found in war (see, e.g., the Rab-šāqê's [henceforth, Rabshakeh] speech to the Jerusalemites), where the local chief deity is claimed to support the aggressor against the local king. Thereby, the aggressor becomes the protector of the local deity, and the extension of their will—the role ancient Near Eastern kings would normally claim to fulfill with regard to the deities in their lands. By extension, this claim can therefore be regarded as the claim by the invading forces that they are the legitimate rulers of the region.

In the following, I will give examples for these two kinds of "inter-/intra-national divination" from Mari and from the Hebrew Bible. I am not aware of such claims from within the Neo-Assyrian corpus, even if one of the cases preserved in the Hebrew Bible occurs in the part of 2 Kings that narrates the events of the interactions between Judah and the Neo-Assyrian empire. The Hebrew Bible attributes Davidic qualities to a number of non-Judean rulers and it can safely be

---

[3] For some explorations of such ideas see Jonathan Stökl, "(Intuitive) Divination, (Ethical) Demands and Diplomacy in the Ancient Near East," in *Mediating Between Heaven and Earth: Communication with the Divine in the Ancient Near East* (ed. C. L. Crouch, Jonathan Stökl, and Anna Elise Zernecke; LHBOTS 566; London: T & T Clark, 2012), 82–92.

[4] It is customary to use "Addu" for the Syrian form and "Adad" as the Akkadian form of the name of the storm god; see, e.g., Daniel Schwemer, "The Storm-Gods of the Ancient Near East: Summary, Synthesis, Recent Studies," *JANER* 7 (2007): 121–168 and *JANER* 8 (2008): 1–44.

assumed that this way of understanding history theologically was influenced by a more common understanding of the way in which "inter-/intra-national divination" was seen to work. Indeed, this structure is the basis for the claim to universal oversight of history and the world by any deity, and presents therefore one of the pre-conditions to the development of monotheism.

The Roman ritual *evocatio* which is linked to siege warfare presents us with a good structural parallel of how religion is used not only to influence one's own troops but also how it can be used as a tool in warfare—essentially claiming that the local deity is in support of the Romans' action and that, therefore, the locals should not oppose the Romans.[5] The parallel of the ritual only occurred to me after the initial idea regarding the Near Eastern material, but as it will be new to most of the readers of these lines I will start by discussing it to give the basic structural outline. The Mesopotamian and biblical examples—which go beyond the Roman example as they also relate to peace-time diplomacy—will be discussed afterwards. The aim is to uncover one of the contributing factors of the development of the idea of deities claiming universal rulership and authority.

THE ROMAN RITE OF THE *EVOCATIO*

While the historicity of the Roman rite *evocatio* ("calling out, evocation") is not entirely ensured, the idea, the concept of it is well-established in ancient literature so that we can use it as a parallel case for what I am about to suggest also for the ancient Near Eastern data. In the *evocatio* rite itself, the Romans would—whether only in literature or also in reality—perform a ritual in which the local deity was called out of the attacked city and promised a new temple cult in Rome, or in the later forms, at least a new cult in their own city.[6] In either case they were

---

[5] Further structural parallels could be found in the evocation ritual by the Hittites after they had devoted a city to the storm-god, i.e., to total destruction, which in Roman terms would be a separate ritual, the *devotio*. The Hittite ritual, CTH 423, has most recently been edited by Francesco Fuscagni, "Rituale di evocazione per gli dei di un villaggio nemico (CTH 423)," [accessed 17 July 2013]. Available online at: http://www.hethport.uni-wuerzburg.de/txhet_besrit/intro.php?xst=CTH%20423&prgr=&lg=IT&ed=F.%20Fuscagni; Daniel Schwemer, "Fremde Götter in Hatti: Die hethitische Religion im Spannungsfeld von Synkretismus und Abgrenzung," in *Ḫattuša-Boğazköy: Das Hethiterreich im Spannungsfeld des alten Orient. 6. Internationales Colloquium der Deutschen Orient-Gesellschaft 22.–24. März 2006, Würzburg* (ed. G. Wilhelm; CDOG 6; Wiesbaden: Harrassowitz, 2008), 137–58. Most ancient Near Eastern examples cited here are similar but vitally different in that they take place *after* the city has been conquered, and therefore the gods have little choice before the battle is decided. Rather, the outcome of the battle is seen as proof of their decision. In addition, some of the Hittite evocation rituals serve the purpose to call out the deity from wherever they might be at the time so that it can inhabit the new cult-image prepared for them; thus, the rituals may share a name, but their purpose is markedly different.

[6] For the *evocatio*, see Gabriella Gustafsson, *Evocatio Deorum: Historical and Mythical Interpretations of Ritualised Conquests in the Expansion of Ancient Rome* (Acta Universitatis Upsaliensis

called upon to support the Roman case, and thereby the Romans were undermin-
ing the religious basis of the city's resistance against them. A number of historians
of ancient Rome claim that the Romans themselves did not really believe in their
own propaganda, and that it is done purely in order to undermine the morale of
the local population. It seems to me that this does not take sufficiently into account the ambiguity with which the Romans viewed relation between religion and
politics, as can been seen in their interactions with ominous signs. If the Romans
had been as cynical about the institution of augury in general as is sometimes argued, it is very unlikely that they would have maintained the office of augur, and,
indeed, indicted augurs who did not carry out their duties correctly.[7]

The Roman ritual known as *evocatio* invited the local deity to abandon their
local temple and the city and to come to Rome to join the Roman empire. In effect,
the ritual turned the local deity into a Roman deity, and resistance to the Roman
legions was then understood by the Romans not only as rebellion against Roman
military might but also as a religious transgression against a Roman deity. The rite
was performed by priests who "lured" the patron deity to Rome by promising
them a greater cult there than the one they currently enjoyed in their city (Pliny,
Nat. hist. 28.18-19). The earliest attestation of the rite is usually taken to be the
siege of the Etruscan city of Veii in 396 BCE, where the Roman commander invited
Juno—or more precisely Uni—the patron deity of Veii, to join the Romans in order
to later take up her new home in Rome itself (Livy, *Ab urbe condita* 5.21-23).[8] After
the ritual inviting the deity out of their new home, the Romans would determine
whether the deity had accepted their invitation through the use of hepatoscopy.
According to Gabriella Gustafsson, the purpose of the ritual was not as such to in-
vite the deity to Rome, but rather, to sever the links between a city and its patron
deity.[9] While I would argue that it is indeed likely that the severing of the link
between a city and its patron deity was a key aspect, it also seems unlikely that the

---

Historia Religionum 16; Uppsala: Uppsala University Press, 2000); V. Basanoff, *Evocatio: Étude
d'un rituel militaire Romain* (Bibliothèque de l'École des Hautes Études; Sciences religieuses 61;
Paris: Presses universitaires de France, 1947); H. S. Versnel, "*evocatio*," *DNP* 4: 329 ET *BNP* 5:
251-52; Mary Beard, John North, and Simon Price, *Religions of Rome* (Cambridge: Cambridge
University Press, 1998), 1:132-34; John S. Kloppenborg, "Evocatio Deorum and the Date of
Mark," *JBL* 124 (2005): 419-50.

    [7] One modern historian who regards the attitude of the Roman elite about their reli-
gion as cynical is John North (*Roman Religion* [Greece and Rome: New Surveys in the Classics
30; Oxford: Oxford University Press, 2000], 76-77), but see Beard, North, and Price, *Religions of
Rome*, 1: 99-108. It is possible that in the first century CE religious views became more cynical
(Beard, North, and Price, *Religions of Rome*, 1: 117-19).

    [8] See Friedhelm Prayon, "Uni," *DNP*, 12/1: 1003 ET *BNP* 15: 112. The fact that Uni was
identified with Iuno and that both Uni and Iuno were identified with Astarte may be the
reason that initially Astarte of Carthage was not called out (*evocata*) but placated ("exorata"),
thus Beard, North, and Price, *Religions of Rome*, 1: 82-83. Only in the third Punic war did the
Romans "evoke" the goddess of Carthage.

    [9] Gustafsson, *Evocatio Deorum*, 80.

Romans would have understood the fact that the deity had become Roman as insignificant. Indeed, it seems as if Gustafsson is constructing false opposites here when distinguishing between the two interpretations, which are really like two sides of the same coin.

Macrobius discusses the *evocatio* in his Saturnalia:

> *They all departed, abandoning their shrines and altars*
> *The gods who had made this realm stand fast . . .*[10]

This statement concerns both the Romans' most ancient custom and their most secret rites. For it is commonly understood that all cities are protected by some god, and that it was secret custom of the Romans (one unknown to many) that they were laying siege to an enemy city and were confident it could be taken, they used a specific spell [= *carmen*] to call out the gods that protected it, because they either believed the city could otherwise not be taken or—even if it could be taken—thought it against divine law to hold gods captive. That is why the Romans themselves wanted both the god responsible for protecting Rome and the Latin name of the city itself to remain unknown. Yet the god's name was included in some of the ancients' books—though they disagree among themselves—and for that reason the range of opinions on the matter is familiar to those who delve into ancient beliefs and practices. For some believed the god was Jupiter, others Lua, some Angerona, who calls for silence by putting her finger to her lips, still others—whom I'm more inclined to trust—said that she is Ops Consivia. But even the most learned men have not learned the name of the city itself, since the Romans were wary of suffering themselves what they knew they had often inflicted on enemy cities, should the name of their protector-god become known and allow their enemy to summon it forth.

We should see to it, however, that the mistake some have fallen into not confuse us too—I mean the belief that a single spell both summons the gods from a city and devotes the city to destruction. For I have found both spells in Book 5 of Serenus Sammonicus' *Secret History*, and he says that he found them in the very ancient book of a certain Furius.[11] The following is the spell used to call the gods forth when a city is surrounded and under siege:

> *I call upon the one in whose protection are the people and community of Carthage, whether it be a god or a goddess, and upon you above all, who have undertaken to protect this city and people, and ask you all for your favor: may you all desert the people and community of Carthage, leave their sacred places, tem-*

---

[10] Macrobius quotes these words from Virgil's Aeneid (2.351-52). Further on (*Sat.* V.22.7), however, Macrobius writes that Virgil derived the concept of the deities of a conquered city abandoning it from Euripides' play *Trojan Women* (25-27), where similar words are attributed to Poseidon (Macrobius, in fact, says that Apollo speaks them but that is likely to be a slight slip).

[11] According to Robert A. Kaster, *Macrobius: Saturnalia* (Loeb Classical Library 510-12; 3 vols; Cambridge/London: Harvard University Press, 2011-12), II: 67, the text is *IAH* 1:29-30 = fr. 1 *IAR*[6], and the Furius in question is L. Furius Philus, who was a friend of Scipio, the Roman general who conquered Carthage in 146 BCE.

> *ples, and city, and depart from them, and upon this people and community heap*
> *fear, dread, forgetfulness, and come to Rome, to me and my people, with kindly*
> *spirit, and may our sacred places, temples, city be more acceptable and ap-*
> *proved in your sight, and may you be well disposed to me and the Roman people*
> *and my army. If you all should do these things so that we know and understand*
> *them, I vow that I will make temples and games for you.*

The same words should be used in offering a sacrificial victim and inspecting the meaning of entrails, so that they give a guarantee of the future. On the other hand, once the divinities have been called forth, cities and armies are devoted to destruction with the following words, which only dictators and generals are able to use for the purpose. (*Sat.* III.9.7-8)[12]

It follows that by either inviting the foreign deity to Rome or by at least persuading the deity to give up their concern for their city, the Romans were in effect claiming that the deity was either one of their many patron deities, which means that the conflict they were engaged in was really a domestic conflict, as the city of a patron-deity that was Roman surely was conceived to belong to the Roman Imperium. Or at the very least, the deity was no longer linked to the attacked city, so that its inhabitants could no longer consider themselves protected by their patron deity—a powerful incentive to stop fighting the Romans.[13]

DIVINING ACROSS BORDERS IN MARI

There are two main examples for "inter-/intra-national divination" in the Mari texts. In the first, Addu of Kallassu demands that Zimri-Lim provide him with a piece of real estate almost as a reward for divine support during Zimri-Lim's campaign to regain his ancestral throne. The other is the claim by Yarim-Lim that "the gods" had told him that he may not hand over some local kings who were seeking asylum in Yamḫad. The second is not, strictly speaking, addressed to Zimri-Lim of Mari, but to Yarim-Lim of Yamḫad, and therefore is not really an example of international divination. But it is included here because the deity addresses issues between the two kings that hover between the international and intra-national. We begin our discussion with this latter example.

The Asylum Affair

We have a significant amount of diplomatic correspondence from Mari.[14] Shortly after a conflict with their overlord, King Zimri-Lim of Mari, some of his

---

[12] The translation is from Kaster, *Macrobius: Saturnalia* vol. II: 65–69.

[13] The fact that the *evocatio* was often followed by a *devotio* in which the city was razed and its inhabitants sold as slaves does not, in and of itself, change the basic image drawn above.

vassal-kings fled into the neighboring kingdom of Yamḫad. Yamḫad had been a large kingdom for a while with considerable control of the region around Aleppo, including the upper Euphrates and the lucrative trade routes to the Phoenician coast.[15]

We do not know the exact background to the letters in question, but in a letter to Yarim-Lim Zimri-Lim accuses Dadi-Ḫadun, one of his vassal-kings, of having called him "brother" rather than "father," as would have been appropriate (FM 7 1).[16] What might seem insignificant to the casual modern reader is in fact an expression of insubordination, as "brother" in the diplomatic nomenclature of the ancient Near East referred to someone of equal status. A vassal would be addressed as "son," and an overlord as "father." In other words, the vassal king is not accused of a minor offense but of failing to recognize Zimri-Lim's overlordship, which is tantamount to insurrection. This vassal-king seems to have fled to Yamḫad in an attempt to avoid Zimri-Lim's revenge. Zimri-Lim writes to Yarim-Lim, addressing him as "my father" (*abīya*) and requests that Dadi-Ḫadun[17] be handed over to him.

In his response to Zimri-Lim, Yarim-Lim acknowledges the seriousness of the offense, interrogates Dadi-Ḫadun, and orders him to write letters to Zimri-Lim, addressed as "to my father and lord" (*ana abīya u bēlīya*). He even makes him and other vassal-kings swear an oath of allegiance to Zimri-Lim in the temple of Addu at Aleppo.

In a different letter, however, we get some further details. FM 7 8 contains the report by another of Zimri-Lim's courtiers, Dariš-libur, to his king. He writes that at first Yarim-Lim said that he will not extradite the vassal-kings who are looking for refuge in his kingdom.[18] Indeed, when Zimri-Lim and Dariš-libur remain insistent, Yarim-Lim says:

---

[14] On the diplomatic correspondence in the Old Babylonian period see, e.g., Jack M. Sasson, "On Reading the Diplomatic Letters in the Mari Archives," in *Amurru 2: Mari, Ébla et les Hourrites: Dix ans de travaux, Deuxième Partie, Actes du colloque international (Paris, mai 1993)* (ed. Jean-Marie Durand and Dominique Charpin; Paris: ERC, 2001), 329–38; Bertrand Lafont, "Relations internationales, alliances et diplomatie au temps des royaumes amorrites," in *Amurru 2: Mari, Ébla et les Hourrites*, 213–328; and most recently the insightful essay by Andrew R. Davis, "'Answer me Properly!': Diplomatic Strategy and Subterfuge in the Treaty Texts from Mari," *Ancient Near Eastern Studies* 50 (2013): 243–54.

[15] For a (political) history of the Old Babylonian period see Dominique Charpin, "Histoire politique du Proche-Orient Amorrite (2002-1595)," in *Mesopotamien: Die altbabylonische Zeit* (ed. Pascal Attinger, Walther Sallaberger, and Markus Wäfler; OBO 160/4; Fribourg: Academic Press/Göttingen: Vandenhoeck & Ruprecht, 2004), 25–480.

[16] For this letter see Jean-Marie Durand, *Florilegium marianum VII: Le culte d'Addu d'Alep et l'affaire d'Alahtum* (Mémoires de N.A.B.U. 8; Paris: SEPOA, 2002), 4–7.

[17] According to Wolfgang Heimpel, *Letters to the King of Mari: A New Translation, With Historical Introduction, Notes, and Commentary* (MC 12; Winona Lake: Eisenbrauns, 2003), 533, Dadi-Ḫadun is identical to Dadi-Ḫadnu.

[18] For an edition of the letter and the others in this dossier (FM 7 1–9), see Durand, *Le culte d'Addu d'Alep*, 3–29.

Has Zimri-Lim forgotten the command of Addu? Indeed, I fear that Zimri-Lim does
not know that in the Land of Addu a refugee cannot be extradited! (lines 25-29)

The expression "command of Addu" (*ṭēm Addu*) suggests that this information was
acquired through some form of divination. While the oracle—whether gained
through prophecy or a different divinatory discipline must remain open—was directed at the customs of the kingdom of Yamḫad, and primarily a matter for interior policy, it had obvious ramifications for Yamḫad's foreign policy. The fact that
Yarim-Lim attempted to maintain the right to asylum in his kingdom even though
the people seeking asylum had started an insurrection against his protégé Zimri-Lim indicates that the regard for the "command of Addu" was genuine.[19]

   It is impossible for us to know whether Yarim-Lim's final change of heart regarding this matter—he does extradite the rebellious chiefs to his vassal Zimri-Lim—is the result of another oracle or whether he simply decided to ignore the
divine command by his chief deity.[20] For our question it is interesting, however, to
see that divinatory oracles were used not only for interior politics but also to justify behavior that would otherwise be difficult to understand.

The Alaḫtum Affair

   Zimri-Lim had a real-estate portfolio in the kingdom of Yamḫad throughout
his reign.[21] The reason for his purchase of villages in his neighbor's kingdom appears to have been to make the court in Mari independent of deliveries of luxury
goods, particularly of wine and oil. At some point in the tenth year of his reign (=ZL
9′) when Ḫammurapi had succeeded his father Yarim-Lim as king of Yamḫad, he
acquired a village called *Alaḫtum*.[22] In spite of the change of king around the time

---

   [19] It is interesting to note that the contemporary Hammurapi also uses religious reasoning in his diplomatic correspondence, see Davis, "'Answer me Properly!'" 249–50, who
quotes ARM 26 469, in which Hammurapi tells Zimri-Lim that he cannot swear the oath for a
diplomatic alliance between them because the day that was set aside for that is ominous in
connection with the moon-god Sîn.

   [20] As is evident by the fact that Mari and Ešnunna agreed on a peace-treaty in spite of
oracles to the contrary (ARM 26 197, 199, 202), divinatory oracles could be ignored, or at
least over-ridden if the circumstances demanded it. See Dominique Charpin, "Le contexte
historique et géographique de prophéties dans les textes retrouvés à Mari," *BCSMS* 23 (1992):
22–25; Jack M. Sasson, "The Posting of Letters with Divine Messages," in *Florilegium marianum
II: Recueil d'études à la mémoire de Maurice Birot* (ed. Dominique Charpin and Jean-Marie Durand; Mémoires de N.A.B.U. 3 / Supplément à N.A.B.U. 1994 no. 2; Paris: SEPOA, 1994), 305-
306.

   [21] For a historical mise-en-scene of the entire "*Alaḫtum*-affair" see Durand, *Le culte
d'Addu d'Alep*, 59–148. Charpin, "Histoire politique," 230 suggests that Alaḫtum is Alalaḫ, and
that is a possibility, but none that can be proven positively, see Durand, *Le culte d'Addu d'Alep*,
65–66.

   [22] This Ḫammurapi should not be confused with the king of Babylon of the same name

of Zimri-Lim's purchase, everything appears to have gone smoothly. Indeed, Nur-Sin, a Mariote emissary to the court of Ḫammur-Rapi of Yamḫad had already organized the cultivation of the fields around Alaḫtum. But the Queen-Mother Gašera seems to have chosen that moment in time to complain to Ḫammurapi, her son, that she had not agreed to the sale/relinquishing of some of her land. Nur-Sin writes a long somewhat despondent letter to his king Zimri-Lim in which he informs him of the proceedings (FM 7 36).

The letters containing prophetic messages from Addu to Zimri-Lim, also sent by Nur-Sin should be read in this context. Nur-Sin writes that he has been approached by male and female prophets (*āpilum/āpiltum*) of Addu of Kallassu, and that their message is for Zimri-Lim.[23] In the message, Addu demands to be given a piece of real estate near Alaḫtum—in all likelihood the piece demanded by Gašera. In return for obeisance, symbolized by the gift of this piece of real estate, Addu promises to support Zimri-Lim, and to give him "land upon land." In case Zimri-Lim should decide not to give the land, Addu threatens Zimri-Lim with being deposed.

We would expect this kind of message, especially using the language of parental protection in a royal oracle within a state, as we find them, for example, in some of the prophetic oracles from the Neo-Assyrian empire.[24] But we might not expect a deity from one country to utter oracles of—conditional—support for a foreign king. Effectively, Mari relied on the support from Yamḫad so that one could argue that Addu of Aleppo and Addu of Kallassu were not addressing a foreign king as such but that they were operating within their sphere of influence. On the surface, this model differs somewhat from the episode of Rabshakeh (2 Kgs 18-19, Isa 36) and Pharaoh Necho (2 Chr 35). There the attacker marching through the attacked country claims that the local deity gave them the authority to do so (even if this situation is transmitted in texts of the invaded nation). Here we see the king of Yamḫad and his deity Addu claiming authority over Mari, but the text originates with Aleppine prophets and is transmitted by a Mariote ambassador. No (direct) military threat accompanies these actions, nor is it the Mariote goddess Ekallatum or a Mariote form of Addu who speaks. What these two somewhat different forms of divinatory communication share, however, is the claim to power and influence over a foreign area as expressed through divine authority.[25]

---

at the same time. See Charpin, "Histoire politique," 230–31 for some further information. Since we have no Old Babylonian texts from Aleppo itself all our knowledge is dependent on outside sources. Charpin, "Histoire politique," 230 suggests that Alaḫtum is Alalaḫ; while that is possible, it cannot be proven positively, see Durand, *Le culte d'Addu d'Alep*, 65–66.

[23] FM 7 39.

[24] E.g., SAA 9 2.5, where lines iii 26'-28' read: [26']*anāku abbuka ummaka* [27']*birti agappīya urtabbīka* [28']*nēmalka ammar* ("I am your father [and] your mother! Between my wings I will raise you! I will see your success!").

[25] Dominique Charpin, "Prophètes et rois dans le proche-orient Amorrite: nouvelles données, nouvelles perspectives," in *Florilegium marianum VI: Recueil d'études à la mémoire*

Aaron Tugendhaft sees a similar model at play in the related letter FM 7 38.[26] In this letter, Nur-Sin transmits a prophetic oracle from Addu of Aleppo to Zim-ri-Lim in which the deity claims that he supported Yaḫdun-Lim, Zimri-Lim's ancestor on the throne of Mari, in all his battles until Yaḫdun-Lim abandoned Addu. According to the oracle, Addu's revenge to this betrayal was swift and enacted by the Šamši-Adad, the king of the short-lived Empire of Upper Mesopotamia. The deity goes on to demand that he be consulted on all decisions regarding military campaigns. Tugendhaft's interprets this as indicating that the Aleppine court gets to decide whom Mari should attack and when.[27] While Tugendhaft's interpretation is likely to be correct within the scope of Old Babylonian realpolitik my aim in this paper is a study of theological constructions, and from that perspective Addu of Aleppo claims that his authority transcends the borders of the kingdom of Aleppo.[28]

A further letter, FM 6 18, sent to Zimri-Lim by his vassal Sumu-Lanasi contains the opposite case.[29] Sumu-Lanasi attributes Zimri-Lim's successful bid to power not to Addu of Aleppo but to "the god of your father," presumably Itur-Mer. But Sumu-Lanasi does not stop there. A few lines below he attributes also his own successful capture of his ancestral throne to Itur-Mer.[30] Sumu-Lanasi thereby puts himself in precisely the position that the message of Addu of Aleppo aims to establish between Yarim-Lim and Zimri-Lim.

CROSS-BORDER DIVINATION IN THE HEBREW BIBLE

The Pharaoh as Prophet?

2 Chronicles 35 retells the narrative of Josiah's reform also found in 2 Kgs 23 and his death at the hands of Pharaoh Necho in Megiddo, adding one episode that

---

d'André Parrot (ed. Dominique Charpin and Jean-Marie Durand; Mémoires de N.A.B.U. 7; Paris: SEPOA, 2002), 7-38, see in particular pages 23-25 and 28-31.

[26] See Aaron Tugendhaft, "Baal and the Problem of Politics in the Bronze Age" (Ph.D. diss., New York University, 2012), 63-120. FM 7 38 has the museum number A.1968 and is sometimes referred to it as that in the secondary literature. For the text see Durand, Le culte d'Addu d'Alep, 134-37. I would like to thank Aaron Tugendhaft for making available to me a copy of his excellent thesis prior to publication.

[27] Tugendhaft, "Baal and the Problem of Politics," 99-100.

[28] Charpin, "Prophètes et rois," 31 and Durand, Le culte d'Addu d'Alep, 2-3.

[29] Tugendhaft, "Baal and the Problem of Politics," 82-85 discusses this text and points out the brilliant rhetorical strategy employed by Sumu-Lanasi.

For the text, see Jean Robert Kupper, "Dans les jardins de Carkémish," in Florilegium marianum VI: Recueil d'études à la mémoire d'André Parrot (ed. Dominique Charpin and Jean-Marie Durand; Mémoires de N.A.B.U. 7; Paris: SEPOA, 2002), 195-200.

[30] Lines 18-22 read: "Now, the god [of my lord] Zimri-Lim is strong and he has set me on the throne of the house of my father."

is of interest for our enterprise here. In vv. 21–22, Necho sends word to Josiah that he does not want to attack the Judeans; rather, his army is marching northward in order to attack the Babylonians. He adds "it is God's will that I hurry. Refrain, then, from interfering with God who is with me, that he not destroy you" (v. 21). The following verse shows Josiah stubbornly refusing to heed Necho's warning: "But Josiah would not let him alone; instead, he sought[31] to fight him, heedless of Necho's words from the mouth of God; and he came to fight in the plain of Megiddo." It is clear, as all the commentators say, that the Chronicler inserted the episode in order to explain why Josiah, the faultless king, died in battle shortly after his reforms.[32]

Presumably, the Chronicler painted a picture that at least the author himself thought credible enough: the idea that God would transmit a divinatory message to Josiah via Necho and his messengers must therefore have been acceptable to his readers. As a consequence we can take seriously the theo-political construction that the Judean deity YHWH can communicate with the Judean king via another king.[33] It is almost as if Necho was co-opted into the Judean court as one of Josiah's prophets. The fact that Necho is Pharaoh makes this observation all the more peculiar, as he stands for the oppressing "house of slavery" (בית עבדים; Exod 20:2). As we shall see, however, the Chronicler's Pharaoh is not the only unlikely candidate to be granted a status close to that of a servant of YHWH. He shares that status with Cyrus, Nebuchadnezzar, and the Assyrian Rabshakeh.

---

[31] This term is normally translated as "he disguised himself." I see no reason to assume that the authors of a text as late as 2 Chronicles 35 were not capable of the somewhat more complicated syntax with להלחם בו depending on התחפש, even if the finite verb would normally be much closer to the dependent infinitive

[32] Whether or not these reforms ever took place is not at issue, since we are concerned with the literary construction here. On Josiah's reform see Ze'ev Herzog, "Perspectives on Southern Israel's Cult Centralization: Arad and Beer-sheba," in *One God, One Cult, One Nation: Archaeological and Biblical Perspectives* (ed. Reinhard G. Kratz and Hermann Spieckermann; BZAW 405; Berlin: de Gruyter, 2010), 169–99; Rainer Albertz, "Why a Reform Like Josiah's Must Have Happened," in *Good Kings and Bad Kings* (ed. Lester L. Grabbe; LHBOTS 393 / ESHM 5; London: T & T Clark, 2005), 27–46; Christoph Uehlinger, "Was There a Cult Reform Under King Josiah? The Case for a Well-Grounded Minimum," in *Good Kings and Bad Kings*, 279–316.

[33] The overwhelming majority of commentators is of the opinion that the deity mentioned here is Judah's god YHWH. Compare e.g. Ralph W. Klein, *2 Chronicles: A Commentary* (Hermeneia; Minneapolis: Fortress, 2012), 525-26. But see Sara Japhet, *I & II Chronicles* (OTL; London: SCM, 1993), 1056, who thinks that the god in 2 Chr 35:21 refers to the statue of a deity whom Necho brought along from Egypt, while in v. 22 'God' refers to Judah's deity. H. G. M. Williamson, *1-2 Chronicles* (NCBC; Grand Rapids: Eerdmans, 1982), 410-11 does not comment on the question at all.

Rabshakeh as YHWH's Prophet

2 Kings 18–19 and Isaiah 36–38 both contain a narrative of the siege of Jerusalem in 701 BCE by the Assyrians. The chief cupbearer (*rāb-šāqê*) says to the Judean officials, "do you think I have marched against this land to destroy it without YHWH? YHWH himself told me, 'Go up against that land and destroy it'" (2 Kgs 18:25; similarly Isa 36:10).

In effect, what Rabshakeh says (on behalf of Sennacherib) to the Judeans is that their deity commanded the Assyrians to take Jerusalem. This tactic, which was also used by the Romans is regarded as a means of psychological warfare, an attempt to undermine the locals' conviction that their deity is protecting them.[34] It is also, of course, the inverse of the principal by which a nation could understand its own loss of independence. There are several examples in ancient Near Eastern texts in which a defeat and subsequent loss of the statue of their deity was rationalized as the deity wanting to go on vacation to see the sights or to go on a business trip or that the deity was angry with the local population for one reason or another.[35] Rabshakeh, therefore, tries to convince all those who are listening to him speaking in "Judean" (v. 26) that from a religious point of view, their city is already lost and that giving up would be to obey YHWH, their own deity.

The model by which a deity commands the hand of a foreign king used to be thought of as something peculiar to the Hebrew Bible, particularly when applied to Nebuchadnezzar II as "YHWH's servant" (עבד יהוה; Jer 25:9, 27:6, and 43:10) and Cy-

---

[34] Peter Dubovský, *Hezekiah and the Assyrian Spies: Reconstruction of the Neo-Assyrian Intelligence Services and its Significance for 2 Kings 18–19* (BibOr 49; Rome: Pontifical Biblical Institute, 2006, 19–20, 229–38 argues that the Neo-Assyrians do the same thing in their conflict with Hezekiah. On pp. 161–88 he discusses the use of psychological warfare in the campaigns by Tiglath-Pileser III and Sargon II in Babylonia. In the cases of the Neo-Assyrian interventions in Babylonia, Dubovský includes several different kind of actions, not all of which I would refer to as psychological warfare. Bribing of enemies with promises of future tax relief (pp. 161–68) is certainly part of the actions of a secret service, but addresses to the masses to undermine their confidence in their rulers and gods seems to me to be closer to actual forms of psychological warfare.

[35] See, e.g., J. J. M. Roberts, "Nebuchadnezzar I's Elamite Crisis in Theological Perspective," in *Essays on the Ancient Near East in Memory of Jacob Joel Finkelstein* (ed. Maria deJong Ellis; Memoirs of the Connecticut Academy of Arts and Sciences 19; Hamden: Published for The Academy by Archon Books, 1977), 183–87. Morton Cogan assembled some Neo-Assyrian references to local deities supporting the Assyrians rather than the local population in his *Imperialism and Religion: Assyria, Judah and Israel in the Eighth and Seventh Centuries BCE* (SBLMS 19; Missoula: Scholars Press, 1974), 9–21. I would like to thank Jacob Wright for pointing this reference out to me. On this question see also his "The Deportation of Jerusalem's Wealth and the Demise of Native Sovereignty in the Book of Kings," in *Interpreting Exile: Displacement and Deportation in Biblical and Modern Contexts* (ed. Brad E. Kelle, Frank Ritchel Ames, and Jacob L. Wright; Atlanta: Society of Biblical Literature, 2011), 105–33, especially 121–24.

rus as "his/my anointed" (ל/משיחו; Isa 45:1).[36] The notion was that this revolutionary new idea allowed Judeans to maintain their ethnic identity and thereby enabled Yahwistic religion to prosper. As intimated above, we know that the idea was a common ancient Near Eastern thought model that allowed theologians to rationalize defeat. What is special in the case of the Hebrew Bible in this context is that Deutero-Isaiah seems to develop this idea in the context of a monotheistic understanding of YHWH.[37] The different theological context gives the same basic structure its new and far-reaching impact.

Returning to the question of prophetic divination used as a means of warfare, we can state that referring to YHWH is a form of psychological warfare akin to the use of leaflets or propaganda radio in more recent conflicts.[38] Unlike the more modern forms of warfare, appeal to the deity serves to underline the attacker's claim. From the point of view that the Judeans had a treaty with the Assyrians and that Hezekiah rebelled against the stipulations of that treaty, it is likely that the Assyrian's claim that YHWH commanded him to wage war against Judah would make factual and "historical" sense as well. If Judah had some form of contractual understanding with Assyria, it is likely that the treaty included treaty curses. In such a circumstance, both Judean and Assyrian ideologues and theologians would have understood the Assyrian's action as the carrying out of the curses, which would have been understood to have been enforced by at least Assur and YHWH.[39] Thus, Rabshakeh's claim that YHWH himself told him to "go up against that land and destroy it" would be exactly what both sides should expect after the Judean breach of the agreement. The fact that Rabshakeh explicitly mentions it (at least in

---

[36] In Isa 45:1 the Septuagint has the better text: τῷ χριστῷ μου = למשיחי. For a short discussion of the matter and some secondary literature regarding the references to Jeremiah as the servant see Jonathan Stökl, "Nebuchadnezzar: History, Memory and Myth-Making in the Persian Period," in *Bringing the Past to the Present in the Late Persian and Early Hellenistic Period: Images of Central Figures* (ed. Ehud Ben Zvi and Diana Edelman; Oxford: Oxford University Press, 2013), 257–69; for a discussion of the implications of Isa 45:1, see Joseph Blenkinsopp's contribution to this volume (page 135).

[37] Saul M. Olyan, "Is Isaiah 40-55 Really Monotheistic," *JANER* 12 (2012): 4 has recently questioned the monotheistic nature of Dtr-Isa, but in my view it is easier to assume that idioms from the polytheistic past are still being used in a monotheistic environment. A good example of this kind of thing can be seen in Psalm 82, which undoubtedly uses the imagery of the divine council, but only in order to demote all its members apart from YHWH.

[38] On the use of radio as a means of propaganda in the Second World War see, e.g., M. A. Doherty, *Nazi Wireless Propaganda: Lord Haw-Haw and British Public Opinion in the Second World War* (International Communications; Edinburgh: Edinburgh University Press, 2000).

[39] As is well-known, the Sefire treaty includes treaty curses sworn by and enforced by the deities of both sides, Sefire A 14-42, see Joseph A. Fitzmyer S.J., *The Aramaic Inscriptions of Sefire* (Rev. ed.; BibOr 19/A; Rome: Pontifical Biblical Institute, 1995). In his study of Assyrian Religion in its imperial enterprise, Cogan points to several texts in which Neo-Assyrian rulers claim that deities had abandoned rulers, e.g., OIP 2 64: 22–24 ("their gods abandoned them, rendering them helpless" referring to the several rebellious cities on the border to Qummuḫ; Cogan, *Religion and Empire*, 11).

the literary memory of the events as transmitted in 2 Kings) suggests that he thought that it would give him a strategic advantage.

CONCLUSIONS

Above, we have looked at several cases in which divination, prophetic and probably technical, was used or referred to in the diplomatic correspondence of several ancient kingdoms and empires. This shows that the earliest prophetic texts known to us today show how divination is used in inter-state relations. In cases of conflict, such as we see the message of Rabshakeh to the Judeans, as well as the Roman religious-military rite of the *evocatio*, the foreign power claims that the local patron deity is communicating with them, and that the patron deity commands them to take control of the city and its inhabitants.

Divine support in the form of an oracle to take command of a deity's earthly dominion is usually claimed by usurpers or other kings whose succession is less than obvious.[40] Zimri-Lim is a good example for this, as he had to conquer his ancestral throne before he could become king of Mari. Similarly, when the Romans claimed that the patron deity of a city supports them, they are essentially claiming the city to be part of their rightful dominion. Likewise, Rabshakeh claims that by breaking their loyalty oath to the Assyrians, the Judeans had essentially forfeited the right to self-governance (even if that is not exactly what happened—but we have to keep in mind that the story is transmitted to us via Judean writings and memory).

The situation is slightly different in the case of Necho and the examples from Mari, as the lines of communication and the transmitted message are different. Necho is the most obscure of the cases debated here. YHWH uses Necho as a megaphone to tell Josiah not to attack him. If the story had been transmitted in Egyptian texts we could claim that this act by YHWH in effect transmitted political authority over Judah to Necho. But the fact that it is used by the Chronicler to explain Josiah's untimely death—particularly after Manasseh's unexpectedly long life—indicates that it is not Necho's authority that is strengthened but YHWH's, whose control over history was thought to extend to include Necho and the Egyptians. Rather than the Egyptians taking over Judah, it therefore symbolizes YHWH taking over Egypt.

The Old Babylonian correspondence between Yarim-Lim, king of Yamḥad (Aleppo), and Zimri-Lim, king of Mari, regarding the asylum seekers can be understood as an attempt by Yarim-Lim to protect the religious and cultural tradition to

---

[40] For this, see, e.g., Stephanie Dalley, "Old Babylonian Prophecies at Uruk and Kish," in *Opening the Tablet Box: Near Eastern Studies in Honor of Benjamin R. Foster* (ed. Sarah C. Melville and Alice Louise Slotsky; CHANE 42; Leiden/Boston: Brill, 2010), 85–97; Jonathan Stökl, "Ancient Near Eastern Prophecy," in *Dictionary of the Old Testament: Prophets* (ed. J. Gordon McConville and Mark J. Boda; Downers Grove: IVP Academic, 2012), 16–24.

offer asylum within his kingdom—presumably Zimri-Lim himself had benefited from exactly this tradition after Šamši-Adad conquered Mari early in Zimri-Lim's life. Zimri-Lim, however, wants to make sure that there is no further insurrection against his rule by the tribal groups and their chiefs in his kingdom; therefore, he wants to make sure that he can punish these chieftains. While Yarim-Lim holds out for some time, in the end he gives in and extradites the chieftains. Yarim-Lim uses a divine command as an explanation for holding out against Zimri-Lim's request, meaning that he argues that he is bound to uphold the right to asylum by "Addu's command." Yarim-Lim invokes Addu's command not only because Addu is his patron deity, but also because Zimri-Lim himself is bound to the deity and his support when he acquired his ancestral throne.

This is expressed by Nur-Sin's letters to Zimri-Lim, in which various hypostases of Addu remind Zimri-Lim of this support and claim various rewards for their support. There is the piece of real estate, Alaḫtum, and there is the typical bit of royal ideology that the king ought to protect the rights of those wronged. The fact that Aleppine forms of Addu can communicate with Zimri-Lim in the way that they do indicates that they understood him as a king under their command, which in turn essentially turns the communication between them and Zimri-Lim into a domestic political affair.

We have seen that divine communication, by whichever means, is used in international politics in the ancient Near East in order to change the power dynamics from one in which two unrelated neighbors interact with each other to one in which both sides claim support in some shape from the local patron deity. This, in turn, changes the power dynamics of foreign politics into those of internal politics, which is used to legitimize the actions of both parties. To put it bluntly: Rabshakeh ceases to be a representative for the foreign Assyrian king and turns into a representative of the Assyrian king, who is the earthly representative of YHWH. Thus, divination used in foreign affairs can have significant ramification for the rhetoric, but also the actions taken by each side.

4
Revisiting Biblical Prophecy, Revealed Knowledge Pertaining to Ritual, and Secrecy in Light of Ancient Mesopotamian Prophetic Texts

Alan Lenzi

Five years ago, in my work on secret knowledge in ancient Mesopotamia and Biblical Israel, I suggested a fundamental distinction between the treatment of secret, revelatory knowledge in ancient Mesopotamian sources and the same in biblical sources.[1] In the Mesopotamian sources, revealed knowledge was kept secret, guarded by a small cadre of elite scribal scholars who served the king. In the biblical representations[2] of such, revealed knowledge was not guarded; rather, it was openly available to all who could read or hear it. I aligned this distinction in the treatment of revealed knowledge to the geopolitical standing of Mesopotamia vs. ancient Israel/Judah: Mesopotamian texts came from a sphere with a long-standing tradition of political and military hegemony; biblical texts arose from politically minor and subservient powers. In formulating these conclusions, I compared the treatment of the most important revealed textual corpora in the two spheres: the scholarly revelatory traditions in Mesopotamia that served the royal

---

[1] I wish to thank Jeff Cooley, Jonathan Stökl, and Tyler Yoder for their critical comments on a previous draft of this essay. I alone, however, bear responsibility for the ideas and formulations contained herein.

[2] I use the words "representation" and "presentation" here purposefully to distinguish between the historical reality in ancient Judah/Israel and the literary presentation. This is a distinction that I employed in SAAS 19 but, in retrospect, did not maintain carefully enough in the chapter on prophecy (chapter 4). See the third section below.

courts (i.e., extispicy, exorcism, celestial divination, etc.)[3] and the literary representation of Judean/Israelite ritual legislation in the Bible (i.e., materials in the Priestly source, Deuteronomy, and Ezekiel—disregarding in some respects their original *Sitz im Leben*).[4]

Because the biblical ritual legislation was revealed to a prophet—a kind of diviner—in all three major corpora (i.e., Moses, as presented in Exodos 6–7 and Deuteronomy 5, and Ezekiel, as presented in Ezekiel 1–3), I examined biblical representations of prophets to understand how this informed the authorization of mediators of revealed knowledge pertaining to ritual in the Bible. For the present purposes, the point of interest in my treatment of prophets is the one I based on the work of John Holladay. In his article "Assyrian Statecraft and the Prophets of Israel" Holladay claimed that the role and practices of Neo-Assyrian imperial messengers, starting at the end of the ninth century BCE, informed the (historical) role and function of the so-called writing prophets in Israel and Judah.[5] According to Holladay, the Hebrew Bible generally depicts the so-called *classical prophets* as messengers of an imperial king who are sent to convey a message to the vassal king, that is, the kings of Judah and Israel, as one sees in the Deuteronomistic History and to some extent Chronicles.[6] This model changed slightly in the late ninth century BCE, according to Holladay, when Neo-Assyrian political policy shifted away from dealing with kings alone to dealing with whole vassal populations. Thus, instead of addressing the king in royal correspondence, the Neo-Assyrian king sometimes addressed whole populations in the salutation of his letters. In addition to cursing or threatening to replace rebellious kings and their royal households in a treaty, the Neo-Assyrian treaties also cursed whole populations, even threatening to deport them from their homeland (which the army in fact did on numerous occasions). And most importantly for our present concern: instead of sending messages addressed to the vassal king alone, the Neo-Assyrian imperial messengers ad-

---

[3] These corpora were considered revelations from Ea, god of wisdom and magic, delivered to the scribes by the ancient sages, the *apkallu*, via scribal transmission.

[4] See Alan Lenzi, *Secrecy and the Gods: Secret Knowledge in Ancient Mesopotamia and Biblical Israel* (SAAS 19; Helsinki: The Neo-Assyrian Text Corpus Project, 2008).

[5] See John S. Holladay, Jr., "Assyrian Statecraft and the Prophets of Israel," *HTR* 63 (1970): 29–51; repr. in *Prophecy in Israel: Search for Identity* (ed. David L. Petersen; Issues in Religion and Theology 10; Philadelphia: Fortress, 1987), 122–43. Holladay supports his ideas about Assyrian statecraft by appeal to a number of Assyrian documents, many of which are now available in new editions in the State Archives of Assyria series. As my brief presentation of Holladay's argument is only intended as background for the present article, I do not reproduce his citations or provide updates for them here.

[6] For substantiation of this point, see Lenzi, *Secrecy and the Gods*, 260–61. With regard to Chronicles, one must note the important distinction between prophets and prophecy and the association of only the former with the human king, as argued by William Schniedewind, *The Word of God in Transition: From Prophet to Exegete in the Second Temple Period* (JSOTSup 197; Sheffield: Sheffield Academic Press, 1995), 80–129.

dressed their messages to the entire vassal population.[7] This shift in political policy toward vassal populations, according to Holladay, influenced the manner in which the ancient Hebrew prophets functioned (in history) and accounts for a noticeable shift in the addressees of the so-called writing prophets (in biblical literature). Like the Neo-Assyrian messengers, the ancient Hebrew prophets (who would become "writing prophets"), beginning with the historical Amos in the eighth century BCE, brought their message to the entire vassal people—not the vassal king alone.

I used Holladay's 'Neo-Assyrian imperial messenger as model for the prophetic office' idea to explain the *literary* presentation of the open treatment of revealed knowledge in the Hebrew Bible.[8] Since, according to the biblical presentation, Judah and Israel were vassals to Yahweh, their divine king, and were ultimately geopolitically marginal compared to their Mesopotamian imperial neighbors, I concluded that the Judean and Israelites kings as presented in the Bible "were not supposed to formulate secret plans of their own. They along with the people in general were only to receive the divine orders" from their imperial divine king "that when ready for implementation would be delivered openly by his messengers, the prophets, to the vassal people."[9] Given this perspective on the prophets and the fact that all revealed knowledge pertaining to ritual is framed as coming from prophets, one can easily understand why this knowledge was not to be kept secret, but communicated openly to all.

In formulating these foundational ideas about biblical prophecy and the open mediation of revealed knowledge about ritual, however, I failed to take into account a broader view of ancient Near Eastern prophecy and to maintain a clear distinction between the literary presentation of the biblical prophets and the historical reality of the ancient Hebrew prophets.[10] Thus, I return to the topic of secrecy and prophecy in the Hebrew Bible in light of Mesopotamian prophetic texts: their manner of initial presentation, their communication to others, and their treatment as written texts. The most important questions in this regard include

---

[7] Although Holladay notes an example of this from actual Assyrian documents (citing Nimrud Letter ND 2632, recently re-edited as SAA 19 98, see Mikko Luukko, *The Correspondence of Tiglath-Pileser III and Sargon II from Calah/Nimrud* [SAA 19; Helsinki: The Neo-Assyrian Text Corpus Project, 2012], 104–105), the parade example is found in 2 Kings 18:17–19:9a, 36–37, the speech of Rabshakeh.

[8] It is important to note that Holladay's thesis is a historical one not simply a literary one. That is, he believes the Assyrian shift in political policy affected the actual historical prophets and the way they functioned in society. His point was not one that simply affected the literary presentation of the prophets by redactors of the prophetic books. In my previous treatment, I was concerned only with the literary presentation of the prophets but I did not make this clear and did not sufficiently distinguish the historical acceptance from the literary utility of Holladay's model.

[9] Lenzi, *Secrecy and the Gods*, 268. See pp. 221–71 for my treatment of biblical prophecy and pp. 273–305 for my discussion of the ritual corpora and the presentation of their intermediaries as prophets.

[10] For the latter point, see the third section of this study below.

the following: Was Mesopotamian prophecy secret knowledge? To whom was prophecy spoken and in what context? Were prophecies in some way restricted or guarded from unauthorized listeners? When the prophecies were recorded in writing, were the written texts restricted or guarded from unauthorized readers? I then return to the biblical corpus to consider how the answers to these questions impact the interpretation of biblical prophecy, its relationship to secrecy that I advocated previously,[11] and, most importantly, our understanding of the Bible's distinctively open treatment with regard to the biblical corpora pertaining to ritual.

PROPHECY AND SECRECY IN ANCIENT MESOPOTAMIA

I begin with a simple question: Was prophecy considered secret knowledge in ancient Mesopotamia? I think the proper answer is both yes and no: yes, in that Mesopotamian prophetic oracles disclosed the secrets of the gods and thus were considered secret in terms of the messages' origins; but no, in that the prophetic oracles were not treated as a secret after their initial revelation.

An Old-Babylonian prophetic text from Iščali (FLP 1674) provides the only direct evidence for the idea that prophetic oracles were considered secret at the time of their revelation. The oracle reads as follows:

1. LUGAL *i-ba-al-pi-el*
2. *um-ma* ᵈ*ki-ti-tum-ma*
3. *ni₅-iṣ-re-tum ša* DINGIR.MEŠ
4. *ma-aḫ-ri-ya ša-ak-na*
5. *aš-šum zi-ik-ru-um*
6. *ša šu-mi-ya i-na pí-ka*
7. *ka-ya-nu ni₅-iṣ-re-et* DINGIR.MEŠ
8. *ap-ta-na-at-ti-a-ak-kum*
9. *i-na mi-il-ki*
10. *ša* DINGIR.MEŠ *i-na ši-ip-ṭì*
11. *ša an-nim ma-tum*
12. *a-na be-li-im*
13. *na-ad-na-at-ku-um*

---

[11] The Hebrew Bible is not univocal in its descriptions of prophetic activity. That is manifestly clear upon a cursory reading (and was the impetus for Holladay's study mentioned above). At the heart of the definition of prophecy (and thus biblical prophecy) is the notion that prophets received and transmitted divine messages to others (see Martti Nissinen with C. L. Seow and Robert K. Ritner, *Prophets and Prophecy in the Ancient Near East* [SBLWAW 12; Atlanta: Society of Biblical Literature, 2003], 1). As this specific concept is the point of discussion in the present context, I treat biblical prophecy, for the purposes of this paper, as a conceptually uniform block of material, about which one may generalize. See likewise Martti Nissinen, "Biblical Prophecy from a Near Eastern Perspective: The Cases of Kingship and Divine Possession," in *Congress Volume Ljubljana 2007* (ed. A. Lemaire; VTSup 133; Leiden: Brill, 2010), 441–68, 444.

14. *ši-in ma-tim e-li-tim*
15. *ù ša-ap-li-tim ta-pa-ṭà-ar*
16. *ma-ak-ku-ur ma-tim e-li-tim*
17. *ù ša-ap-li-tim te-pé-ed-de*
18. *ma-ḫi-ir-ka ú-ul i-˹ma˺-aṭ-ṭì*
19. *e-em ma-tim ša qa-at-ka*
20. *ik-šu-du a-ka-˹al˺*
21. *˹ta˺-ne-eḫ-tim i-˹ka˺-[ni-(-šum)]*
22. *iš-di* ᵍⁱˢGU.ZA-*ka*
23. *a-na-ku* ᵈ*ki-ti-tim*
24. *ú-da-na-an la-ma-˹sa˺-[am]*
25. *˹na˺-ṣe-er-tam aš-ta-ak-na-ak-˹kum˺*
26. *ú-zu-un-ka li-ib-ba-ši-a-am*

King Ibalpiel, thus says Kititum: The secrets of the gods are set before me. Because the mention (lit. memory) of my name is constantly in your mouth, I continually reveal (lit. open) the secrets of the gods to you. On the counsel of the gods (and) by the judgment of Anu, the land is given to you to rule. You will ransom (lit. "loosen the sandal of") the upper and lower land. You will . . . (?) the possessions of the upper and lower land. Your market will not diminish; the food of peace will be firmly established for any country that you conquer (lit. your hand reaches). I, Kititum, will fortify the foundation of your throne. I have appointed a protective spirit to you. May your ear be (attentive) to me! [12]

The first two sentences clearly indicate that prophetic oracles, like oracles acquired by means of extispicy (see below), belong to the secrets of the god. That is, prophetic oracles are secret because they derive from realms of the divine sphere to which human access is severely restricted.

The Iščali text, as previously stated, is the only direct evidence we have for the secret origins of prophetic revelations. However, there are texts that describe the *ad hoc* oracular results[13] of other forms of divination (e.g., extispicy and astrology)

---

[12] The translation is my own, but it has benefitted from Nissinen's (see his *Prophets and Prophecy in the Ancient Near East*, 94–95). My translation of the verb *tapaṭṭar* in line 15 and the expression *akal tanēḫtim* in lines 20–21 follows Nissinen's understanding, who bases himself on Maria deJong Ellis, "The Goddess Kititum Speaks to King Ibalpiel: Oracle Texts from Ishchali," *MARI* 5 (1987): 235–66, here 263. But I do not follow them in their rather tenuous derivation of *tepedde* in line 17 from *padû/pedû*, "to spare, to release, to relent, to stop" (Nissinen, *Prophets and Prophecy in the Ancient Near East*, 95; Ellis, "The Goddess Kititum Speaks," 263). *Padû/pedû* is usually used with gods or cosmic powers as the subject. The three attestations where this is not the case are somewhat obscure and do not offer a parallel to justify the translation "amass" (Nissinen, 94) or "loosen/ransom" (Ellis, 240, 258) in the present context (see CAD P, 6–7). Thus, I prefer to leave it untranslated for now. For my previous discussion of this text in light of divinatory practice and secret knowledge, see Lenzi, *Secrecy and the Gods*, 58–62.

[13] *Ad hoc* oracular results ought to be distinguished from the canonical omen collections. The former are temporary, as they are linked to a particular situation. The latter are

as a secret of the gods. Since prophecy is a form of divination, these may provide indirect support for the secret origin of Mesopotamian prophetic oracles. Note, for example, the following statement, occurring in a Standard Babylonian *ikribu*-prayer as well as ritual texts of the diviner:

inaddin Šamaš ana mār bārê pirišti Šamaš u Adad

Šamaš will give to the diviner the secret of Šamaš and Adad.[14]

Such a statement indicates clearly that the results of extispicy were considered secret knowledge from the divine realm. Similar to this, a colophon attached to astrological tablet Ki.1904-10-9, 94 suggests that observing celestial omens resulted in the revelation of secrets from the divine realm, too. The text reads:[15]

26. *ta-mar-ti* DINGIR.MEŠ GAL.MEŠ *ni-ṣir-ti* AN u KI
27. *ta-mar-ti mu-kal-lim-ti ni-ṣir-ti um-ma-a-ni*

The observation (i.e., viewing the astral appearance) of the great gods (is) the secret of heaven and earth. The reading of commentary (on it is) the secret (texts or prerogatives) of the scholars.

The idea that prophecy, like other forms of divination, revealed secret divine knowledge is not very surprising. In fact, we might have deduced it without explicit textual support from two obvious facts: the divine mind was considered inscrutable and the divine realms, whether the heavens or the netherworld, whence divinatory oracles derived,[16] were generally conceived as inaccessible to humans.

---

part of an authoritative textual corpus that functions as an interpretive apparatus for various omina, observed or induced. See Lenzi, *Secrecy and the Gods*, 67.

[14] Heinrich Zimmern, *Beiträge zur Kenntinis der babylonischen Religion* (AB 12; Leipzig: J. C. Hinrichs, 1901), no. 88, rev. 3; see also no. 1–20, lines 18, 26, 119 and no. 24, line 38. I cite the text above in normalization because the orthography of the various texts attesting it differs from one text to another. For a broader discussion of divination and secrecy, see Lenzi, *Secrecy and the Gods*, 27–66. The present texts are discussed on p. 57.

[15] The citation follows Hermann Hunger, *Babylonische und assyrische Kolophone* (AOAT 2; Kevelaer: Butzon & Bercker / Neukirchen-Vluyn: Neukircherner Verlag des Erziehungsvereins, 1968), no. 519. Hunger's lines 26–27 are rev. 9'–10'. For my earlier discussion of this text, see Lenzi, *Secrecy and the Gods*, 212–13. Although my conceptual understanding remains the same, the present rendering has benefitted from Frahm's brief discussion in his *Babylonian and Assyrian Text Commentaries: Origins of Interpretation* (GMTR 5; Münster: Ugarit-Verlag, 2011), 47. Frahm makes the point that the statement takes advantage of the different meanings of *tāmartu*, "appearance, observation, viewing, reading" (see CAD T, 111). He also notes alternative renderings of the passage in the secondary literature in n.191. Parenthetically, these celestial omen observations, as the citation suggests, were textualized and became the object of scholarly hermeneutical activity. Frahm explores these hermeneutical activities of ancient Mesopotamian scribal scholars extensively in his work.

[16] For the mythology of extispicy and the resulting oracle's connection to the netherworld, see Piotr Steinkeller, "Of Stars and Men: The Conceptual and Mythological Setup of

Thus, whatever insight or knowledge that purported to originate with the gods and their abodes would have been considered privileged information.[17]

As stated earlier, I believe it is important to separate the secret *origins* of prophecies (or other oracular results, for that matter) from their *treatment* among humans, including both at the time of their initial communication to others and their subsequent treatment as a written text (if applicable).[18] The question at root is this: Did the secret origins of prophecy in the divine sphere also require that the disclosed message continue to be treated as secret subsequent to its revelation among humans? To gather evidence for this broad question, I ask the following more specific questions: To whom was prophecy spoken and in what context? Were prophecies in some way restricted or guarded from unauthorized listeners? And perhaps most importantly, when prophecies were recorded in writing, are there any indications that the resulting written texts were restricted or guarded from unauthorized readers?

Although there are a handful of texts from other locales, the lion's share of Mesopotamian prophetic texts, as is well-known, comes from the Old Babylonian site of Mari and the first millennium context of the state archive of Assyria in Ni-

---

Babylonian Extispicy," in *Biblical and Oriental Essays in Memory of William L. Moran* (ed. A. Gianto; BibOr 48; Rome: Pontifical Biblical Institute, 2005), 11–47. For the relationship of prophets to the divine council in ancient Mesopotamia, see Martti Nissinen, "Prophets and the Divine Council," in *Kein Land für sich allein: Studien zum Kulturkontact in Kanaan, Israel/ Palästina und Ebirnâri für Manfred Weippert zum 65. Geburtstag* (ed. U. Hübner and E. A. Knauf; OBO 186; Fribourg: Universitätsverlag / Göttingen: Vandenhoeck & Ruprecht, 2002), 4–19. Nissinen appeals to ARM 26 196, ARM 26 208, FLP 1674 (cited above), SAA 3 13, SAA 9 9: 16–21, SAA 13 139, Prism B v 15–vi 16, and SAA 12 69 to support his claims. Jonathan Stökl has re-assessed the texts and concluded that the Mesopotamian prophets did not stand in the divine council themselves (as in the Hebrew Bible); rather, the prophet conveys the divine message from the deity who was actually in the divine council to hear it. See his *Prophecy in the Ancient Near East: A Philological and Sociological Comparison* (CHANE 56; Boston/Leiden: Brill, 2012), 224–26. In either case, the prophecy derives from a typically inaccessible divine realm directly or indirectly by way of a prophet.

[17] See, e.g., *Babylonian Theodicy*, lines 58, 82–87, and 256–64 (W. G. Lambert, *Babylonian Wisdom Literature* [Oxford: Clarendon Press, 1960; repr. Winona Lake: Eisenbrauns, 1996], 75, 77, and 87, who cites Gudea Cylinder A, vii 4 as a parallel to line 256 in the notes on p. 309) and *Ludlul Bēl Nēmeqi* I 29–32, II 33–38 (Amar Annus and Alan Lenzi, *Ludlul bēl nēmeqi: The Standard Babylonian Poem of the Righteous Sufferer* [SAACT 7; Helsinki: The Neo-Assyrian Text Corpus Project, 2010], 16, 20). One could also note, though somewhat less directly relevant, the heavenly ascent of Adapa, the first of the famed *apkallu*, in the myth that bears his name and its role as a foundation myth for cultic officials, who have access to the gods and yet do not enjoy divine privileges (such as immortality and clear insight into the divine mind). See Mario Liverani, *Myth and Politics in Ancient Near Eastern Historiography* (ed. and introduced by Zainab Bahrani and Marc Van De Mieroop; Ithaca: Cornell University Press, 2004), 3–23 for this interpretation.

[18] This is a distinction I develop in *Secrecy and the Gods*, passim.

neveh.[19] As I will show in the following brief overview of this material, there is no clear evidence that Mesopotamian prophecy was generally treated in a secretive manner by people after a prophet's initial revelation of it.

We begin with a consideration of the locations within society where prophecies were originally pronounced. Is there any indication that the original oral conveyance of prophetic oracles occurred in settings that would have somehow kept the messages secret or would have restricted in some way those who heard its contents? Although there are clues that messages had a somewhat restricted circulation, there is no clear evidence that the original oral conveyance was considered secret, to be heard by only a select few.

Many of the Mesopotamian prophecies, especially among the Mari texts, were received and pronounced by prophets[20] in the temple of a deity, probably in front of the divine image.[21] This might suggest an exclusive group among the divine message's initial audience. But it is very likely that the individuals charged with various cultic and mundane tasks in the temples would have been within earshot of such pronouncements. Thus, messages delivered in this setting might be considered limited in audience but still relatively public.[22] In some Mari prophetic texts the prophets delivered their message orally to a royal servant or royal family

---

[19] See Nissinen, *Prophets and Prophecy in the Ancient Near East* for a convenient collection of nearly all of the relevant texts. The most up-to-date list appears now in Stökl, *Prophecy in the Ancient Near East*, 29–34 for the Old Babylonian sources and 104–109 for the Neo-Assyrian ones.

[20] I use the term "prophet" without regard to the intermediary's gender. There were both male and female prophets in ancient Mesopotamia. I also use the term indiscriminately, whether the speaker was an *āpilu*, *ma/uḫḫû*, *raggintu*, etc. For a reference to an overview of these various titles and functions, see note 63 below.

[21] For this observation, see Karel van der Toorn, "From the Oral to the Written: The Case of Old Babylonian Prophecy," in *Writings and Speech in Israelite and Ancient Near Eastern Prophecy* (ed. E. Ben Zvi and M. H. Floyd; SBLSymS 10; Atlanta: Society of Biblical Literature, 2000), 219-34, 221-23 and "Mesopotamian Prophecy between Immanence and Transcendence: A Comparison of Old Babylonian and Neo-Assyrian Prophecy," in *Prophecy in its Ancient Near Eastern Context: Mesopotamian, Biblical, and Arabian Perspectives* (ed. M. Nissinen; SBLSymS 13; Atlanta: Society of Biblical Literature, 2000), 70-87, 80. Texts that report an oracle that also explicitly state that the recounted oracles were delivered in a temple include the following: ARM 26 195: 5–7, ARM 26 199: 52b–54, ARM 26 202: 7–9, ARM 26 212: 7–10, ARM 26 213: 5–7, ARM 26 214: 5–7, ARM 26 219: 4′–6′, ARM 26 233: 14–16 (although recounting a dream in which Dagan speaks, the speaking occurs in the temple), and ARM 26 237: 22–23. ARM 26 215: 15–16, which states the prophet "arose before Dagan" (*pān Dagan itbī-ma*) in a context already concerned with cultic matters, strongly implies that the prophet spoke in front of the divine image in the temple. ARM 26 200, in which the *šangû* of the Annunītum temple conveys an oracle to the king, also strongly implies the prophet delivered the oracle in a temple. Among Neo-Assyrian texts, see the letter SAA 13 37: 7–11. The general practice of hearing prophecy in the temple is mentioned in ARM 26 196: 8–12.

[22] Note that Stökl classifies the messages described in ARM 26 200, 213, 214, 215, and 219, all delivered in a temple, as "unequivocally public messages" (*Prophecy in the Ancient Near East*, 84).

member (PN *illikam-ma kīam iqbêm/iqbi*, "PN came and spoke to me"), who then conveyed the message to the palace via letter.[23] This sort of transmission process may suggest some level of discretion but nothing more than was given to the non-prophecy-related topics treated in the very same letters.[24] Thus again, the prophecies were not treated in a particularly secretive manner. Finally, we have a few prophecies, including some from the Neo-Assyrian corpus,[25] that were delivered in a very public setting: at the city gate in front of the assembled elders (ARM 26 206: 13–16, 32–34; the latter lines include an explicit statement that the prophet did not speak his oracle in private or secret [*ina šimištim ul iqbêm*]; on which, see below), at the gate to the royal palace (ARM 26 208: 7–8, 371: 9–16), in the midst of assembled citizens (ARM 371: 18–20, SAA 10 352, rev. 1–2),[26] with a witness standing alongside (FM 7 39: 6–8, 46–47, 60–61), or in public ritual contexts (possibly ARM 26 216, FLP 1674 [from Iščali],[27] and SAA 9 3.2[28]). These last several texts clearly show that some

---

[23] See, e.g., A.1968, ARM 26 197, 198, 199, 206, 208, 210, 220, 221, 243, and 414. Note, however, ARM 26 194, in which the prophet himself seems to be the sender of the letter. As Charpin has noted, this letter may have been written by Utu-kam, the scribe sent at the prophet's request, as mentioned at the end of ARM 26 414. The former tablet then accompanied the latter tablet to the king (see Dominique Charpin, "Prophètes et Rois dans le Proche-Orient Amorrite: Nouvelles Données, Nouvelles Perspectives," *Florilegium marianum* 6 [2002]: 14–15. I thank Jonathan Stökl for this reference.)

[24] For example, ARM 26 196 seems to deal with a prophetic oracle, which is immediately followed by a report about grain.

[25] Unfortunately, we do not know the *Sitz im Leben* of most of the Neo-Assyrian oracles due to the fact that the collected prophetic oracles from the Neo-Assyrian royal archive at Nineveh, published in SAA 9, do not preserve a clear indication of the oracles' original places of pronouncement. (I leave aside the rather vague statements about an intermediary's city of origin [as in, e.g., SAA 9 1.1: 28′ or SAA 9 2.2: 35′, among several others] as irrelevant to the issue of the *Sitz im Leben* of the actual prophetic pronouncement.) But many interpreters have concluded that these oracles were delivered in a public setting. Representative of this view is Jonathan Stökl, who writes, "[h]aving very little evidence to go on for the *Sitz im Leben* of prophecy in the Neo-Assyrian empire, it is impossible to prove whether it was situated in the public sphere or not, but based on anthropological parallels, as well as both biblical and Old Babylonian evidence, it is likely that Neo-Assyrian prophecy was public as well" (Stökl, *Prophecy in the Ancient Near East*, 112. He cites several other scholars from the literature who agree with this view).

[26] Note also the much later Hellenistic Astronomical Diary (AD 3 -132 B), which recounts a prophet giving an apparently very provocative public prophecy in Babylon. For a brief discussion of the text, see Martti Nissinen, "A Prophetic Riot in Seleucid Babylonia," in *"Wer darf hinaufsteigen zum Berg YHWHs?" Beiträge zu Prophetie und Poesie des Alten Testaments, Festschrift für Sigurður Örn Steingrímsson zum 70. Geburtstag* (ed. H. Irsigler; Arbeiten zu Text und Sprache im Alten Testament 72; St. Ottilien: EOS Verlag, 2002), 62–74.

[27] William L. Moran argues that this oracle was delivered at a royal enthronement ceremony (see his "An Ancient Prophetic Oracle," in *Biblische Theologie und gesellschaftlicher Wandel: Für Norbert Lohfink* [ed. G. Braulik, W. Groß, and S. McEvenue; Freiburg: Herder, 1993], 252–59, 254).

prophecies were not at all intended to be treated as secret information to be heard by a select few.

One might suggest that the public pronouncement in ARM 26 206: 32–34, which states rather emphatically that an oracle was not delivered in private (*ina šimištim*) but in the assembly of the elders, is exceptional and thus suggests the opposite as the norm, namely, that prophecies were typically treated as knowledge best kept private—thus, a secret known only by a few royal servants and the king.[29] This is a possible but unlikely interpretation. It is true that the very public pronouncement described in ARM 26 206 is atypical in our rather limited number of sources; temple pronouncements or oral deliveries to a royal servant or family member are much more common. But I think resting the idea that prophecies were treated as secret knowledge in need of guarding on this one instance is more than the phrase can bear, especially in light of the prophecies that were delivered in a very public manner. It is much more likely that the writer of this letter was merely commenting on the oracle's atypical, very public delivery. Thus, as the examples in the previous paragraph indicate, we have no conclusive evidence that the initial oral delivery or conveyance of the oracles was somehow restricted, protected, or kept secret.

After the initial oral delivery, the message normally needed to be transmitted to its intended audience, usually the king.[30] According to our available evidence, which is textual and thus skewed, no doubt, prophetic messages were typically transmitted via letter by a royal servant or family member to the king (compare Amos 7:10).[31] Some of the Neo-Assyrian oracles, after their delivery to the palace

---

[28] SAA 9 3.2 may be an oracle used in the public enthronement of the Assyrian king. Note that the addressee in line 1 is specified as the citizens of the land of Assyria. For the interpretation that SAA 9 3 was used in the enthronement of Esarhaddon, see, e.g., Simo Parpola, *Assyrian Prophecies* (SAA 9; Helsinki: Helsinki University Press, 1997), LXX; Martti Nissinen, *References to Prophecy in Neo-Assyrian Sources* (SAAS 7; Helsinki: The Neo-Assyrian Text Corpus Project, 1998), 26–28; and idem, "Spoken, Written, Quoted, and Invented: Orality and Writtenness in Ancient Near Eastern Prophecy," in *Writings and Speech in Israelite and Ancient Near Eastern Prophecy*, 251–53. Stökl, *Prophecy in the Ancient Near East*, 138–140 discusses the controversy and gives references to alternative views.

[29] This idea is suggested though not clearly affirmed by Beate Pongratz-Leisten, who writes, "Man könnte dies als Hinweis auf den generellen Ausschluß der Öffentlichkeit aus der Orakelpraxis werten, der hier durchbrochen wird" (*Herrschaftswissen in Mesopotamien: Formen der Kommunikation zwischen Gott und König im 2. und 1. Jahrtausend v.Chr.* [SAAS 10; Helsinki: The Neo-Assyrian Text Corpus Project, 1999], 66).

[30] Obviously, this only happened if the king were not himself already present at the time of the message's pronouncement.

[31] For the process of transmission, see Nissinen's article, "Spoken, Written, Quoted, and Invented," passim and van der Toorn, "From the Oral to the Written," 225–28. ARM 26 201 explicitly refers to sending the king a tablet containing a prophecy (see also, e.g., ARM 26 197: 4–5, 206: 28–31, and 217: 27–28). In fact, however, all of the Mari prophecies are second hand accounts delivered to the king via letter by one of his servants or a family member. The practice of conveying prophetic oracles to the king in writing in a timely manner seems to

by letter (probably),[32] were preserved as individual oracle reports in the state archives (e.g., SAA 9 7 and 8) while others were re-copied and organized on larger so-called *Sammeltafeln* for preservation (see, e.g, SAA 9 1, 2, and perhaps 4).[33] Are there any hints of restrictions on who could receive such messages from the prophets, carry the letters containing the messages, or be present when such were read? These were precisely the issues in the Mari letters that surrounded extispicies and conveying the secret results to others.[34] With regard to prophecy, however, there is no clear evidence that such letters, reports, or archived documents containing prophecies were considered confidential,[35] were protected from interception, or were guarded from unauthorized eyes or ears.

As evidence to the contrary of this assertion, one might point to ARM 26 414, a letter in which a prophet is quoted as saying, "Send me a discreet (*naṣram*)[36] scribe! I will have him write down the message which Šamaš has sent me for the king."[37] If the translation is accurate, this prophet intends to restrict access to his message, limiting its exposure to the (discreet) scribe who will compose the letter conveying it and the king, who was the intended recipient of the oracle.[38] But it is not at all clear that he demanded this discretion from the scribe as a matter of professional principle, i.e., because prophecy was a restricted form of divinatory knowledge.[39] In fact, it seems more likely that he made the request for a discreet scribe simply because he believed the particular topic of *this* oracle was sensitive and needed to be treated with care. Moreover, this one instance of a guarded prophecy does not

---

have been an expectation that faithful servants wanted to satisfy. Among the Mari texts, see FM 7 39: 34–45, written from the servant's perspective, and ARM 26 196: 7–10, which is a servant's quotation of a royal order. Prophecies were reported to the king via letter in Neo-Assyrian times as well. See SAA 10 24, 352; SAA 13 37, 139, 144, 148; and SAA 16 59, as listed in Matthijs J. de Jong, *Isaiah among the Ancient Near Eastern Prophets: A Comparative Study of the Earliest Stages of the Isaiah Tradition and the Neo-Assyrian Prophecies* (VTSup 117; Leiden/Boston: Brill, 2007), 176–77. He also suggests that SAA 9 10 and 9 11 are letters (172, 176, though on the latter page he calls SAA 9 10 a report). Note also the expectation in the succession treaty of Esarhaddon (SAA 2 6 §10) that faithful servants report malevolent prophecies to the king.

[32] So, e.g., Stökl, *Prophecy in the Ancient Near East*, 130 and de Jong, *Isaiah among the Ancient Near Eastern Prophets*, 172.

[33] For the most recent discussion of the issues surrounding tablet form, content, and genre of the SAA 9 prophetic texts, see Stökl, *Prophecy in the Ancient Near East*, 131–41.

[34] See Lenzi, *Secrecy and the Gods*, 28–45.

[35] As is asserted by van der Toorn, "Old Babylonian Prophecy," 229.

[36] For this translation and references to alternatives, see Nissinen, *Prophets and Prophecy in the Ancient Near East*, 75, note d.

[37] The translation is Nissinen's (*Prophets and Prophecy in the Ancient Near East*, 75). The Akkadian text reads: [31]1 LÚ.DUMU É ṭup-pí na-aṣ-ra-am [32]tú-ur-da-am-ma ṭe₄-ma-am ša ᵈUTU [33]ana LUGAL iš-pu-ra-an-ni lu-ša-[á]š-ṭe₄-er (see Durand, AEM I/2, 294).

[38] See likewise Jean-Marie Durand, *Les documents épistolaires du palais de Mari* (vol. 2; LAPO 17; Paris: Cerf, 1998), 254.

[39] Contra van der Toorn, "Old Babylonian Prophecy," 229.

negate the fact that many other prophecies indicate a public or semi-public initial audience.

Instances in which prophetic messages have more extensive chains of transmission, written and oral, would also suggest that maintaining the secrecy of prophetic messages was not a typical concern for the servants who passed prophetic messages on to the king. For example, ARM 26 202 is a letter to the king from a man whose father has written to him. In the letter the father reports the words of a prophet he had heard in a temple. One might interpret such a round-about manner of transmission as evidence that the king was sometimes quite out of the prophetic-information loop!

I grant that there is a *prima facie* reasonableness to the view that prophecies were a kind of state secret, especially given the close association prophecy had to kingship and thus *Herrschaftswissen*.[40] But as we have seen, there is no solid evidence to support the idea that prophetic oracles were considered secret knowledge in need of guarding from unauthorized hearing (at the time of initial pronouncement) or reading (in written copies), as were, for example, the learned corpora of the scribal scholars, who practiced exorcism, extispicy, celestial divination, lamentation, and medicine.[41] Moreover, none of the Neo-Assyrian archived prophecies (in SAA 9) bears the *Geheimwissen* colophon, as is the case with other divinatory texts belonging to the secret scholarly corpora.[42]

One might object, at this point, with some warrant that I am comparing *ad hoc* oracular reports to highly developed learned corpora transmitted for generations among practitioners of the other divinatory crafts, especially extispicy and celestial divination. So one might ask me, Are you asking too much from the wrong genre? Are you comparing apples and oranges? I am comparing different genres, but I do not think this means I am asking too much of them.

We are missing proper comparanda for prophecy and other divinatory techniques (i.e., extispicy and celestial divination) on one level of comparison, the "corpus" level. Prophecy differed from the other forms of divination in that it was highly intuitive. It did not develop a learned corpus that might have been guarded or kept secret because it did not need one. Surely this is significant (see below).

But even when we compare the reported/recorded prophecies to the more comparable written reports of haruspices and celestial diviners, by which they communicated their *ad hoc* divinatory results to the king, we still see a difference between prophecy and these other forms of divination. From the Mari letters, for

---

[40] For this point, which hardly needs support, see, e.g., Martti Nissinen, "Biblical Prophecy from a Near Eastern Perspective," especially 445–49; Pongratz-Leisten, *Herrschaftswissen in Mesopotamien*, 47–95; and her treatment in "When the Gods Are Speaking: Toward Defining the Interface between Polytheism and Monotheism" in *Propheten in Mari, Assyrien und Israel* (ed. M. Köckert and M. Nissinen; FRLANT 201; Göttingen: Vandenhoeck & Ruprecht, 2003), 132–68, 160–62.

[41] See Lenzi, *Secrecy and the Gods*, 67–134.

[42] See Lenzi, *Secrecy and the Gods*, 135–219.

example, we know that extispicy and the reports that resulted were not open to just anyone; rather, access to this information was restricted to specific personnel.[43] Also, the written extispicy reports that we have from the Neo-Assyrian times look like official internal memoranda. They follow a standard form and include the diviner's and the reporter's names, both of whom worked for the king.[44] The same is true of the astrological reports in SAA 8. These come from the king's scholars, men who were in rather frequent contact with him. All of this is quite different from the way many of the prophecies were reported. As stated above, the prophecies were often reported by a royal family member or official in letters, which often included any number of other topics. The prophets themselves, it seems, did not have easy access to the king like the more scholarly diviners.[45] Furthermore, in contrast to the occasional public or semi-open promulgation of prophetic messages, we have an astrological report (SAA 8 338: 7–rev. 4) in which a celestial diviner named Ašaredu admonishes the king that

7. [ṭ]up-šar-ru-ti i-na KI.LAM
r1. ul iš-šem-mi EN LUGAL.MEŠ
r2. UD-mu šá pa-ni-šú maḫ-ru
r3. re-šá-a liš-ši-ma lu-up-ru-us-ma
r4. a-na LUGAL be-lí-ia lu-uq-bi

The scribal art [which here refers to celestial divination] should not be heard in the market place. Let the lord of kings summon me on a day agreeable to him and I will investigate and speak to the king, my lord.[46]

The same words also occur in another report written by Ašaredu, SAA 8 342: 7–rev. 2 (broken context). The presence of this statement in two different reports (though by the same diviner) suggests the sentiment is not an isolated thought but perhaps a common saying or a common assumption among celestial diviners: their professional concerns are not public fare.[47] Thus, the reporting of prophecy and the reporting of the results of more technical forms of divination differed in a manner that supports the above generalizations with regard to the attachment of secrecy—or rather, its lack of attachment—to prophecy.

---

[43] See Lenzi, *Secrecy and the Gods*, 39–45.

[44] See SAA 4 279–354 for the extispicy reports from the reign of Assurbanipal.

[45] The scholars had a different relationship to the king than the various kinds of prophets. For example, SAA 10 7: 6–14 describes scholars entering into a treaty with the king: "The scribes, the haruspices, the exorcists, the physicians and the augurs staying in the palace and living in the city will enter the treaty on the 16th of Nisan (I)." We never read about prophets affirming their loyalty in this manner.

[46] The translation follows Hunger's in SAA 8 (p. 194). Context leaves little doubt that Ašaredu is talking about the results of celestial divination here and not the scribal art abstractly when he uses the word ṭupšarrūtu.

[47] See likewise Lenzi, *Secrecy and the Gods*, 102–103.

ANCIENT JUDEAN/ISRAELITE PROPHECY VS. BIBLICAL PROPHECY IN LIGHT OF ANCIENT NEAR EASTERN EVIDENCE

The results of recent work comparing ancient Near Eastern prophecy and prophetic texts with the biblical prophetic materials have highlighted several important issues that I briefly present here as further background before turning to the issues of secrecy, prophecy, and revealed knowledge pertaining to ritual in the Bible. It should be noted that the following statements are presented as results of scholarship rather than arguments for positions. Each builds upon the previous.

First, a distinction between prophets/prophetic oracles in historical space and time and the scribal, literary presentation of prophets/prophetic materials in the historiographical and prophetic books of the Hebrew Bible is essential. In light of a century and a half of critical biblical scholarship, this hardly needs justification; but the distinction is not always clearly maintained in comparative treatments.[48] With Martti Nissinen, I call the former "ancient Hebrew prophecy" and refer to the latter as "biblical prophecy."[49]

Second, ancient Hebrew prophets and prophecies, as scholars have recently reconstructed them in light of comparative evidence, are remarkably similar to what we see in the ancient Near East.[50] There are of course some differences (e.g., the ancient Hebrew prophets seem to have had access to the king much more readily than prophets in Mesopotamia did).[51] But by and large, the ancient Hebrew prophets were part of the *Herrschaftswissen* apparatus as were their colleagues in the East.

Third, the biblical prophetic books, the most important fraction of "biblical prophecy" for the present purpose, are a scribal product that underwent a long and complex editorial history, unlike all other ancient Near Eastern prophetic texts, that extended into the Persian and Hellenistic periods (and perhaps be-

---

[48] See note 2 above for my earlier difficulty in this regard.

[49] See note 52 below. Although the categories seem clean and neat, there are a plethora of issues that can be raised that resist simple answers. See Ehud Ben Zvi's reflections on the matter from the perspective of orality and writtenness in his essay, "Introduction: Writings, Speeches, and the Prophetic Books—Setting an Agenda," in *Writings and Speech in Israelite and Ancient Near Eastern Prophecy*, 1–29.

[50] See, e.g., Nissinen, "Biblical Prophecy from a Near Eastern Perspective," 450–51; the important, recent comparative study of de Jong, *Isaiah among the Ancient Near Eastern Prophets*, 352–56 (which presents the summary of his results); and his "Biblical Prophecy—A Scribal Enterprise: The Old Testament Prophecy of Unconditional Judgement considered as a Literary Phenomenon," *VT* 61 (2011): 39–70, especially 51–53 for the present point.

[51] The prophets' access to the king was probably comparable to what we know about the Mesopotamian scholars' access. See, e.g., Nissinen, "Biblical Prophecy from a Near Eastern Perspective," 451; de Jong, *Isaiah among the Ancient Near Eastern Prophets*, 355; and Jack Sasson, "About 'Mari and the Bible'," *RA* 92 (1989): 97-123, 118–19. Other differences between ancient Mesopotamian and *biblical* prophecy will be presented below.

yond).[52] Since understanding the literary presentation of the prophets in the Hebrew Bible and its relationship to secrecy lies at the heart of the present study, we might expect that this unique literary history will loom large in our understanding of any other elements in the biblical prophets that we might deem distinctive.

Fourth, as several scholars have noted, biblical prophecy contains far and away much more criticism of king and society than other ancient Near Eastern prophetic sources.[53] This criticism, however, is not only a quantitative matter; it is also a qualitative one, for unlike any other ancient Near Eastern prophetic text, the biblical prophetic books depict prophets announcing the deity's radical and total rejection of king and people. As de Jong states it, "[a]s far as we can see now, no prophet in the ancient Near East ever announced the unconditional divine repudiation of his own society."[54]

And fifth, this radical repudiation of the prophets is an artifact of the post-monarchical editing of the prophetic books.[55] As de Jong's summary captures the idea well, it is worth citing at length:

> Commissioned to be Yahweh's mouthpieces of unconditional and total destruction, they stand outside the system; they do not belong to the 'prophets and

---

[52] Nissinen has repeatedly noted the connection between the long editorial history of the prophetic books and the importance of distinguishing "ancient Hebrew prophecy" from "biblical prophecy." See, e.g., his "What is Prophecy? An Ancient Near Eastern Perspective," in *Inspired Speech: Prophecy in the Ancient Near East: Essays in Honor of Herbert B. Huffmon* (ed. J. Kaltner and L. Stulman; JSOTSup 378; London/New York: T & T Clark, 2004), 17-37, 29-31 and "The Historical Dilemma of Biblical Prophetic Studies," in *Prophecy in the Book of Jeremiah* (ed. H. M. Barstad and R. G. Kratz; BZAW 388; Berlin: de Gruyter, 2009), 103-20. A representative statement: "The Hebrew Bible . . . is a canonical composition *sui generis* in the ancient Near East, the result of the editorial history of several centuries and, hence, temporally distant from the prophets appearing on its lines. The Hebrew Bible not only documents the prophetic phenomenon in [the] Southern Levant but also the emergence and early development of the concept of prophecy. This fundamental difference of the Hebrew Bible from other Near Eastern documents of prophecy must be recognized, otherwise we fail to understand what we are comparing" ("The Historical Dilemma," 114).

[53] See Martti Nissinen's important article on prophetic criticism/dissent, "Das kritische Potential in der altorientalischen Prophetie," in *Propheten in Mari, Assyrien und Israel* (ed. M. Köckert and M. Nissinen; FRLANT 201; Göttingen: Vandenhoeck & Ruprecht, 2003), 1-33, 31-32, with similar comments in his "Biblical Prophecy from a Near Eastern Perspective," 453. See also Lenzi, *Secrecy and the Gods*, 269-70.

[54] "Biblical Prophecy—A Scribal Enterprise," 43.

[55] See Nissinen's connection of the two issues in the works cited in note 53 above. For a defense of this view in a comparative perspective with references to the secondary literature, see de Jong's programmatic essay, "Biblical Prophecy—A Scribal Enterprise." As a point of entry into the issues of producing and reading the prophetic books *as written texts* in post-monarchic, Achaemenid Yehud, see the remarks in Ben Zvi, "Introduction: Writings, Speeches, and the Prophetic Books—Setting an Agenda" (cited in n. 49) and the various essays in *The Production of Prophecy: Constructing Prophecy and Prophets in Yehud* (ed. D. Edelman and E. Ben Zvi; BibleWorld; London: Equinox, 2009).

priests' that are part of the system. They are not 'diviners pro status quo', but isolated figures, contra society, ordered to speak the word of Yahweh. They do not
speak for their contemporaries, but instead for future generations. This portrayal
is part of the scribal, *ex eventu* explanations in the prophetic books. It informs us of
exilic and post-exilic thought, not about prophecy as a socio-historical phenomenon in Israel and Judah. As far as the protagonists of the biblical prophetic books
are presented as being 'totally different' from the prophets, priests, and diviners,
i.e. the whole range of divination, they are to be understood as *ex eventu* images.
The *ex eventu* imagery is part of the explanation of the disastrous events of the
downfall of the Israelite and the Judean states as being due to divine anger, a
commonplace explanatory motif in the ancient Near Eastern world.[56]

These perspectives represent my point of departure for the ideas developed
below.

THE TRANSFORMATION OF PROPHECY IN RESPONSE TO EMPIRE
AND THE OPENNESS OF REVEALED KNOWLEDGE PERTAINING TO RITUAL

As I have shown in the second section of this study, Mesopotamian prophetic
revelations were secret in origin (i.e., they were from the divine realm, generally
inaccessible to humans) but were not treated as such during and after their initial
revelation (i.e., pronouncement, oral conveyance, and textual preservation). This
is precisely what I concluded about biblical prophecy in my earlier work.[57] If prophetic oracles were not kept secret in Mesopotamia after their revelation, then the
problem of explaining the distinctively open communication of prophetic oracles
in the biblical corpus evaporates and my explanation based on Holladay's model of
the imperial messenger (which is problematic on other grounds in light of contemporary comparative prophetic studies[58]) is unnecessary. Thus, the specific idea

---

[56] "Biblical Prophecy—A Scribal Enterprise," 66–67.

[57] Lenzi, *Secrecy and the Gods*, 266.

[58] Holladay's specific argument for the broad audience of biblical prophetic oracles,
rooted as it is in Neo-Assyrian political policy, is problematic for at least three reasons. First,
Holladay was working at the level of the historical eighth-century prophets when our approach to the prophets should be first and foremost a literary one. Holladay's specific explanation therefore may be too early to explain a feature we know only in the biblical prophetic
literature. Second, biblical prophecy (as literature) is not unique in addressing prophecies to
the people in general. Even though our sources attesting such addressees are rather few,
prophecies from the broader ancient Near East were also addressed to the people at times.
Thus, Holladay's question is ill-posed. The question is not so much, Why do the biblical prophetic books (not the historical prophets, as he originally framed it) address the people?
Rather, the question is, In light of the fact that such is rare in other ancient Near Eastern
prophetic sources, why is it the norm in the Bible? Third, Holladay was working with a historical reconstruction, a prophet addressing his entire community and announcing total
destruction, that comparative work has made historically unlikely. There is no parallel for
this kind of behavior among ancient Near Eastern prophets living under an indigenous king.

related to prophecy and empire that I used previously for explaining the distinctively open treatment of revealed knowledge about *ritual* does not work. Yet the question remains: Why is revealed knowledge about ritual in the Hebrew Bible open to all without any clear sign of restriction or secrecy attached to it? This is quite different from the guarded and restricted ritual and divinatory corpora of the Assyrian and Babylonian scholars who served the king. Since each biblical ritual corpus is revealed to a person presented as a prophet (Moses and Ezekiel), the answer to this question must still be related to the issue of prophecy. In the following I posit a two-prong explanation for the open treatment of revealed knowledge pertaining to ritual in the Bible. One prong is rooted in a general notion about prophecy in the ancient Near East; the other, in the specific transformation of prophecy (turning it into "biblical prophecy") that occurred during the several centuries of successive imperial presence in the Levant—the very same centuries that witnessed the production of the Bible itself.

We begin first with a generality about prophecy. The absence of secrecy with regard to the *treatment* of prophecies in ancient Mesopotamia may support what has already been recognized about prophecy in general vis-à-vis the Mesopotamian political authorities, namely, that prophecy was difficult to control.[59] Even though our documentation indicates that prophecy served the king, we have no codified rules, outside of the Succession Treaty's stipulations (SAA 2 6 §10) against treasonous prophecy,[60] about its proper exercise. We have no indication that prophets received an indoctrinating education or training, as did the Neo-Assyrian scribal scholars of the court.[61] In principle, there was no limit on the topics that a prophet could address, and prophecies could be spoken at almost any time, almost

---

Comparative work would suggest that biblical prophetic materials are better explained as part of a re-orientation of the prophetic materials to a post-monarchical situation in which total destruction is explained *ex eventu* in terms of divine wrath.

[59] See Pongratz-Leisten, *Herrschaftswissen in Mesopotamien*, 94–95 for this point more broadly considered.

[60] For a discussion of this section of the treaty and its implications for prophetic dissent, see Nissinen, *References to Prophecy in Neo-Assyrian Sources*, 156–62 and his earlier work "Falsche Prophetie in neuassyrischer und deuteronomistischer Darstellung," in *Das Deuteronomium und seine Querbeziehungen* (ed. T. Veijola; Schriften der Finnischen Exegetischen Gesellschaft 62; Helsinki: Finnische Exegetische Gesellschaft; Göttingen: Vandenhoeck & Ruprecht, 1996), 172–95, which is available in English in an abridged version as "Prophecy Against the King in Neo-Assyrian Sources," in *"Lasset uns Brücken bauen. . .": Collected Communications to the XVth Congress of the International Organization for the Study of the Old Testament, Cambridge 1995* (ed. K.-D. Schunck and M. Augustin; BEATAJ 42; Frankfurt am Main: Lang, 1998), 157–70.

[61] Certain literary features in the prophetic evidence have moved some to speak of the intellectual status of the prophets (see, e.g., Pongratz-Leisten, *Herrschaftswissen in Mesopotamien*, 73). Still, we have no evidence of the prophet's formal educational curriculum. Further, given the rigors of scholarly education, it is unlikely the prophets were expert scribes. They could have easily acquired some knowledge of literature by hearing texts read aloud (see Nissinen, "Spoken, Written, Quoted, and Invented," 247).

anywhere, by almost anyone:[62] a professional intermediary attached to the court, a cultic official in the temple, or the occasional person on the street at the city gate—represented quite sparsely in our written record.[63] Finally, and importantly, there was no guarantee that the message would always be favorable to the king or coincide with his plans.[64] As many have pointed out before, mostly pro-royal prophecies from various intermediaries have been preserved in excavated (royal) archives. This no doubt accounts for our limited data about several of the above points.[65] But there is enough extant evidence to warrant the conclusion that authorities did not always easily control the prophets, whether institutionally-affiliated or not.[66] Of course, the idea that prophecy is difficult to control is as common in the Bible's depiction of it as it is probably exaggerated. Examples hardly need be given.[67] The ancient Mesopotamian sources provide historical data that clearly show ancient Near Eastern prophecy's potential to address the public, and to do so in a way that did not always support central authorities.[68] I think this is an

---

[62] I do not want to be understood to be affirming the ubiquity of lone prophetic dissidents, wandering around without any institutional support. Quite to the contrary! Such a view has overly influenced biblical scholars. The norm throughout the ancient Near East, including ancient Judah and Israel, would have been institutionally-affiliated prophets. See Nissinen, "What is Prophecy? An Ancient Near Eastern Perspective," 23. Although the lone dissident, often a lay-prophet, seems to have been a rarity, we should not entirely ignore this critical potential. I think this potential (among other things) lies at the root of what would eventually become "biblical prophecy."

[63] For a recent discussion with extensive references to the secondary literature of the sociological positions and institutional relationships, if any, of the āpil(t)um, ma/uhhû(m), and raggimu/raggintu, assinnu, and qammatum, see Stökl, Prophecy in the Ancient Near East, 39–69 (Old Babylonian), 111–127 (Neo-Assyrian). For examples of prophecies from a "person on the street" see, ARM 26 210, SAA 10 24, and SAA 16 59.

[64] On this last point, see, e.g., Pongratz-Leisten, Herrschaftswissen in Mesopotamien, 88–92, who cites both SAA 16 59 and SAA 10 24 as evidence. See also de Jong's discussion of the role of Isaiah in Hezekiah's court against the backdrop of ancient Near Eastern prophecy. While discussing Isaiah 28:7b–10, he states "[t]here are no examples of comparable controversies among prophets from Mari and Assyria, but it is clear that prophetic oracles could play a role in political advice that competed with opposite views," citing SAA 16 59 and ARM 26 199 for support (Isaiah among the Ancient Near Eastern Prophets, 349, and n.334). Both of these texts are briefly discussed along with several other texts in Nissinen, "Das kritische Potential in der altorientalischen Prophetie."

[65] See my previous discussion in Secrecy and the Gods, 269–70.

[66] I do not mean to imply that the other divinatory professions were always and easily manipulated by the king.

[67] See Nissinen's comparative thoughts on the Succession Treaty of Esarhaddon and the measures against false prophecy in Deut 13 in his essay "Falsche Prophetie in neuassyrischer und deuteronomistischer Darstellung," cited in note 60 above.

[68] In other words, comparative data indicates that the Hebrew Bible's post-monarchical depiction of the prophets is probably exaggerated, but this depiction is still rooted to some degree in historical reality.

important element in understanding the transformation of prophecy described below.

Building on this, we must also take into consideration the fact that Judah and Israel existed under a continuous foreign imperial occupation from the late eighth century on into the late Hellenistic period, which coincides with the time of the Bible's composition and editing. During these centuries, new genres of literature were introduced and old ones re-oriented. To understand this process, I draw on the work of Seth Sanders,[69] who has effectively described a transformation in the writing of biblical history, law, and prophecy involving a "shift in horizons," which he traces from West Semitic inscriptions to biblical texts. This "shift in horizons," as he calls it, involves a process of texts turning away from the king and royal household as protagonists toward the people in light of a new imperial situation.[70] According to Sanders, when West Semitic kings came in contact with the eastern imperial powers beginning in the mid-eighth century, the kings adopted some of their monumental royal genres and expressed them in local vernacular languages (e.g., the Moabite stone) in an attempt to "identify this writing with the people whose language it was" and "to domesticate West Semitic political culture by materializing and monumentalizing its language."[71] In other words, the petty West Semitic kings adopted the signs and symbols of empire for themselves to buttress their local hegemony. "But," Sanders continues, "local media experts—writers and craftspeople—seemed to take the king at his word: some of the new vernaculars actually became identified with the people they were claimed to represent."[72] And thus occurred a transformation of genres and a shift in horizons that began in West Semitic inscriptions and found its most important representation in the historiographical, legal, and prophetic texts of the Hebrew Bible. As Sanders observes:

> At root, the late Iron Age shift in horizons is a shift in these genres' participants: For whom does the text speak? To whom is it addressed? And who are its protagonists? In each case we see evidence of the genre being reshaped under particular political conditions to meet the assumptions of a new audience [namely, the people rather than the king—ACL]. The newly written discourses . . . address a West

---

[69] Seth Sanders, *The Invention of Hebrew* (Urbana/Chicago: University of Illinois Press, 2009). The brief summary here, which draws on Sanders' conclusions, cannot do justice to his entire argument, perhaps the most controversial part of which is his idea of the distinctive West Semitic political culture of kinship and collective assemblies (that existed prior to imperial incursions from the East) in which communal decisions were made. These distinctive political roots, he argues, are the underlying factor for the transformations of (what we now see as familiar) biblical genres that he describes, including the shift from king to people as protagonists, under the influence of the dominant imperial cultures.

[70] One will note the similarity with the observation that Holladay presented as his opening problematic: a shift in prophetic address from king to people. Holladay was not incorrect to look to the new imperial context for answers, though his specific proposal is not sufficiently compelling.

[71] Sanders, *Invention of Hebrew*, 158.

[72] Sanders, *Invention of Hebrew*, 159.

Semitic culture of kinship and political communication transformed by, and transforming, a historical context of imperialism.[73]

The transformation of prophecy, as Sanders recognizes, is the most important of these generic transformations in the Bible because it frames both law and history.

> Rather than assuming that the king had the right to speak for a people, we see a different expectation: that the ideal interlocutor for a people is a prophet. Biblical law is handed down by a prophet, and biblical history is framed as the working-out of prophecy. It is as prophecy above all that biblical genres of discourse reflect on, and empower, their own mediation.[74]

Without necessarily denying Sanders' point about early West Semitic political culture as an important factor, I suggest that prophecy occupied this foundational role because it always had the potential to address large audiences openly in the ancient Near East (though rarely in practice, according to our sources) and to do so in a manner that did not necessarily support the central (imperial) powers.[75] This latent potential in prophecy made it best suited to the biblical scribes' transformative task and desire for a shift in horizon (and addressee). In the process of developing this latent potential in ancient Near Eastern prophecy, the biblical scribes transformed what was once ancient Hebrew prophecy into what we now read as biblical prophecy directed to the people. The application of this view of prophecy to the mediation of the biblical corpora pertaining to ritual explains the open communication of that material as presented in the biblical text. As I concluded before, "the biblical ritual texts," unlike those in Mesopotamia, "in keeping with the open promulgation of prophetic oracles, were potentially open to all."[76] Through this assertion of prophetic mediation, the scribes authorized their corpora as divine knowledge and gave what was once the presumed possession of priests (the ritual corpora) the potential to become the possession of any reader/hearer.

In explaining the application of the biblical view of prophecy to the corpora pertaining to ritual in my previous work, I made the argument that the prophetic mediation of the revealed ritual corpora of the Hebrew Bible was a scribal myth-making strategy, the scribes' attempt to legitimize their texts (and thus themselves) as authoritative.[77] Sanders opposes this view. But his statement in opposition to it also encapsulates well the ideas he presents with regard to the transformation of prophecy, thus I cite it at length. He writes:

---

[73] Sanders, *Invention of Hebrew*, 160.

[74] Sanders, *Invention of Hebrew*, 164–65.

[75] Sanders himself seems to recognize this. See Sanders, *Invention of Hebrew*, 165, though I do not agree with him that prophecy was "always formally independent of kingship" in its performance and "as writing . . . had always been a state secret."

[76] Lenzi, *Secrecy and the Gods*, 305.

[77] Lenzi, *Secrecy and the Gods*, 273–305.

The scribal adoption of the prophetic mantle has often been seen as an act of "legitimation," the creation, indeed the forgery, of a basis of authority that did not exist in objective fact. But if we read the biblical discourses of history, law, and prophecy as inaugurated in the transformation of early Iron Age Assyrian-based genres of power into late Iron Age West Semitic-based forms of political communication, we can see them differently: not as legitimation or authority-forging but as taking on a traditional discursive task of summoning and addressing a people. What has changed in the Iron Age is the political condition of sovereignty: it is no longer vested in the military power of the assembled kin or the state. Thus the people are now addressed through the circulation of texts, as a public.[78]

Rather than contradicting the legitimation view, Sanders' perspective, in my opinion, complements and extends it. The negotiation of social authority is always a reciprocal act between groups. Would-be leaders, for example, present themselves and their ideas to the people as worthy of authority. That is, they must present themselves as legitimate bearers of authority. The people, on the other hand, who we assume are not blind sheep, must decide whether or not to grant the authority to the seeker of it. If the would-be leader is persuasive, the people will respond to their summons. We would expect both sides to use traditional resources in this negotiation process. Thus, a scribe's donning of prophetic authority for the purposes of giving persuasive weight to an edited version of a prophetic or ritual corpus (what I called mythmaking) need not necessarily assume duplicitous intentions, as the word "forgery" would suggest. This may have been part of acceptable scribal practice.[79]

CONCLUSION

My conclusions here support my original conclusions in *Secrecy and the Gods*. But in forming them I have reassessed and rejected the support I once found in Holladay's Neo-Assyrian messenger model of prophecy, which he believed explained the shift in audience from king to people in the so-called writing prophets. I previously used Holladay's idea to understand the open treatment of prophecies in the Bible and thereby to explain why prophetically-mediated revealed knowledge pertaining to ritual in the Bible, in contradistinction to such knowledge in Mesopotamia, bears no indication of ever having been treated as secret knowledge. But upon examining the ancient Mesopotamian prophetic texts more thoroughly in the present study, I find no evidence that prophecy was ever treated as secret knowledge in ancient Mesopotamia despite the fact, as in the Bible, it was

---

[78] Sanders, *Invention of Hebrew*, 165.

[79] For thoughts about the possibility of scribal editors and amplifiers identifying with characters of biblical texts and thereby adopting for themselves "a quasi-prophetic status" as they re-arranged and amended the text, see Ben Zvi, "Introduction: Writings, Speeches, and the Prophetic Books," 14.

considered a divinely revealed secret in terms of its origin. Because prophetic oracles were not kept secret in ancient Mesopotamia after their revelation, the problem of explaining the distinctively open communication of prophetic oracles in the biblical corpus disappeared, and my explanation based on Holladay's model became unnecessary. But the question remained as to why the Bible's revealed knowledge pertaining to ritual was not treated as secret knowledge like it was in Mesopotamia. The answer formulated here is based on a richer understanding of prophecy, rooted in both comparative study of prophetic texts (and its potential for public dissent) and recent thinking about the distinctive political culture of ancient Judah/Israel (and its development in the shadow of empire), and thus the scribes responsible for the Bible. My conclusion is differently framed but fundamentally the same as what I argued for earlier: prophecy authorized the mediators of revealed knowledge pertaining to ritual and formed the basis for its open publication to the people.

Prophecy and empire, or better, prophecy under empire, became an important catalyst in the production of biblical literature, with its strong theological advocacy for an alternative covenant with their divine (rather than their human) imperial lord. Secrecy may insulate a central authority's power from gainsayers or create an empowering mystique around a marginal group. In the Bible, as I concluded before, secrecy only serves an authorizing function for divine secret knowledge (whether prophetic or ritual); the knowledge itself is delivered openly, available to all who would hear it. This pervasive biblical sentiment is perhaps best expressed in the words of Ps 25:14, with its strong parallelism between Yahweh's סוֹד ("secret counsel") and his covenant:[80]

> The secret counsel (סוֹד) of Yahweh belongs to those who fear him,
> His covenant, in order to make them (i.e., those who fear him) know.

---

[80] For my previous statement about this verse, see Lenzi, *Secrecy and the Gods*, 265–66.

5

Chaoskampf against Empire: Yhwh's Battle against Gog (Ezekiel 38–39) as Resistance Literature

C. A. Strine

Introduction

The tale of Yhwh's conflict with Gog of Magog in Ezekiel 38–39 has long perplexed scholars. Commentators remain at odds about the identity of Gog himself perhaps more than any other question. Stated simply, for whom or what does that enigmatic figure stand as a cipher? Modern identifications have been especially speculative, ranging from the Ottoman Turks (Martin Luther's proposal) to Napoleon (a popular option in 19th century Britain) to Russia (a view that was very prominent in some American circles during the cold war and persists even until this day).[1]

In order to address this question, it is sensible to follow the recent trend in Ezekiel studies that situates Ezekiel 38–39 within its larger context, whether that be construed as the preceding oracles (Ezekiel 34–37), the following temple vision (Ezekiel 40–48), or as a middle section of a larger narrative that includes all three parts. A number of recent studies have explored the complex relationship between the Greek and Hebrew texts of Ezekiel, with particular attention to the substantial differences between Papyrus 967 (hereafter 𝔓967) and the MT around and within these chapters.[2] That work is complemented by studies concentrating on how Eze-

---

[1] See Andrew Mein, "The Armies of Gog, the Merchants of Tarshish, and the British Empire," in In the Name of God: The Bible in Colonial Discourse of Empire (ed. C. L. Crouch and Jonathan Stökl; BibIntSup 126; Leiden: Brill, 2013), 133–50.

[2] Ashley S. Crane, Israel's Restoration: A Textual-Comparative Exploration of Ezekiel 36–39 (VTSup 122; Leiden: Brill, 2008); Ingrid E. Lilly, Two Books of Ezekiel: Papyrus 967 and the Masoretic Text as Variant Literary Editions (VTSup 150; Leiden: Brill, 2012).

kiel 38–39 relates to other canonical texts. For instance, Anja Klein and William Tooman have argued in related but different ways that Ezekiel 38–39 comprises an interpretation of earlier texts within Ezekiel (Klein's focus) and beyond it (Tooman's primary contribution).[3]

Tooman concludes on this basis that Ezekiel 38–39 is a product of the Hellenistic period that seeks to integrate Ezekiel with other texts that it viewed as authoritative.[4] He maintains that the "reuse of antecedent Scripture is key to its purpose and meaning,"[5] which is "to supplement Ezekiel in an effort to harmonize the book with a wider body of traditional religious literature, literature found in today's canon within the Torah, Prophets, and Psalms."[6] Tooman's argument relies upon identifying the reuse of locutions from other canonical texts in Ezekiel 38–39. Though there are a number of places one can legitimately differ with Tooman, and on that basis find themselves at odds with his conclusion about the date and provenance of Ezekiel 38–39,[7] he demonstrates conclusively that understanding the Gog of Magog oracle requires the interpreter to apprehend its allusions to other texts.

---

[3] Anja Klein, *Schriftauslegung im Ezechielbuch: redaktionsgeschichtliche Untersuchungen zu Ez 34–39* (BZAW 391; Berlin: de Gruyter, 2008); William A. Tooman, *Gog of Magog: Reuse of Scripture and Compositional Technique in Ezekiel 38–39* (FAT II/52; Tübingen: Mohr Siebeck, 2011).

[4] Tooman, *Gog of Magog*, 274.

[5] Tooman, *Gog of Magog*, 35.

[6] Tooman, *Gog of Magog*, 37.

[7] Not only do I find several of the connections that Tooman identifies problematic (e.g., Num 24), those links he deems determinative for the date of Ezekiel 38–39 are tenuous. Tooman places Ezekiel 38–39 in the 4th to 2nd centuries BCE based heavily on connections to Joel 1:6; 2:27, and Isaiah 62:2; 66:19 (p. 271). Tooman himself admits the Joel 1:6 link is remote (p. 98). Joel 2:27 neither includes the key divine title (Holy One) Tooman is examining nor shares the same syntax as Ezek 39:7. Though Isa 62:2 is similar to Ezek 39:21 (it includes גוים and ראה), neither it nor Isa 52:10 (which he also mentions) uses the same phrase as the Gog oracles. Finally, Tooman maintains that Isa 66:19 is a source for the groups named in Ezekiel 38–39 (Put, Tubal, and Tarshish) and also that it inspires the phrases "my glory among the nations" as well as "all the nations will see" in Ezek 39:21. Each point is questionable: Ezekiel had access to all the group names from other texts (Gen 10 and elsewhere in Ezekiel), so this cannot be determinative of a date after Third Isaiah; in Ezek 39:21 YHWH puts (נתן) YHWH's own glory amongst all the nations and they see (ראה) his judgments, whereas in Isa 66:19 the nations (lacking כל) declare (נגד) YHWH's glory. To be sure, Tooman is justified to see similarities between Ezek 39:21 and Isa 66:19, but there is insufficient evidence to conclude the direction of dependance necessary for dating the Gog oracles later than Third Isaiah.

Tooman's other basis for dating the Gog oracles is the "comparative evidence that GO is a second temple text" (p. 271). Although he does mention Dan 9 (immediately dismissing it from the discussion, p. 200, n. 6), he does not address either Ezekiel 20 or Neh 9—both of which parallel Ezekiel 38–39's indebtedness to a wide variety of earlier texts, a propensity to adopt and adapt their locutions (on which, see Risa Levitt Kohn, *A New Heart and a New Soul* [JSOTSup 358; London: Sheffield Academic Press, 2002] and Mark J. Boda, *Praying the Tradition: The Origin and Use of Tradition in Nehemiah 9* [BZAW 277; Berlin: Walter de Gruyter, 1999]), and attempts to fill perceived gaps in the sources (e.g. Ezek 20:23-25). If these texts also qualify

As an aside in his argument, Tooman rejects the notion that Ezekiel 38–39 is "an [oracle against a foreign nation], perhaps even a coded indictment of Bablyon."[8] For Tooman, that view rests upon three faulty premises. First, such arguments deny that YHWH's battle with Gog should be classified as apocalyptic. Those same commentators assume there is a connection between apocalyptic and eschatology observes Tooman, so that they deduce that the incongruities between Ezekiel 38–39 and other so-called apocalyptic texts exclude the possibility that the Gog oracle describes events in a far off future. Finally, advocates of the oracles against the nation interpretation maintain that a non-apocalyptic, non-eschatological Ezekiel 38–39 must deal with events and figures from the sixth century BCE, requiring that a historical, sixth-century political enemy of Judah known to Ezekiel and the Judahites in Babylonia lies behind Gog and his armies.

Tooman is correct to question these premises. Of course a prophetic text speaks to its "age," but identifying the "age" of the text only circumscribes the possibilities for its referent and leaves numerous options open. Tooman is also correct to take exception with classifying Ezekiel 38–39 as a foreign nation oracle. But there are at least two other objections that he does not mention. First, while determining whether the text is apocalyptic and/or eschatological is difficult, resolving the issue is irrelevant; Anathea Portier-Young has shown that apocalyptic literature can be used to resist a real, historical empire just like other genres.[9] Indeed, her work will be an important guide in reassessing Ezekiel 38–39 in due course. Second, Ezekiel 38–39 is eschatological, but only insofar as John Barton defines that term as the view "that history (national, international, or even cosmic) has an end or goal which will one day arrive, and the path towards which passes through various distinct phases or epochs."[10] It is impossible to say if Ezekiel 38–39 envisions its cataclysmic events as imminent or distant because all indications of timeframe within it are imprecise at best.

Conceding Tooman's points and adding these others do not preclude Ezekiel 38–39 from being a coded indictment of Babylon; it means that different premises are needed to substantiate that view. I shall argue in this essay that Ezekiel 38–39 is a coded indictment of Babylon on three different premises. First, the sixth-century

---

as thematic pastiche, and there are numerous reasons to think they do, then this evidence that a similar strategy to that employed in Ezekiel 38–39 was already prevalent during the 5th and perhaps even 6th centuries BCE challenges Tooman's second argument for the Hellenistic date of Ezekiel 38–39.

Tooman has justifiably opened a debate about the provenance of the Gog oracles in view of its allusions to other texts—including other texts in Ezekiel—but he has not demonstrated conclusively that Ezekiel 38–39 dates to the 4th century BCE or later.

[8] Tooman, *Gog of Magog*, 133; Klein, *Schriftauslegung*, 115.

[9] Anathea Portier-Young, *Apocalypse against Empire: Theologies of Resistance in Early Judaism* (Grand Rapids: Eerdmans, 2011).

[10] John Barton, *Oracles of God: Perceptions of Ancient Prophecy in Israel after the Exile* (London: Darton, Longman and Todd, 1986), 218.

Judahite exiles, just like numerous other subaltern communities across history, resist their overlords with disguised messages that are difficult to detect and intentionally vague even when recognized.[11] Second, acknowledging the importance of reading Ezekiel 38–39 as an integral part of a larger whole, discerning Gog's identity is only possible when the oracles about him and his hordes are read in conjunction with the material that follows in Ezekiel 40–48. Third, building on Tooman's work, Gog's identity only comes into focus when one accounts for the way Ezekiel 38–39 alludes to other texts inside and outside the Hebrew Bible in its description of him. To state this positively, Ezekiel 38–39 is part of the concluding section of the book that intends to resist Neo-Babylonian ideology; but, because of the asymmetric power structure and the threat of a punitive response by the dominant group, it must do so in a veiled manner. Ezekiel 38–48 draws on the form and content of the *Chaoskampf* tradition in order to craft a narrative in which YHWH is portrayed as the victorious deity who defeats chaos, which is embodied in another deity. Instead of a dragon, a sea monster, or a god controlling death, Ezekiel 38–39 personifies chaos in Babylon's patron deity, Marduk. Asserted openly, that seditious message is sure to provoke punishment, so it is advanced in polysemous language, ambiguous images, and through the narrative substructure of Ezekiel 38–48. These chapters constitute a counterdiscourse meant to encourage its audience to resist Babylonian control and to trust patiently in YHWH's promise to deliver them.

My argument proceeds in three stages. First, I discuss the precedent for the presence of a disguised transcript of resistance against the Babylonian empire in Ezekiel. Second, I present evidence that Gog is a foreign deity rather than a foreign human figure. Third, I compare the narrative structure and cosmic imagery of Ezekiel 38–39 with those of other *Chaoskämpfe*, highlighting evidence that indicates *Enū-ma eliš* and Marduk are the models for the plot of Ezekiel 38–48 and Gog, respectively.

PRECEDENT FOR THIS ARGUMENT

To begin, it is sensible to provide a rationale for reading Ezekiel 38–39 as an intentionally ambiguous text intended to resist the Neo-Babylonian empire. The

---

[11] For arguments supporting a sixth century, Babylonian provenance for a large majority of the text in Ezekiel see, *inter alia*, R. E. Clements, "The Chronology of Redaction in Ezek 1–24," in *Ezekiel and His Book: Textual and Literary Criticism and their Interrelation* (ed. J. Lust; BETL 74; Leuven: Peeters, 1986), 283–94, and the summary discussions in Paul M. Joyce, *Ezekiel: A Commentary* (LHBOTS 482; London: T & T Clark, 2007), 3–16, and C. A. Strine, *Sworn Enemies: The Divine Oath, the Book of Ezekiel, and the Polemics of Exile* (BZAW 436; Berlin: de Gruyter, 2013) 18–21. This model, though popular, is not a consensus; Karl-Friedrich Pohlmann, *Der Prophet Hesekiel/Ezechiel* (2 vols; ATD 22; Göttingen: Vandenhoeck & Ruprecht, 1996–2001), represents well the arguments for a long development of the book occurring primarily during the Persian period.

precedent follows from two features of Ezekiel: its indubitable links to other ancient Near Eastern texts and evidence that the book resists Babylonian ideology in a similar fashion elsewhere.

It is hard to overstate the importance of reading Ezekiel against the backdrop of other ancient Near Eastern texts. For instance, Daniel Bodi illuminated YHWH's departure from the Jerusalem temple by demonstrating its similarity to the Mesopotamian poem *Erra and Išum*.[12] Daniel Block expanded these insights to show that Ezekiel resembles other Mesopotamian accounts of divine abandonment.[13] More recently, John Kutsko observed that Ezekiel is indebted to Assyrian and Babylonian practices of cult image spoliation and refurbishment[14] and Margaret Odell's commentary discusses how the book carefully attends to Assyrian and Babylonian influence, showing that it uses these cultural resources which were "voluntarily adopted by the Judahite elite" for various purposes.[15] Closest to the present concerns, Paul Fitzpatrick establishes numerous connections between Ezekiel 38–39 and the *Chaoskampf* myths from across the ancient Near East.[16]

Supporting these insights, there is growing evidence the author(s) of Ezekiel knew at least some of the cuneiform texts that formed the core of Mesopotamian scribal training. Abraham Winitzer, for example, demonstrates similarities between Babylonian scribal techniques and Ezekiel's sign action of lying on his left and right side (Ezek 4:4–6). Elsewhere, Winitzer shows that *Gilgameš* is important background for Ezekiel 28. It is notable that he identifies this connection both through the reuse of particular words but also by observing "that Ezekiel knew *Gilgameš* and *applied its storyline* allegorically in the composition of his oracles."[17] This is a point to which I shall return later.

---

[12] Daniel Bodi, *The Book of Ezekiel and the Poem of Erra* (OBO 104; Göttingen: Vandenhoeck & Ruprecht, 1991). For an English translation of the poem see Benjamin R. Foster, *Before the Muses: An Anthology of Akkadian Literature* (3d ed.; Bethesda: CDL Press, 2005), 880–911 and Stephanie Dalley (*COS* 1.113:404–16).

[13] Daniel I. Block, *Gods of the Nations: Studies in Ancient Near Eastern National Theology* (2d ed.; ETS Studies; Grand Rapids: Baker Academic; Leicester: Apollos, 2000). See also Donna Lee Petter, "The Book of Ezekiel: Patterned After a Mesopotamian City Lament?" (Ph.D. diss., University of Toronto, 2009).

[14] John F. Kutsko, *Between Heaven and Earth: Divine Presence and Absence in the Book of Ezekiel* (Biblical and Judaic Studies from the University of California, San Diego 7; Winona Lake: Eisenbrauns, 2000); see also idem., "Ezekiel's Anthropology and Its Ethical Implications," in *The Book of Ezekiel: Theological and Anthropological Perspectives* (ed. Margaret S. Odell and John T. Strong; SBLSymS; Atlanta: Society of Biblical Literature, 2000), 119–41.

[15] Margaret S. Odell, *Ezekiel* (Macon: Smith & Helwys, 2005), 5–9, esp. 8–9.

[16] Paul E. Fitzpatrick, *The Disarmament of God: Ezekiel 38–39 in Its Mythic Context* (CBQMS 37; Washington: Catholic Biblical Association of America, 2004).

[17] Abraham Winitzer, "Assyriology and Jewish Studies in Tel Aviv: Ezekiel among the Babylonian Literati," in *Encounters by the Rivers of Babylon: Scholarly Conversations between Jews, Iranians and Babylonians in Antiquity* (ed. U. Gabbay and and S. Secunda; Tübingen: Mohr Siebeck, forthcoming). Emphasis added. For further evidence that Ezekiel knew such esoteric

If it is justifiable to conclude that Ezekiel knows and creatively employs features from such Mesopotamian texts, it remains necessary to show that the book uses that knowledge for the purpose of resisting imperial power. This is exemplified in Ezekiel 17.[18]

Ezekiel 17 exhibits a two-fold structure on both the literary and conceptual level.[19] After the opening allegory (17:1–10), the remainder of the passage (17:11–21) interprets Jerusalem's judgment on two levels: vv. 16–18 explain that the king of Babylon carries out the punishment in the human realm while vv. 19–21 indicate that YHWH simultaneously accomplishes these deeds in the divine realm (17:19–21). Alongside its structure, the cosmological imagery of Ezekiel 17 makes the Babylonian king YHWH's earthly agent. Note that YHWH appears as the divine agent who fights and repels chaos, the complex of themes often called the Chaoskampf. Verse 10 is exemplary: it specifies that the vine representing the Judahite king will be struck and withered by an east wind. The רוח הקדים is a storm element, a prominent set of divine weapons in the Chaoskampf. Though the east wind is only mentioned here in Ezekiel 17, the image fits with descriptions of YHWH using a storm (שׁאה; 38:9), a storm wind (רוח סערות; 13:11), and even clouds (ענן; 38:9) elsewhere.[20]

This east wind strikes a vine planted "beside many waters," (על מים רבים; 17:5),[21] which is Zedekiah, the Babylonian installed king of Judah, who is sworn to be a loyal vassal to Babylon (17:6, 13–14). The story plays on Zedekiah's role as a vassal (17:5–6, 13–14): the מים רבים are the chaos waters manifest in the threatening power of Egypt (cf. Ezekiel 19; 31) so that when Zedekiah turns his allegiance to the other great eagle Zedekiah aligns himself with the very מים רבים against which

---

Mesopotamian texts, see Jonathan Stökl, "The מתנבאות of Ezekiel 13 Reconsidered," *JBL* 132 (2013): 61–76.

[18] For a detailed treatment of the issue, see Strine, *Sworn Enemies*, 228–43.

[19] Moshe Greenberg, *Ezekiel 1-20: A New Translation with Introduction and Commentary* (AB 22; Garden City: Doubleday, 1983), 317–20.

[20] These elements are comparable to the sirocco, a hot wind characteristic of the dry season (cf. A. Fitzgerald, *The Lord of the East Wind* [CBQMS 34; Washington: Catholic Biblical Association of America, 2002], 175–77). Ezekiel 13 also describes YHWH using storm elements, namely, a driving rain (גשׁם שׁטף; 13:11) and great hailstones (אבני אלגביש; 13:13); these are characteristic of the rainstorms that occur during the wet season. See Fitzgerald, *East Wind*, for a detailed discussion of the various storms and storm imagery in the Hebrew Bible.

[21] Though scholars consistently interpret על מים רבים in v. 5 as non-adversarial—indicative of the positive character of the vine's seedbed (Walter Zimmerli, *A Commentary on the Book of the Prophet Ezekiel, Chapters 1-24* [transl. R. E. Clements; Hermeneia; Minneapolis: Fortress, 1979], 362; Greenberg, *Ezekiel 1-20*, 310; Daniel I. Block, *The Book of Ezekiel: Chapters 1-24* [NICOT; Grand Rapids: Eerdmans, 1997], 531; Joyce, *Ezekiel*, 136), this reading fails both to account for the point of the allegory and also to recognize that everywhere else in Ezekiel the image marks its referent as a force of chaos to be resisted. Margaret Odell is correct to remark that although the מים רבים "appears to be innocuous . . . its use elsewhere suggests that it has a more sinister connotation" (Odell, *Ezekiel*, 240).

he is meant to defend (v. 8).[22] Judah and its king no longer serve as a buffer against Egypt on behalf of Babylon, but transform into the advanced front of the Egyptian threat. YHWH responds by enlisting the Babylonian king to judge Zedekiah because the defiant Judahite king is now a force of chaos, not order.

This last point is crucial: the cosmological imagery of Ezekiel 17 implicitly challenges an ideology with which it disagrees by (re)appropriating those very same cosmological images. The text re-imagines the way the world is arranged: it labels Zedekiah as a force of chaos and the Babylonian king a force of order, albeit under the aegis of YHWH, not Marduk.[23] The interpretation of the allegory in vv. 11–24 clarifies this last point. The withering east wind of v. 10 corresponds to YHWH's net in v. 20 that captures the Judahite king Zedekiah.[24] The net is not selected haphazardly, but appears here because it evokes Enūma eliš. There, Marduk uses it, the wind, and his bow and arrow in order to kill Tiamat. Enūma eliš IV 93–104 recounts Marduk's battle with Tiamat:

Tiamat and Marduk, sage of the gods, drew close for battle,
They locked in single combat, joining for the fray.

The Lord spread out his net, encircled her,
The ill wind he had held behind him he released in her face.
Tiamat opened her mouth to swallow,
He thrust in the ill wind so she could not close her lips.

The raging winds bloated her belly,
Her insides were stopped up, she gaped her mouth wide.
He shot off the arrow, it broke open her belly,
It cut to her innards, it pierced the heart.

He subdued her and snuffed out her life,
He flung down her carcass, he took his stand upon it.[25]

---

[22] So, read vv. 7–8 thus: "Behold, there was another great eagle—with great wings and much plumage. Look, this vine bent its roots toward him and its branches reached out to him so that he caused it to be nourished. In a good field, by many waters it was planted to grow branches and to produce fruit to be a noble vine." Verses 9–10 are the rhetorical question that make this clear: can it turn from its assigned role thus and succeed? Of course not.

[23] C. L. Crouch and C. A. Strine, "YHWH's Battle against Chaos in Ezekiel: The Transformation of Judahite Mythology for a New Situation," JBL 132 (2013): 883–903. See also Jer 25:9; 27:6; 43:10 where Nebuchadnezzar is called "servant of YHWH" and the discussion of this language in Konrad Schmid, "Nebukadnezars Antritt der Weltherrscheft und der Abbruch der Davidsdynastie: Innerbiblische Schriftauslegung und universalgeschichtliche Konstruktion im Jeremiabuch," in Die Textualisierung der Religion (ed. Joachim Shaper; Tübingen: Mohr Siebeck, 2009), 150–66, esp. 159–63.

[24] Block, Ezekiel 1–24, 536–39.

[25] See the "Epic of Creation" in Foster, Before the Muses, 460–61, Tablet IV 93–104 (cf. Tablet IV 35–44). Textual arrangement in four verse stanzas follows that of Philippe Talon, The Standard Babylonian Creation Myth: Enuma Eliš: Introduction, Cuneiform Text, Transliteration, and Sign List with a Translation and Glossary in French (SAACT 4; Helsinki: The Neo-Assyrian Text

A net is a common tool, one that has many uses beyond divine combat to be sure.[26] Still, its sudden appearance as YHWH's weapon in Ezek 17:20, in a context where YHWH employs the Bablyonian king as a human servant and defeats enemies depicted as chaos, closely parallels the account of Marduk defeating Tiamat in *Enūma eliš*. It is the combination of these factors, not the appearance of the net alone, that encourages the conclusion that Ezekiel portrays YHWH in images reminiscent of Marduk.

Chapter 17 culminates with more evidence that *Enūma eliš* IV is part of its backdrop. In the concluding verse (v. 24) YHWH restores Judah so that "all the trees of the field"—an image of foreign kings as a metonymy for their nations[27]—"shall recognize that 'I am YHWH: I make low the exalted tree and I make high the lowly tree . . . I am YHWH: I have spoken and I will act" (Ezek 17:24; cf. 21:31). Compare that statement to *Enūma eliš* IV 5–8:

> O Marduk, you are the most important among the great gods,
> Your destiny is unrivalled, your command is supreme!
> Henceforth your command cannot be changed,
> To raise high, to bring low, this shall be your power.[28]

The cluster of allusions in Ezekiel 17 not just to *Enūma eliš* generally but to Tablet IV in particular reinforces the previous deduction, namely, that this assembly of images tacitly presents YHWH in Marduk's distinctive role. Said another way, Ezekiel 17 replaces Marduk with YHWH as the divine king.[29]

Corpus Project, 2005), 93. Note as well Tablet VI 80–84, where the net is placed with the bow in the presence of the gods as demonstration of Marduk's feat. Thorkild Jacobsen (*The Treasures of Darkness: A History of Mesopotamian Religion* [New Haven: Yale University Press, 1976], 167–91) offers a succinct description of the story and of the role of the net and bow (p. 182).

[26] For the various uses of *saparru*, the term used in *Enūma eliš* IV, from ensnaring animals to meteorological phenomenon, see CAD S, 161–63. A similar role is ascribed to the net (CAD S, 161–62, s.v. saparru 1b, 5b) of the gods in their judgment of Assurbanipal's enemies, demonstrating the applicability of this image for Ezekiel 17 (Maximilian Streck, *Assurbanipal und die letzten assyrischen Könige bis zum Untergange Ninevehs* [Vorderasiatische Bibliothek 7.2; Leipzig: Hinrichs, 1916], 37). The image is not limited to deities, as Esarhaddon claims the concept for himself in one of his inscriptions (Rykle Borger, *Die Inschriften Asarhaddons, Königs Von Assyrien* [AfOB 9; Graz: Im Selbstverlag des Herausgebers, 1956], 58).

Standard Akkadian has three other terms meaning net: *pūgu*, *šētu*, and *šuškallu*. These terms appear in various contexts from hunting animals (e.g., *šētu* A, CAD Š/2, 340) to the oncoming of debilitating drowsiness (e.g., CAD Š/3, 383), but also feature in descriptions of capturing enemies. The plurality of roles these terms for net can play is a real factor in considering the likelihood of a link between Ezekiel 17 and *Enūma eliš*, but the variation does not obscure the strong parallel between the two texts.

[27] Greenberg, *Ezekiel 1–20*, 316; Block, *Ezekiel 1–24*, 552.

[28] Foster, *Before the Muses*, 457.

[29] Thus, Block is correct to comment, "this oracle is . . . about the cosmic sovereignty and fidelity of Yahweh" (*Ezekiel 1-24*, 552).

This seditious message is conveyed in polysemous language. Ezekiel 17 creates ambiguity with its image-rich text and through the implicit statement made by its structure. Upon scrutiny from the dominant group, the subversive message could be attributed to general knowledge of kingship metaphors and to unintentional structural parallels. One could argue that the polemical interpretation is accidental, not indicative of subversive intent. It is this possibility of interpreting Ezekiel 17 innocuously that allays the threat of a penal response by the dominant group. Indeed, one might even claim that Ezekiel 17 portrays the Babylonian king, Marduk's earthly representative, in positive terms while unreservedly condemning the Judahite king for rebellion against Babylon. On that construal Ezekiel 17 agrees with Babylonian rhetoric rather than challenges it.

If this sounds like speaking out of both sides of one's mouth, that is both true and fundamental to my argument. James C. Scott demonstrates that subaltern groups are widely characterized as cunning or deceptive as a result of the way in which their anti-imperial views seep into public statements in the form of disguised expressions.[30] Scott describes this as a "verbal facility" that allows the oppressed "to conduct what amounts to a veiled discourse of dignity and self-assertion within the public transcript."[31] The modes of concealment are "limited only by the imaginative capacity of subordinates" and "[i]t is impossible to overestimate the subtlety of this manipulation."[32] Ambiguity, in other words, protects the subjugated voice. It "permits subordinate groups to undercut the authorized cultural norms" in such a way that "the excluded (and in this case, powerful) audience may grasp the seditious message in the performance but find it difficult to react because that sedition is clothed in terms that can also lay claim to a perfectly innocent construction."[33]

The vulnerability of the Judahite exiles to Babylonian power did not permit them "the luxury of direct confrontation."[34] Therefore, to identify anti-imperial messages in Ezekiel it is imperative to heed Scott's guidance that "[i]f we wish to hear this side of the dialogue we shall have to learn its dialect and codes."[35] Ezekiel 17 indicates that allusion to and transformation of *Enūma eliš* is one way in which the book encodes its counterdiscourse.

---

[30] James C. Scott, *Domination and the Arts of Resistance: Hidden Transcripts* (New Haven: Yale University Press, 1990).

[31] Scott, *Domination*, 137.

[32] Scott, *Domination*, 139.

[33] Scott, *Domination*, 159.

[34] Scott, *Domination*, 136.

[35] Scott, *Domination*, 138.

GOG AS A FOREIGN DEITY

Prior to discussing how Ezekiel 38–39 encodes its message of resistance, it is necessary to discuss a common position, namely, that Gog of Magog must represent a human figure.[36] Careful reconsideration of the way in which Ezekiel 38–39 portrays Gog favors identifying him as a foreign deity.

There are three features which suggest that Gog should not be associated with a strictly historical figure. First, it is important to recognize that Gog hails from Magog, a place of uncertain location. Magog is a symbolic space, probably one that the author(s) did not conceive as mappable and did not intend to be identified definitively.[37] A similarly symbolic meaning applies to Gog's horde, which is comprised of armies from nations that represent the known world.[38] Although either feature could be used in a hyperbolic description of a human king or army, the non-geographic and non-historical nature of the images opens the question of whether this language points towards a historical or ahistorical referent.

A second feature also points away from Gog being a human figure. Ezekiel 38:9 depicts Gog advancing "like a devastating storm" (שֹאָה; cf. Isa 10:3; Zeph 1:15) and "like a cloud that covers the earth" (כֶעָנָן לְכַסוֹת הָאָרֶץ). These images evoke both Baal the "rider upon the clouds" (e.g., KTU 1.3 iii 36–38, 1.4 iii 10–11, 17–18, etc.; cf. Ps 104:3) and Marduk, who deploys the four winds along with numerous other storm elements (Enūma eliš IV 42–58). Although such cosmic language described kings in the Neo-Assyrian period,[39] that sort of description does not feature in the Neo-Babylonian period.[40] While it remains possible that Ezekiel attributed this cosmic imagery to a human figure, both the wider Mesopotamian usage and the way in which Ezekiel 17 employs similar storm imagery only to characterize Judah's patron deity indicate that Gog's cosmic features denote his divine identity.

Thirdly, Ezekiel's appropriation of the foe from the north theme is ahistorical in character. Brevard Childs observes that Ezekiel's idiosyncratic use of the great army approaching from the north "has been elevated into the trans-historical. . . . Gog has become the representative of the cosmic powers of the returned chaos

---

[36] The possibility that Gog represents a divine figure has been advanced in the past. For instance, Johannes Hermann proposed a connection between Gog and the deity Kakka who appears in Tablet III of Enūma eliš (Johannes Hermann, Ezechiel übersetzt und erklärt [KAT 11; Leipzig: Deichert, 1924], 244), although his argument is unconvincing.

[37] Cf. Corrine Carvalho, "The God That Gog Creates," Forthcoming.

[38] Whereas Odell maps the nations into an alliance of northern and southern countries (Odell, Ezekiel, 466–71), Tooman places them in a circular arrangement that covers all points of the compass (Tooman, Gog of Magog, 147–50). In either case, the effect is the same: Gog is supported by a horde indicative of worldwide domination.

[39] See C. L. Crouch, War and Ethics in the Ancient Near East: Military Violence in Light of Cosmology and History (BZAW 407; Berlin: de Gruyter, 2009), 35–64.

[40] David S. Vanderhooft, The Neo-Babylonian Empire and Babylon in the Latter Prophets (HSM 59; Atlanta: Scholars Press, 1999), 40–41.

which Yahweh destroys in the latter days, powers that cannot be described as historical."[41] Childs correctly recognizes that Gog is something other than a historical human character and is instead a figure who represents cosmic chaos, the very definition of the divine adversary in the *Chaoskampf*.

If these three points support identifying Gog as a deity, what is to be made of YHWH assigning Gog a burial site in Israel (39:11)? Surely a deity does not have a physical grave. Note, however, how the text states that Gog is buried in the valley of the Oberim (גי העברים) east of the sea (קדמת הים). Francesca Stavrakopoulou remarks that this location "points to the mythic-symbolic function of a valley as the intersection of the earthly realm and the underworld."[42] Bearing in mind that deities are depicted descending into and ascending from the subterranean home of the dead in other ancient Near Eastern myths (e.g., *The Descent of Ishtar to the Underworld*; Baal's defeat by Mot), it is not at all clear that Gog's gravesite indicates that he is a human. Indeed, the name Oberim evokes "the Ugaritic word *'brm*, which denotes the deified dead," according to Stavrakopoulou, but that can only be conjecture. Nonetheless, it is likely that there is a double entendre in Gog's fallen army being called המון (39:11; cf. 39:15), which can mean crowd or horde, but is also a common way to describe chaos.[43]

None of these points alone proves that Gog is a deity, but the cumulative effect of these features is, as Fitzpatrick notes, to present "Gog as the antithesis of creation."[44] It also justifies asking, "Does a human or divine Gog better fit in the plot of Ezekiel 38–39?" Here, an argument from symmetry may be advanced, namely, that identifying Gog as a foreign deity balances the battle between YHWH and Gog. If YHWH's adversary represents a foreign human king, then the battle is between a divine power and a human power. YHWH's victory might be complete, but the defeat of a mere human being and his armies is hardly an awe-inspiring act for a deity. By contrast, if the battle pits YHWH against a foreign deity who can summon cosmic forces and human armies from every corner of the known world, then the outcome is legitimately in doubt. Victory, in this scenario, is both remarkable and capable of producing the awe and wonder of YHWH that Ezekiel 38–39 stresses is the point of the battle (i.e., 38:16, 23; 39:6, 7, 21). Fitzpatrick grasps this dynamic when he reckons that Ezekiel 38–39, like the broader ancient Near Eastern *Chaoskampf* tradition, presents deities battling with one another.[45]

Fitzpatrick expands this line of argument to support his view that the Gog oracle is "a new ending to the Israelite cosmogonic myth" that offers fulfillment to

---

[41] Brevard S. Childs, "The Enemy From the North and the Chaos Tradition," *JBL* 78 (1959): 187–98 (196). Cf. Klein, *Schriftauslegung*, 132–40.

[42] Francesca Stavrakopoulou, "Gog's Grave and the Use and Abuse of Corpses in Ezekiel 39:11-20," *JBL* 129 (2010): 67–84 (77).

[43] Stephen L. Cook, *Prophecy and Apocalypticism: The Postexilic Social Setting* (Minneapolis: Fortress Press, 1989), 93.

[44] Fitzpatrick, *The Disarmament of God*, 87.

[45] Fitzpatrick, *The Disarmament of God*, 105–08.

the Israelite creation myth.[46] Though he correctly apprehends the importance of the *Chaoskampf* for understanding Ezekiel 38–39, he overplays creation as the key theme of the *Chaoskampf*. Neither in Ezekiel 38–39 nor elsewhere in the book does YHWH create the heavens and earth. John Day demonstrated that "there are passages in the Old Testament which associate Yahweh's conflict with the dragon and the sea with the creation of the world,"[47] but none of those instances are in Ezekiel. Furthermore, Day showed that the concern for creation was appropriated from the West Semitic, not the Mesopotamian, manifestation of the *Chaskampf*.[48] W. G. Lambert established almost a half-century ago with respect to *Enūma eliš*, the exemplar of that tradition, that its primary concern is to affirm Marduk as the deity who "held all might and all right."[49] This cosmic projection of Nebuchadnezzar I's *Realpolitik* concentrates on the theme of supremacy, not creation. Likewise, this is the explicitly stated result that Ezekiel 38–39 predicates of those who witness YHWH's defeat of Gog (cf. 38:16, 23; 39:6, 7, 21). The focus of the Gog oracle is not creation, but a divine struggle for cosmic authority.[50]

EZEKIEL 38–48* AS CHAOSKAMPF MYTH

Susan Niditch has noted the similarities between the temple vision of Ezekiel 40–48 and "an extremely ancient mythic pattern," namely "that of the victory and enthronement of the deity."[51] "The essential action motifs or plot events of this traditional literary theme," she continues, "consist of (1) a challenge to the deity, (2) a battle, (3) a victory, (4) a procession, (5) the enthronement/building of a 'house,' and (6) a feast."[52] Niditch then focuses on the way that this pattern replicates "the Babylonian *Enuma elish*, which depicts Marduk's victory over Tiamat, and . . . the Canaanite epic of Baal and Anat, which tells of Baal's victory over the Sea and of his temporary defeat by and eventual victory over Death."[53]

Without disregarding the likelihood that there are influences on Ezekiel 38–48 that lie beyond these two texts, the previously noted connections to *Enūma eliš* elsewhere in Ezekiel and the shared concern for the supremacy of one particular

---

[46] Fitzpatrick, *The Disarmament of God*, 194.

[47] John Day, *God's Conflict with the Dragon and the Sea: Echoes of a Canaanite Myth in the Old Testament* (COP 35; Cambridge: Cambridge University Press, 1985), 61.

[48] Day, *God's Conflict*, 61.

[49] W. G. Lambert, "The Reign of Nebuchadnezzar I: A Turning Point in the History of Ancient Mesopotamian Religion," in *The Seeds of Wisdom: Essays in Honor of T. J. Meek* (ed. W.S. McCullough; Toronto: University of Toronto Press, 1964), 4.

[50] Or, as Klein remarks (*Schriftauslegung*, 140), "Gog is not only the last enemy in the book itself, but in the overall shape of the book also presents the victory of YHWH over this enemy as the ultimate demonstration of his sovereignty."

[51] Susan Niditch, "Ezekiel 40–48 in a Visionary Context," *CBQ* 48 (1996): 208–24 (221).

[52] Niditch, "Ezekiel 40–48," 221; cf. Fitzpatrick, *The Disarmament of God*, 181–92.

[53] Niditch, "Ezekiel 40–48," 221.

deity in both texts supports revisiting and expanding Niditch's deduction. In addition, Winitzer's assessment that the plot structure of *Gilgameš* informs the story in Ezekiel 28 offers a precedent for a renewed analysis of how Ezekiel 38–48 interacts with the plot structure of *Enūma eliš*, an equally prominent Mesopotamian text.[54] And, finally, the absence of evidence that Gog is modeled on the dragon or the sea, the cosmic antagonists in the Baal Cycle,[55] points away from the West Semitic version of the *Chaoskampf* and towards its Mesopotamian exemplar.

It remains necessary to establish the text for analysis. The existence of 𝔓967 provides the rare occasion on which the diachronic growth of a canonical text is traceable. The Old Greek (hereafter OG) tradition represented by 𝔓967 has Ezekiel 37 following the Gog oracles in Ezekiel 38–39, before concluding with Ezekiel 40–48 in a form that matches the MT with few exceptions. Space prohibits any detailed discussion of the issues, so it must suffice to mention that the work of Johan Lust, Ashley Crane, and Ingrid Lilly gives ample evidence that 𝔓967 attests an older arrangement of the book than the MT.[56] It is logical to work with the OG arrangement in view of the aims of this essay and, for the remainder of it, Ezekiel 38–48* shall refer to the textual arrangement in 𝔓967 where Ezekiel 38–39 comes before Ezekiel 37, which is then followed by Ezekiel 40–48.

The plot of Ezekiel 38–48* can be summarized as follows:[57]

38:1–13	Preparation for Battle (with description of Gog's army)
38:14–23	Description of the Coming Battle
39:1–8	Battle between Gog and YHWH
39:9–20	Disposal of Gog and his horde
39:21–24	Summary of the Message for Israel in these Events
39:25–29	Promise to Restore Israel
37:1–14	(Re)Creation of Humanity
37:15–28	Unification of Tribes

---

[54] Winitzer, "Assyriology and Jewish Studies in Tel Aviv," forthcoming.

[55] On the distinctive nature of these enemies in the West Semitic tradition embodied at Ugarit, see Day, *God's Conflict*, 7–12. For further discussion of similarities between East and West Semitic traditions and possible tradents see Jean-Marie Durand, "Le mythologème du combat entre le Dieu de l'Orage et la Mer en Mésopotamie," *MARI* 7 (1993): 41–61.

[56] See Crane, *Israel's Restoration*, and Lilly, *Two Books*, for full treatments of the issue. For an overview of Johan Lust's work on the topic see, *inter alia*, J. Lust, "Ezekiel 36–40 in the Oldest Greek Manuscript," *CBQ* 43 (1981): 517–33; idem., "The Sequence of Ez 36–40 and the Omission of Ez 36,23c–38 in Pap. 967 and in Codex Wirceburgensis," *BIOSCS* 14 (1981): 45–46; idem., "The Use of Textual Witnesses for the Establishment of the Text. The Shorter and Longer Texts of Ezekiel," in *Ezekiel and His Book: Textual and Literary Criticism and Their Interrelation* (ed. J. Lust; BETL 74; Leuven: Peeters, 1986), 7–20; and idem., "Major Divergences Between LXX and MT in Ezekiel," in *The Earliest Text of the Hebrew Bible: The Relationship between the Masoretic Text and the Hebrew Base of the Septuagint Reconsidered* (ed. A. Schenker; SBLSCS 52; Atlanta: Society of Biblical Literature, 2003), 83–92.

[57] For variations on this outline, see Daniel I. Block, *The Book of Ezekiel: Chapters 25–48* (NICOT; Grand Rapids: Eerdmans, 1998) and Tooman, *Gog of Magog*, 134–37.

40–47:12   Temple Vision
47:13–48:34   Assignment of places for leaders/tribes
48:35   Arrival of YHWH

Lest it be obscured in the detailed discussion that follows, note that the plotline of Ezekiel 38–48* resembles Tablets IV to VI of *Enūma eliš*: a battle between deities ends with the death of the losing deity who is dismembered and disposed of (IV 85–V 62), after which humanity is created (VI 1–38) as a prelude to the climactic construction of a temple to honor the victorious deity (VI 45–79). Ezekiel 38–48* does not follow the plot of *Enūma eliš* exactly, but the similarities are conspicuous and far stronger than between Ezekiel and any other extant text from the ancient Near East.

The first section (38:1–13) describes how Gog and his horde prepare for the coming battle. Gog is identified as the prince, head of Meshech and Tubal, and the nations composing his horde are named. At an indeterminate time in the future (מימים רבים) Gog will advance against the mountains of Israel with the wicked intention to plunder the land. This section resembles *Enūma eliš* IV 30–58: Marduk, just enthroned on his royal dais and having proved his power by creating and destroying a constellation, is adorned with "unstoppable weaponry" (IV 30) for his fight against Tiamat. It is probably not incidental that YHWH's battle with Gog will occur at the navel of the earth (טבור הארץ; v. 12), an image reminiscent of Nebuchadnezzar II's rhetoric that portrays Babylon (Marduk's cultic home) as the center of the world.[58]

When 38:4 speaks of Gog's hordes as horses and horsemen, their "clothing and weapons (vv. 4b–5) are itemized in some detail, using locutions culled from Ezek 21, Ezek 27, and, especially, from Ezek 23" writes Tooman.[59] Pinpointing the allusion to Ezek 23:12, Tooman remarks that the imagery adds "nothing to the plot or argument of [the Gog oracle]" and only serves to direct the audience's mind back to this earlier material. Tooman is unable to explain how Ezekiel 38 interprets or reformulates this material as his model predicts it should. His error is in seeking an explanation at all. The image is not reinterpreted but stealthily connects Gog's hordes with the foreign armies of Ezekiel 23: the Assyrians and the Babylonians (23:12–18).[60]

Ezekiel 38:9 supports this assessment. There Gog takes the form of "a devastating storm" (שואה; cf. Isa 10:3; Zeph 1:15) and "a cloud that covers the earth" (כענן לכסות הארץ). These images are redolent of the *Chaoskampf* generally, but in the context of an allusion to Mesopotamian armies they recall that Marduk sets flashing lightning before his face (*birqu*; IV 39), then fashions a storm (*imḫullu*), an evil wind (*šāru lemnu*), a tempest (*meḫû*), and cyclone (*ašamšutu*; all four in IV 45), and finally, as his greatest weapon, prepares a deluge (*abūbu*; IV 49).

---

[58] Vanderhooft, *Neo-Babylonian Empire*, 45–49.

[59] Tooman, *Gog of Magog*, 152–53.

[60] So also, Klein, *Schriftauslegung*, 129–30.

Still more persuasive evidence that a Mesopotamian army lies behind Gog's hordes comes in Tooman's own contention that "the pieces and parts of 38.7-13 follow the order of elements in [Isa 10 and Jer 49] (almost) perfectly."[61] Isaiah 10 condemns Assyria, who is the rod of Yhwh's anger, for exceeding its remit and conceiving arrogant plans of conquest (cf. Ezek 38:10-13). Jeremiah 49 is even more specific: the verbal similarities are to Jer 49:28-33,[62] a pericope that recounts Nebuchadnezzar's assault and plunder of Kedar and Hazor. Tooman concludes that "[t]he characterization of Nebuchadnezzar's thoughts as a scheme, an evil plan, is used to depict Gog as well."[63] The depiction is not just of Gog, but of Gog and his human army; in symmetry with Yhwh and the people of Israel, the text presents Gog as the foreign divine power symbolizing chaos who is represented in the human realm by these imperial armies.

The next section (38:14-23) offers a prologue to the battle between Gog and Yhwh. Gog and his army, advancing like a cloud that darkens the land, are met by Yhwh, whose raging anger manifests in an earthquake, a destroying sword, pestilence, and other elements from a cataclysmic storm. This corresponds to Enūma eliš IV 60-86. Marduk sets out towards Tiamat and sets his face against her. A conversation ensues between them about the actions that have brought them to this point, with Marduk's final statement indicating that it is a prelude to the real drama: "Come within range, let us duel, you and I!" It is worth noting the reason that Marduk gives for the ensuing battle, specifically Tiamat's disrespect towards Anšar (IV 83-84). Another motivation goes unspecified, namely, that Marduk's willingness to fight Tiamat is tied to his plan to be enthroned as the divine king. Both points correspond to the motivation for Yhwh's battle with Gog: "I will magnify myself, and cause myself to be hallowed, and I will be known in the eyes of many nations. And they will know that I am Yhwh" (38:23). Or, as Tooman remarks, "[t]here is no concern for Israel. . . . God acts for the sake of his reputation."[64]

Though there are some terms in 38:14-23 that bear a passing resemblance to the depiction of Marduk in the Enūma eliš,[65] it is in Ezek 39:1-8 that the most im-

---

[61] Tooman, Gog of Magog, 157.

[62] Tooman, Gog of Magog, 158; cf. Klein, Schriftauslegung, 135.

[63] Tooman, Gog of Magog, 158.

[64] Tooman, Gog of Magog, 164-65.

[65] Gog's forces, a great horde and a vast army, all ride horses (38:15). This is comparable to Marduk's forces, which are headed by an awesome storm that is described as a terrible chariot, a four-team steed of horses called Slaughterer, Merciless, Overwhelmer, and Soaring (EE IV 50-51). Ezekiel 38:22 presents Yhwh's judgment in three dyads: pestilence and blood, rain and hailstones, and fire and brimstone. The first two come from elsewhere in Ezekiel; the third, similar to the judgment on Sodom and Gomorrah in Gen 19:24, is not wholly dissimilar from EE IV 40, which explains that Marduk covers his body with a raging fire (nablu muštaḥmeṭu) in order to battle Tiamat. While the brimstone has no obvious counterpart in EE IV, the abundance of storm imagery is not unconnected to the great deluge (abūbu; EE IV 75) and the various other storm images in this section.

portant links occur. The section opens with YHWH declaring that "I am against you" (cf. IV 60) and saying that YHWH will cause Gog to turn round, to drive on, to go up from the far reaches of the north, and to come to the mountains of Israel, where the battle will take place. This statement has exercised scholars who are uncomfortable with YHWH controlling Gog in this fashion. But a different, perhaps less problematic, approach is suggested by *Enūma eliš* IV 87–90, where Marduk's challenge to Tiamat throws her into a wild rage that results in her coming forth for battle. Perhaps Ezek 39:1–2 envisions a similar situation in which YHWH's declaration of intent (הנני אליך גוג; v. 1b) merely instigates Gog's procession to the battleground (thus the causative form of עלה in v. 2).

Tooman also demonstrates that 39:1–8 draws from Isa 14.[66] That oracle explicitly condemns the king of Babylon for his oppressive acts, though it is widely believed to be a reappropriation of an oracle originally directed against Assyria. Because Tooman decides on other evidence that Ezekiel 38–39 is subsequent to the work of Deutero-Isaiah, he presumes the author of the Gog oracles follows Deutero-Isaiah's lead here.[67] Absent that debatable assessment of the Gog oracle's date,[68] it is equally plausible that Ezek 39:1–8 knows the Neo-Assyrian period material in Isa 14 and precedes Deutero-Isaiah in reappropriating it against Babylon. As I shall argue below, because Ezekiel is largely shaped by the asymetric power structure of the mid sixth-century BCE—when Babylonian hegemony made explicit resistance perilous—it refashions themes from Isa 14 to condemn the Babylonians covertly. Deutero-Isaiah, a product from an era when Babylonian power was waning and overt resistance to it was less treacherous, is, by contrast, free to name Babylon explicitly.[69] Differing socio-political circumstances explain the conceptual agreement and rhetorical divergence of the two texts.

Further evidence that Ezek 39:1–8 has *Enūma eliš* as background comes from the brief but decisive description of YHWH defeating Gog in v. 3. This concise summary declares that YHWH will strike Gog's bow from his left hand and cause the arrow to fall from Gog's right hand. Neither weapon appears in the earlier description of Gog, so their introduction here necessitates an explanation. Consider Marduk's slaying of Tiamat, in which he impedes her with a net and uses the winds to open her mouth, at which point (IV 101–102):

He shot off the arrow, it broke open her belly,
It cut to her innards, it pierced the heart.[70]

---

[66] Tooman, *Gog of Magog*, 169–75.

[67] For instance, Klein, *Schriftauslegung*, 128, concludes that Ezek 39:3 draws on the oracles against Egypt in Ezekiel 29–30, especially 29:5 and 30:22.

[68] See note 7 above.

[69] Cf. Strine, *Sworn Enemies*, 258–62.

[70] Foster, *Before the Muses*, 460.

Paired with the evidence from Ezek 17 and the other indications that *Enūma eliš* provides context for the Gog oracle, it hardly seems accidental that YHWH's defeat of Gog includes disabling the very weapon with which Marduk kills Tiamat.

Ezekiel 39:9–20 advances the narrative with three events: the people burn the weapons of their now dead enemies (vv. 9–10), Gog and his horde are interred in גי העברים (vv. 11–16), and then the bodies of Gog and his horde are devoured by the birds and animals (vv. 17–20). Although Tooman recognizes that "this episode is unique,"[71] he searches for texts that inspire it (e.g., Deut 26:9 and Jer 7:32), only to conclude that the whole is "predicated upon Priestly notions about the defiling effects of corpses on the land."[72] If one follows his initial observation that there is no clear precedent for this scene in the Hebrew Bible and looks outside it, other possibilities emerge. For instance, Stavrakopoulou maintains that "the use and abuse of corpses in this narrative are more importantly indicative of the powerful social, territorial, and ideological function of Gog's grave: its construction, placing, and presence assert Israel's claim to its land and legitimize the exiles' return."[73] Further, she observes that "the biblical description of Gog's grave is reminiscent of the rhetoric of conquest in many third- and second-millennium texts from lower Mesopotamia that describe the construction of vast burial mounds containing the corpses of foreign enemies to mark the successful completion of a military campaign."[74] *Enūma eliš* describes a related practice: Marduk gathers together Tiamat's hordes and sets them in a heap (IV 112) as a sign to others (V 73–76).

If there is a model for the devouring of the corpses in Ezek 39:11–20, it is probably not *Enūma eliš* but the Baal Cycle (KTU 1.6 ii 35–7),[75] though that account differs substantially as well.[76] It is more helpful to foreground Stavrakopoulou's point that the juxtaposition of burial and devouring suggests that the bodies are exhumed in order to be a visual reminder of YHWH's victory.[77] Bearing that in mind, there is a parallel to the way Tiamat's hordes are handled (EE V 75–76):

> He made images [of them] and set them up at the [Gate of] Apsu:
> "Lest ever after they be forgotten, let this be the sign."[78]

Verses 21–29 then bring Ezekiel 39 to its triumphant climax with two distinct points: vv. 21–24 summarize the message for Israel in YHWH's defeat of Gog and vv.

---

[71] Tooman, *Gog of Magog*, 181.

[72] Tooman, *Gog of Magog*, 182.

[73] Stavrakopoulou, "Gog's Grave," 84.

[74] Stavrakopoulou, "Gog's Grave," 78.

[75] cf. Athtart's command to Baal to scatter Yamm (see Mark S. Smith and Wayne Thomas Pitard, *The Ugaritic Baal Cycle: Volume 2: Introduction with Text, Translation and Commentary of KTU/CAT 1.3–1.4* [VTSup 114/2; Leiden: Brill, 2009], 357).

[76] Fitzpatrick, *The Disarmament of God*, 109–12.

[77] Stavrakopoulou, "Gog's Grave," 82.

[78] Foster, *Before the Muses*, 466.

25-29 speak of Israel's return to its land. It is unsurprising that they evince no connection to Enūma eliš. Yet, this is just a brief interlude and more similarities emerge when one looks at the remainder of Ezekiel 38-48*.

In Enūma eliš, Marduk continues on to create humanity (VI 1-38), an act paralleled in Ezek 37:1-14, the next pericope in Ezekiel 38-48*. Marduk proposes the creation of humanity to Ea to reduce the gods labor. Needing raw material, Marduk selects Qingu's blood, allowing this to double as his punishment. Ea is then able to make humans and to impose the burden of the gods upon them (VI 36). Granting that differences remain between this account and Ezek 37:1-14, it is remarkable that the (re)animation of human beings in Ezek 37:1-14 corresponds in its narrative location to Enūma eliš.[79] The collaboration between YHWH and Ezekiel also stands out: like Marduk compels Ea to create humanity from Qingu's blood, so also does YHWH compel Ezekiel to prophesy so that the bones gather together and become animate humans.[80] These similarities stand out all the more when set against the lack of parallels in other potential background texts like the Baal Cycle.[81]

Ezekiel's following sign act predicting the reunification of Israel and Judah (37:15-28) is unparalleled—again no surprise given its content—but that gives way to a slow ascent towards the book's denouement in the temple vision of Ezekiel 40-48. Albeit different in their extent and detail, it is obvious that the account of the Esagila's construction and Ezekiel's vision of a restored temple play comparable roles in the two texts.[82]

To sum up the preceding two sections, Ezekiel 38-48* contains allusions to a number of key images in Enūma eliš while it also exhibits conspicuous parallels to its plot structure. These observations inform the pericope's interpretation in at least three ways. First, these similarities are further evidence that Ezekiel 38-39 portray Gog as a deity, not a human. Recognizing that the text depicts a battle between deities, the Gog oracle is logically read in light of the ancient Near Eastern Chaoskampf tradition. Second, comparing the narrative structure of Ezekiel 38-48* with other Chaoskämpfe, Enūma eliš provides the closest parallel. Third, this structural correlation is supported by key terms and images in Ezekiel 38-39 that portray Gog in images redolent of Marduk (e.g., 38:9), Gog's hordes as a Mesopotamian imperial army (e.g., 38:4), and YHWH in terms reminiscent of Marduk (e.g., 39:3), the divine king.

This evidence is circumstantial and not direct, so it can be interpreted in other ways. Indeed, some will regard the proposed connections as too vague. The final section of this essay advances an argument that accounts for that ambiguity by

---

[79] Fitzpatrick, The Disarmament of God, 178, discusses other connections that have been made between Ezek 37:1-14 and Enūma eliš that strengthen my case.

[80] It may also be significant that the bones form a vast, great army (חיל גדול מאד מאד), which enables them to take on the task that YHWH has heretofore performed, namely, defending the land and fighting back chaos.

[81] Day, God's Conflict, 7-18, esp. 17-18.

[82] Cf. Niditch, "Ezekiel 40-48," 222; and Fitzpatrick, The Disarmament of God, 185-92.

showing that the socio-political setting that prevailed in the sixth century BCE necessitated it.

GOG ORACLES AS DISGUISED TRANSCRIPT OF RESISTANCE

James C. Scott establishes a cross-cultural basis for concluding that subaltern groups shrewdly express their distaste for imperial power in disguised forms. In *Domination and the Arts of Resistance* he remarks that "[i]f subordinate groups have typically won a reputation for subtlety—a subtlety their superiors often regard as cunning and deception" it is "because their vulnerability has rarely permitted them the luxury of direct confrontation."[83] The subversive ideas of subaltern groups are commonly voiced outside the gaze and hearing of the dominant group in what Scott calls a "hidden transcript."

As the hidden transcript develops from unrefined, "raw" expressions of resistance into sophisticated, "cooked" statements of opposition, it finds its way into the open.[84] Neither the hidden transcript nor the disguised version of it that emerges in public is "a language apart," but remains in constant dialogue with the public transcript that is controlled by the dominant group.[85] The hidden transcript stays cloaked and only at highly charged moments does it receive a complete revelation; the hidden transcript is usually voiced as "a partly sanitized, ambiguous, and coded version of the hidden transcript."[86] Although the hidden transcript "is always present in the public discourse of subordinate groups"[87] it remains beyond the reach of the powerful by one of two means: either the messenger is anonymous or the message is disguised.

Anathea Portier-Young explores texts that adopt the former mode of disguise. She offers new evidence that pseudepigraphic apocalyptic literature—particularly Daniel and the Enochic traditions—functions as resistance literature against the hegemony of Antiochus IV.[88] Hegemony, defined as "nonviolent forms of control exercised through cultural institutions, systems of patronage, and the structured practices of everyday life,"[89] has a cosmological dimension that "legitimates claims about truth."[90] Resistant counterdiscourse comes in many forms; among them, she draws attention to "[o]ne form of counterdiscourse" that "answers myth with

---

[83] Scott, *Domination*, 136.
[84] Scott, *Domination*, 119.
[85] Scott, *Domination*, 135.
[86] Scott, *Domination*, 19.
[87] Scott, *Domination*, 19.
[88] See John J. Collins, *The Apocalyptic Imagination: An Introduction to Jewish Apocalyptic Literature* (Grand Rapids: Eerdmans, 1998), esp. 43–144, for a summary of previous scholarship on these texts.
[89] Portier-Young, *Apocalypse*, 383.
[90] Portier-Young, *Apocalypse*, 12.

myth, as in the Book of the Watchers, the Book of Dreams, or Daniel 7." These texts retain categories from the dominant ideology but assign them different values.[91]

The book of Ezekiel, also a product of an intense multicultural, subaltern experience in the Babylonian exile, is a precursor to the phenomenon that Portier-Young identifies in the pseudepigraphic apocalyptic texts. However, it relies on the latter of Scott's modes of disguise: rather than obscuring its messenger by pseudepigraphy, it encodes its subversive ideas in such a way that "the excluded (and in this case, powerful) audience may grasp the seditious message in the performance but find it difficult to react because that sedition is clothed in terms that can also lay claim to a perfectly innocent construction."[92]

Take, for example, the camouflaged ways that Ezekiel 38–39 connect Gog and his hordes with the Neo-Babylonian empire. It begins in 38:4, where the description of Gog's hordes is an allusion to the description of Assyria and Babylon in Ezekiel 23. Tooman presciently writes that this language "*covertly* encourages the reader to transfer the negative associations of Israel's lovers to Gog and his allies."[93] Next, Ezek 38:7–13 uses a cluster of terms to evoke Isa 10 and Jer 49, two oracles that condemn the plundering ways of the Assyrian and Babylonian kings. This implicitly portrays Gog's hordes as a Mesopotamian imperial army subjugating Judah. For an audience attuned to the dialect of disguise in Ezekiel, this adumbrates the correlation of Gog with Marduk in 39:1–8. Reusing locutions from Isa 14[94] while depicting Gog battling YHWH with the very weapons that Marduk uses to kill Tiamat, 39:1–8 responds to the myth of Marduk's divine supremacy by claiming that YHWH will be triumphant.

Alongside these allusions, Ezekiel 38–48* surreptitiously borrows key plot points from *Enūma eliš* in order to advance its counterdiscourse. Instead of Marduk compelling Ea to create humanity from Qingu's blood, YHWH guides the prophet Ezekiel through (re)animating the dry bones into a vast army. At the climax it is YHWH, not Marduk, who is honored with the building of a temple. The basic storyline of *Enūma eliš* is adopted by the book of Ezekiel and adapted into an expression of discontentment with the current state of affairs and an argument for recalcitrant Judahite nationalism.

Without appealing to weak evidence that Ezekiel 38–39 is a foreign nation oracle, or wading into the vexed question of whether the Gog oracle is "apocalyptic" (however conceived and defined), approaching Ezekiel 38–48* in this way reveals how Gog is a coded indictment of Babylon. Gog is a cipher for a historical, sixth

---

[91] Portier-Young, *Apocalypse*, 13–15, who notes that The Book of Watchers seeks to create "a new mythology that inverts motifs from Greek and Babylonian religious traditions."

[92] Scott, *Domination*, 158.

[93] Tooman, *Gog of Magog*, 153. Emphasis added.

[94] The identity of הילל בן שחר in Isa 14:12 is debated, though there is wide consensus that it refers to a deity (see, e.g., John C. Poirier, "An Illuminating Parallel to Isaiah XIV 12," *VT* 99 [1999]: 371–89). In that respect, Isa 14 parallels Ezekiel 38–39 in seeing a direct connection between the defeat of a deity and the defeat of the associated human king.

century BCE enemy of Judah, though not a human figure who *lived* in the sixth century BCE. Gog represents Marduk, patron deity of Babylon, divine counterpart to the human king of Babylon, and cosmic head of its vast army. This ideology, reaffirmed annually in the new year celebration, is a conspicuous tool of hegemony, a prominent nonviolent form of control exercised through cultural institutions by the Babylonians to subjugate the Judahite exiles among others.

Still, Ezekiel 38–48* can be interpreted as non-threatening to the Babylonian imperial edifice. Note that the repopulated land of Israel has boundaries that extend only slightly east of the Jordan river.[95] This restored Israel is hardly a threat to Babylonian power and international control. Furthermore, the allusions to *Enūma eliš* and Marduk in Ezekiel 38–48* remain indeterminate enough that the Judahite exiles could claim no intent to subvert the prevailing Babylonian ideology. Envision a Judahite in Babylon explaining to the powers that be that Ezekiel 38–48* imagines a return and restoration authorized by Marduk and the Babylonian king. That may sound far fetched, but there is a precedent for it in both the Assyrian and Babylonian practice of refurbishing cult images and sending them back to restored temples in order to curry favor with those populations.[96] Under that guise, it is possible to assert that Ezekiel 38–48* does not condemn Babylon, its king, or patron deity, but visualizes a restored Israel serving as a Babylonian ally near the border of its most dangerous enemy, Egypt.[97] Recall that Ezekiel 17 utilizes that very logic.

Scott shows that the modes of concealment are "limited only by the imaginative capacity of the subordinates" so that it is "impossible to overestimate the subtlety of this manipulation."[98] To that he adds that "[t]hese ambiguous, polysemic elements of folk culture mark off a relatively autonomous realm of discursive freedom on the condition that they declare no *direct* opposition to the public transcript as authorized by the dominant."[99] There is no denying Ezekiel's imaginative capacity (e.g., Ezekiel 16; 18; 23). It is also manifest that the book addresses a subordinated population that is facing issues analagous to the groups that Scott analyzed. Recognizing, finally, the plausible interpretation of Ezekiel 38–48* as an indirect challenge to Babylonian hegemony, it is necessary to consider seriously that this material is a disguised counterdiscourse.

Equally, since it is impossible to read Ezekiel 38–39 without inquiring if it does contain an anti-imperial agenda, each commentator must answer that question. Weighing up the broader collection of evidence indicating that the book is largely a product of the first half of the sixth century BCE, that Ezekiel 38–39 is well-integrated into that larger whole, that Ezekiel 17 contains a similar counterdis-

---

[95] See Daniel Block, *The Book of Ezekiel: Chapters 25–48*, 711, for an illustration of the borders of the restored land envisioned in Ezek 47:13–48:34.

[96] See Kutsko, *Between Heaven and Earth*, 113–17, for discussion and further references.

[97] See Crouch and Strine, "YHWH's Battle against Chaos," 889–96, for details.

[98] Scott, *Domination*, 139.

[99] Scott, *Domination*, 157.

course against Marduk and Babylonian ideology, and the allusions between Ezekiel 38–39 and *Enūma eliš* outlined here, I am persuaded that the narrative that stretches from YHWH's defeat of Gog to YHWH's arrival at the restored temple is a *Chaoskampf* that disguises Ezekiel's intent to resist Babylonian forms of hegemony.[100]

The vibrant and varied *Wirkungsgeschichte* of the Gog oracle is explained to some extent by this approach as well. Because it manipulated the themes in the *Chaoskampf* so successfully when crafting its disguise for Gog and his hordes, Ezekiel 38–39 presented a malleable text for future authors to reapply against subsequent imperial powers. The book of Revelation's reappropriation of many images from Ezekiel 38–39 against Rome, to take just one example of this tactic, is easily understandable.

Ezekiel 38–48* contains elusive images, polysemous language, ambiguous metaphors, and narrates a disjointed series of events. These features demand an explanation. *Pace* Tooman, they are not the result of an author's attempt to align Ezekiel with other canonical texts, though many of the allusions he recognizes between them are genuine. Rather, Ezekiel 38–39 works together with chs. 37 and 40–48 to form a *Chaoskampf* that resists an empire. To a Judahite displeased with Babylonian rule, it is a disguised counterdiscourse asserting that YHWH, not Marduk, shall prevail.

---

[100] It is reasonable to suggest that the text has Persian rather than Babylonian hegemony in view. To be sure, Cyrus and his Medo-Persian successors did appropriate Marduk as a divine patron (e.g., the Cyrus Cylinder). Still, the broader evidence for a Neo-Babylonian provenance cited earlier points towards Babylonian hegemony as the intended target.

6
Propagandistic Constructions of Empires in the Book of Isaiah

Göran Eidevall

One way of putting the fundamental question addressed by this paper is: Does the book of Isaiah uphold or undermine empire? There can be no straightforward answer to that question as more than one empire is described in it. Thus, it is necessary to be more specific: *Which* empire are we speaking of? To make things even more complicated we need to add: Which part of the book, Proto-, Deutero- or Trito-Isaiah? And which editorial layer?

Despite all disputes concerning details, a majority of scholars would probably agree that the history of composition and redaction of Isaiah 1–66 covers at least four centuries, from the 8th century through the Persian era. Interestingly, from the point of view of the history of Judah, this lengthy process of textual growth coincides with the period of subjugation to several successive empires: Assyria, Egypt (a short interlude), Babylonia, and Persia. To this list we might add the Ptolemaic and the Seleucid empires, since some late additions to the book, for instance Isa 19:19–25, probably originated in the Hellenistic era. However, the last major redaction, which shaped the book as we now have it, is often dated to the 5th or the 4th century, that is, to the Persian period.[1]

This is the point of departure for the following discussion: All the texts in the book of Isaiah originated in a situation when Judah/Yehud was dominated by an empire. Hence, it is far from surprising that large parts of the text are dominated by discourse on the role or fate of various empires. In my monograph *Prophecy and Propaganda*, I studied images of enemies in the book of Isaiah, including various

---

[1] Thus, e.g., Marvin Sweeney, *Isaiah 1–39: With an Introduction to Prophetic Literature* (FOTL 16; Grand Rapids: Eerdmans, 1996), 51–55.

images of empires.[2] To sum up the results, I found that while the portraits of Assyria, Egypt, and Babylon are strikingly different, they would all seem to serve the propagandistic purposes of leading circles in Jerusalem, since they reflect the Zion-centered perspective which defines the ideology of the book.[3] In my analysis, I stressed the independent, and potentially subversive, character of this ideology. Without using that term, I tended to depict the book of Isaiah as largely "anti-imperial." However, it is possible to problematize such a picture of this prophetic book.

In this paper, I would like to introduce new perspectives, in order to develop the discussion further. In *Prophecy and Propaganda*, I occasionally registered features in the texts that might imply a more positive stance toward a certain empire. How could such signs of ambiguity be integrated into the analysis? Further questions raised by that previous study include: How should one explain apparent instances of "re-use of topoi from the Assyrian propaganda" in depictions of the Neo-Assyrian empire?[4] Or how can the book's conspicuous silence concerning Persia be interpreted?[5] In an attempt to throw new light on these and other issues, I will deploy perspectives and concepts drawn from postcolonial theory. In one very obvious sense, at least, the book of Isaiah can be seen as a "postcolonial" document. It contains texts expressing the experiences of several centuries of imperial domination.

Postcolonial theory has emerged in the context of studies focusing on the dynamics of subjugation and assimilation, resistance and liberation, in the former colonies of European empires.[6] Nevertheless, it appears to be applicable also in the study of ancient empires, and more specifically, in the study of biblical texts composed in the shadow of, for instance, Assyria or Rome.[7] According to Homi Bhabha,

---

[2] Göran Eidevall, *Prophecy and Propaganda: Images of Enemies in the Book of Isaiah* (ConBOT 56; Winona Lake: Eisenbrauns, 2009). I am aware that the term "propaganda" can be seen as to some extent anachronistic. However, I have not found any better alternative.

[3] See Eidevall, *Prophecy*, 130–32, 190–94. On the Zion-centered ideology, see 187–90. This concept was not invented by me. It has been shown by other scholars, as well, that the consistent focus on the fate of Jerusalem creates a sense of unity across the oracular *bricolage* of Isaiah 1–66. Within the world projected by this book, there is *one* center and summit: Zion, the temple mount in Jerusalem. See Antti Laato, *"About Zion I Will Not Be Silent": The Book of Isaiah as an Ideological Unity* (ConBOT 44; Stockholm: Almqvist & Wiksell International, 1998) and Christopher Seitz, *Zion's Final Destiny: The Development of the Book of Isaiah* (Minneapolis: Fortress, 1991).

[4] Eidevall, *Prophecy*, 192.

[5] Eidevall, *Prophecy*, 193–94.

[6] For helpful introductions, see Leela Gandhi, *Postcolonial Theory: A Critical Introduction* (New York: Columbia University Press, 1998); Uriah Y. Kim, "Postcolonial Criticism: Who is the Other in the Book of Judges?" in *Judges & Method: New Approaches in Biblical Studies* (2nd ed.; ed. Gale A. Yee; Minneapolis: Fortress, 2007), 161–82; and R. S. Sugirtharajah, "Charting the Aftermath: A Review of Postcolonial Criticism," in *The Postcolonial Biblical Reader* (ed. R. S. Sugirtharajah; Malden/Oxford: Blackwell, 2006), 7–32.

[7] See Jon L. Berquist, "Postcolonialism and Imperial Motives for Canonization," in *Postcolonialism and Scripture Reading* (ed. L. Donaldson; Semeia 75; Atlanta: Society of Biblical

discourse arising out of colonial situations will typically display *ambivalence*.[8] The cultural identity developed by those who are colonized tends to be characterized by *hybridity*. Bhabha speaks of an "interstitial passage between fixed identifications" which "opens up the possibility of a cultural hybridity."[9] Assimilation to the norms of the colonizing culture is never complete. One may speak of *mimicry*, described by Bhabha as being an imitation of the colonizer's culture, which results in behavior which is "almost the same, *but not quite*."[10] In many cases, and often for obvious reasons, public responses to the oppressive power of the colonizers are not openly subversive. Still, such speeches or texts may have a disturbing effect on the imperial authority, since they move "between mimicry and *mockery*."[11] Inspired by recent studies by Steed Vernyl Davidson (on the book of Jeremiah) and Hans Leander (on the gospel of Mark), I shall make use of Bhabha's terminology in an attempt to read a number of passages in the book of Isaiah as cultural responses to imperial domination.[12] In some cases, though, where such an approach seems less fruitful, I will instead draw on the work of James C. Scott, concerning the function of *hidden transcripts*, as expressions of resistance against empires.[13] Scott describes various techniques that serve to "disguise the message" in a situation of oppressive domination.[14] However, it needs to be stressed that throughout the analysis, a tentative use of postcolonial perspectives will be combined with the use of more conventional exegetical methods.

Toward the end of this paper, I will adopt a synchronic approach, discussing possible implications of the overall structure of Isaiah 1–66. For the most part, though, the order of presentation will be based upon a schematic diachronic sequence of empires dominating Judah. As is well known, the dating of each textual

---

Literature, 1996), 15–35; Uriah Y. Kim, *Decolonizing Josiah: Toward a Postcolonial Reading of the Deuteronomistic History* (The Bible in the Modern World 5; Sheffield: Sheffield Phoenix Press, 2005); Stephen D. Moore, *Empire and Apocalypse: Postcolonialism and the New Testament* (Sheffield: Sheffield Phoenix Press, 2006); and Fernando Segovia, "Biblical Criticism and Postcolonial Studies: Toward a Postcolonial Optic," in *The Postcolonial Biblical Reader* (ed. R. S. Sugirtharajah; Malden/Oxford: Blackwell, 2006), 33–44.

[8] Homi K. Bhabha, "DissemiNation: Time, Narrative, and the Margins of the Modern Nation," in *Nation and Narration* (ed. H. K. Bhabha; London: Routledge, 1990), 291–322; idem, *The Location of Culture* (London: Routledge, 1994), 129–38.

[9] Bhabha, *The Location*, 4.

[10] Bhabha, *The Location*, 86 (emphasis as in the original).

[11] Bhabha, *The Location*, 86 (emphasis added).

[12] See Steed Vernyl Davidson, "Ambivalence and Temple Destruction: Reading the Book of Jeremiah with Homi Bhabha," in *Jeremiah (Dis)Placed: New Directions in Writing/Reading Jeremiah* (ed. P. Diamond and L. Stulman; LHBOTS 529; New York: T & T Clark, 2011), 162–71; and Hans Leander, "With Homi Bhabha at the Jerusalem City Gates: A Postcolonial Reading of the 'Triumphant' Entry (Mark 11.1–11)," *JSNT* 32 (2010): 309–35.

[13] James C. Scott, *Domination and the Arts of Resistance: Hidden Transcripts* (New Haven: Yale University Press, 1990).

[14] Scott, *Domination*, 136–72 (quote on p. 139).

passage is a matter of scholarly dispute. Rather than making the whole discussion contingent on my own reconstruction of the history of composition and redaction, I have chosen to follow the course of the political history of the ancient Near East. From a Judean reader's point of view, I suggest, the logical order of the empires would have been Assyria – Egypt – Babylonia – Persia. In the first section, therefore, all texts *referring* to Assyria will be discussed, even though some of these texts may actually have originated in the Persian era.

ASSYRIA

The prophecies dealing with Assyria can be divided into three groups, each of them associated with a distinctive image of, and attitude to, this empire. Tentatively, these images and attitudes can be linked to successive stages in the historical development of the Assyrian-Judean relations.

First Stage: Loyalty and Mimicry

In the initial stage, associated with the so-called Syro-Ephraimite crisis in the 730s BCE, Assyria is regarded as an ally of sorts. Posing a threat to Judah's rivals in the regional conflict, Israel and Aram, the Assyrian empire becomes *the enemy's enemy*.[15] The brief account in Isa 8:1–4 belongs to this group of texts. The main point is that the centers of the two hostile kingdoms, Damascus and Samaria, are about to be sacked and plundered (8:3). The Assyrian ruler is merely mentioned as the one responsible for this apparently laudable action (8:4). In Isa 7:4–9a and 17:1–3, two oracles which convey a similar message as regards the fate of these neighboring nations, the identity of the attacker is not revealed. This is the case in Isa 28:1–4, as well. However, it is likely that 28:2 refers to an expected (or already effectuated) *Assyrian* invasion of the Northern kingdom: "See, the Lord (אדני) has one who is powerful and strong; like a hailstorm, a destructive tempest, like a storm of mighty, overflowing waters, he will hurl (them) down to earth with violence."[16] Inundation metaphors are frequently attested in official Assyrian propaganda. More precisely, this is how Assyrian kings described their own victorious army: as virtually unstoppable, like overflowing waters.[17]

This first group of texts corresponds roughly to recent reconstructions of the 8th century core of the book of Isaiah, made by other scholars.[18] The "first" Isaiah

---

[15] See further Eidevall, *Prophecy*, 190–92.

[16] Cf. Isa 8:7, where an Assyrian invasion of Judah is described in a similar way.

[17] See Simonetta Ponchia, "Analogie, metafore e similitudini nelle iscrizioni reali assiri: Semantica e ideologia," *Oriens Antiquus* 26 (1987): 223–55, esp. 233–34. See also Peter Machinist, "Assyria and Its Image in First Isaiah," *JAOS* 103 (1983): 719–37, esp. 726.

[18] Whereas Uwe Becker, *Jesaja: von der Botschaft zum Buch* (FRLANT 178; Göttingen: Vandenhoeck & Ruprecht, 1997) has argued that the core comprised 8:1-4*, 17:1-3*, and 28:1-3*, Matthijs de Jong, *Isaiah among the Ancient Near Eastern Prophets: A Comparative Study of the*

appears to have been a prophet of the common Near Eastern type represented by the texts from Mari and Nineveh, delivering oracles in support of the legitimacy of the ruling dynasty, promising divine assistance to the king, and prefiguring the imminent defeat of all his enemies. In other words, Isaiah ben Amoz can be characterized as a Judean "nationalist." From such a perspective, one may ask, was there any reason to prophesy *against* Assyria, as long as this empire was acting as the enemy's enemy?

However, on a closer examination, the portrayal of Assyria in these passages is ambiguous. Beyond the stereotypical image of an invincible military force (likened to a natural force), the texts do not provide any characterization of Assyria—neither critique nor praise. I suggest that this reticence is explicable in the light of what actually happened in the aftermath of the Syro-Ephraimite crisis. Tiglath-Pileser III struck against Israel and Aram, but he did not invade Judah. However, king Ahaz had to pay a price for this "protection." From now on, Judah was an Assyrian vassal state. If the texts in our first group, and especially Isa 8:1-4 and 28:1-4, are read against this backdrop, one can make the following observations. On the surface, these oracles are perfectly compatible with an attitude of loyalty towards the Assyrian overlord. However, this remains implicit, since the texts do not contain any declaration of loyalty. As we have seen, the depiction of the Assyrian army in 28:2 echoes Assyrian propaganda. This can be regarded as a case of uncritical imitation, in a situation when Assyria had demonstrated its terrifying power in the immediate vicinity of Judah. Still, I think it is possible to apply Bhabha's notion of *mimicry* here: "almost the same, but not quite." In one crucial respect, though, the saying in Isa 28:2 deviates from the pattern of the Assyrian royal inscriptions: the Assyrian army is placed directly under the authority of YHWH, the national deity of Judah! The overlord has to obey "the Lord." Thus, although these oracles are far from anti-Assyrian, they would nevertheless seem to carry a subversive potential.

Second Stage: From Mimicry to Mockery

As a consequence of the fall of Samaria in 722 BCE, Judah could no longer be threatened by this neighbor. However, one threat continued to loom large: Assyria. Although the fate of Israel might have deterred him from all such attempts, we know that king Hezekiah joined an anti-Assyrian coalition, possibly assuming that Assyria would be weakened by internal strife in the wake of Sargon's death. As is

---

Earliest Stages of the Isaiah Tradition and the Neo-Assyrian Prophecies (VTSup 117; Leiden: Brill, 2007), would rather ascribe 7:4-9a, 8:1-4, and 17:1b-3 to this first stage of the Isaiah tradition.

well known, Sennacherib's punitive expedition devastated large parts of Judah.[19] In 701 BCE, the Assyrian army was approaching Jerusalem. For some reason, the city was spared. According to the most plausible explanation, indicated by the annals of Sennacherib as well as one of the biblical accounts (2 Kgs 18:14–16), Hezekiah was forced to pay considerable amounts of silver and gold. A second group of texts dealing with Assyria can be related to this event, which takes on a paradigmatic significance within the book of Isaiah as a whole.[20]

According to Isa 8:6–8*, a text that I would place in a transitional stage between the first and the second group, Judah itself will be invaded. Once again, an invasion by the Assyrian army is depicted in terms of an inundation (v. 7). We are told that the overflowing waters will keep rising until the flood "reaches up to the neck" (v. 8). This can be interpreted as a graphic description of the situation in the year 701.[21] Only Jerusalem, the head (i.e., the capital) of Judah, remained intact.[22] Recalling Isa 28:2 (see above), this description of the Assyrian ally-turned-enemy uses the Assyrian rulers' own favorite imagery. It is worth noting that the reference in v. 7 to "the king of Assyria in all his splendor (כבודו)" seems to be void of irony.[23] Rather, as suggested by Peter Machinist, this expression could allude to a central concept in Assyrian royal ideology, *melammu*, denoting the king's "divinely endowed effulgence."[24]

Yet, also in this case it is stressed that YHWH (rather than Assur or the Assyrian king) is in control: "the Lord (אדני) is about to bring up against them the mighty and abundant waters of the River" (Isa 8:7). The final word of this oracle is intriguingly ambiguous. Is "Immanuel" (8:8b) used as a designation of the hopelessly inferior Judean king? I would rather suggest that this designation (referring to the entire nation?) expresses the hope of the colonized on the verge of resignation: "God (YHWH) is with us," on *our* side, despite all signs to the contrary. Thus interpreted, this text illustrates Bhabha's thesis, that the speech of the colonized is inevitably marked by *ambiguity*.

---

[19] For an assessment of the archaeological record, see, e.g., Israel Finkelstein, "The Archaeology of the Days of Manasseh," in *Scripture and Artifacts: Essays on the Bible and Archaeology in Honor of Philip J. King* (ed. Michael D. Coogan, J. Cheryl Exum, and Lawrence E. Stager; Louisville: Westminster John Knox, 1994), 169–187. Concerning the Shephelah, Finkelstein states succinctly: "The settlement system of the eighth century was virtually annihilated by Sennacherib" (p. 173).

[20] See further Eidevall, *Prophecy*, 187–90.

[21] Cf. Laato, *About Zion*, 104. With Sweeney, *Isaiah 1–39*, 171–73, I take the reference to "Rezin and the son of Remaliah" in v. 6 as a gloss which ties this prophecy to the historical context of the preceding passage, 8:1–4, viz. the Syro-Ephraimite conflict. Arguably, Isa 8:6–8 makes better sense as a depiction of the situation in 701 BCE.

[22] As shown by Isa 7:8–9, the cross-cultural metaphor "the capital is the head of the national body" belonged to the repertoire of the Isaianic writers.

[23] This phrase is often regarded as a late addition. So, e.g., Joseph Blenkinsopp, *Isaiah 1–39: A New Translation with Introduction and Commentary* (AB 19; New York: Doubleday, 2000), 240. However, if this is correct, which means that these words were written at a point when the Assyrian threat belonged to a distant past, the awe-struck tone is even more remarkable.

[24] See Machinist, "Assyria," 727.

In Isa 10:5–15, a passage which belongs more firmly to my second group of texts, the focus shifts from the Assyrian army to an anonymous Assyrian ruler. The question of his "real" identity is a moot point. The conquests that are listed in v. 9 were begun by Tiglath-Pileser III and completed some decades later, during the reign of Sargon. However, the situation evoked by this prophecy, an Assyrian threat against Jerusalem (vv. 10–11), would rather seem to point in the direction of Sennacherib. Clearly, as observed by Carol Newsom, "[t]he words attributed to the king in Isaiah 10 telescope the achievements of more than one Assyrian king."[25] Even more importantly, this anonymous king *personifies* the oppressive Assyrian empire.[26] At the outset, the mighty emperor is deprived of his dignity. He is pictured as a tool, a "rod (שבט)" or "staff (מטה)" in the hands of YHWH (v. 5).[27] Such imagery is ambiguous. It may sound respectful, yet it is well suited for daring and disrespectful discourse, something that becomes evident as the author picks up this rhetorical tool/weapon again in v. 15, and wields it with force: "Should the axe vaunt itself over the one who hews with it, or the saw magnify itself against the one who wields it? As if a rod (שבט) would wield him who lifts it, or as if a staff (מטה) should lift the one who is not (made of) wood!" This is an accusation of hubris. In addition, the rhetorical technique of *dehumanization*, common in wartime propaganda, may be at work here.[28] Seemingly without a will of his own (and, perhaps significantly, without a name), the foreign king is *instrumentalized*, reduced to a tool. The royal scepter (for which Hebrew uses both שבט and מטה, cf. vv. 1 and 15!) has, so to speak, been wrought out of his hand. No longer the wielder (subject), he is being wielded (object).

In Bhabha's terminology, this is *mockery*, rather than mere mimicry. Interestingly (but far from surprisingly, in a prophetic book), the foreign ruler is not being ridiculed by a mortal Judean. These words are instead presented as uttered by the national deity of Judah, YHWH. In 10:6–7, YHWH pictures the Assyrian king as disobedient and rebellious, and accuses him of overstepping the limited mandate which he had been given. According to my analysis, this is a way of describing that Assyria's role had changed, from a Jerusalemite point of view. Having acted as the *enemy's* enemy in the 730s, the mighty empire became *Judah's* enemy during the invasion which culminated with the (abortive) siege of Jerusalem in 701. In v. 12, the prophet/author speaks. Here the Assyrian ruler is said to be arrogant. This can

---

[25] Carol Newsom, "God's Other: The Intractable Problem of the Gentile King in Judean and Early Jewish Literature," in *The "Other" in Second Temple Judaism: Essays in Honor of John J. Collins* (ed. D. C. Harlow et al.; Grand Rapids: Eerdmans, 2011), 31–48; quote on p. 39, n. 17.

[26] I disagree slightly with Newsom, "God's Other," 39, as she avers that "the king's psyche is . . . the focal issue." In my opinion, the main topic of this text is rather the nature of Assyrian oppression and exploitation, regardless of the personality of the current ruler.

[27] Instrumental metaphors constitute the framework of the text (vv. 5 and 15). One may speak of an *inclusio*.

[28] See further Eidevall, *Prophecy*, 5–6.

be seen as a *subversive re-use of Assyrian propaganda*. In the royal inscriptions, the enemies of Assyria are regularly described as "insubmissive; insolent; proud; haughty."[29] In other words, his own standard reproach against rebels of all kinds is turned against the Assyrian ruler.

The remainder of Isa 10:1-15 consists of the king's speech (vv. 8-11, 13-14). However, he is not allowed to speak with his own voice. These quotations are fictitious, just like the words of the speaker's enemies in the Psalms. They serve to illustrate the allegations. As noted by Newsom, part of what the king says is true: the cities mentioned in v. 9 had all been captured by the Assyrians.[30] In some respects, moreover, this speech recalls common *topoi* in the Assyrian royal inscriptions. Nevertheless, I suggest that it can be characterized as a piece of *parody*, in the service of Judean propaganda. Judging from his boasting monologue, the Assyrian king is not only arrogant and cruel, he is exceedingly greedy, as well. In vv. 13-14 he portrays himself as an unrestrained plunderer of birds' nests. Arguably, killing fledglings was not considered a heroic deed. This text may have been composed in 701 BCE, or shortly after, but I would guess that it was written in the latter part of the 7th century. The memory of Assyrian oppression would still have been vivid, but there was no longer any reason to be afraid.

A date towards the end of the 7th century, or even later, is commonly posited for the final example to be considered in the second group of texts dealing with Assyria: the legendary account of Jerusalem's miraculous rescue in the year 701, which occupies chapters 36 and 37 in the book of Isaiah.[31] From a rhetorical perspective, I find this text very interesting, since it describes *a propaganda war*. It is all about words. No other weapons are used in this battle over Jerusalem.

The first verbal attack in this drama is delivered by an anonymous Assyrian official bearing the title *rab šāqê* (denoting the chief cupbearer; henceforth this character in the story will be referred to as "Rabshakeh"). His intimidating speeches may have a factual background. According to Kirk Grayson, "the Assyrians came to prefer psychological warfare whenever it was feasible."[32] If diplomacy failed, they would not immediately launch a military attack. Since a siege could turn out to be an expensive affair, they would at first surround the city and shout, in an

---

[29] F. M. Fales, "The Enemy in the Assyrian Royal Inscriptions: The 'Moral Judgement'," in *Mesopotamien und seine Nachbarn: Politische und kulturelle Wechselbeziehungen im Alten Vorderasien vom 4. bis 1. Jahrtausend v. Chr. (XXV. Rencontre Assyriologique Internationale, Berlin, 3. bis 7. Juli 1978)* (ed. H.-J. Nissen and J. Renger; Berliner Beiträge zum Vorderen Orient 1; Berlin: Reimer, 1982), 2:425–35, quote on p. 428.

[30] Newsom, "God's Other," 39.

[31] This narrative is also found in 2 Kgs 18:13 + 18:17–19:37. Whether it was imported from the Deuteronomistic History to the book of Isaiah or the other way round is not immediately relevant for the analysis offered here.

[32] A. Kirk Grayson, "Assyrian Rule of Conquered Territory in Ancient Western Asia," in *Civilizations of the Ancient Near East* (ed. Jack Sasson; Peabody: Hendricksons, 2000), 2:959–68, quote on p. 960.

attempt to persuade the inhabitants to surrender.[33] The response from the Jerusalemite leadership to Rabshakeh's first speech is telling: "Please speak to your servants in Aramaic, for we understand it; do not speak to us in the language of Judah within the hearing of the people who are on the wall" (Isa 36:11, NRSV). Aware of the power of skillfully selected words, they do not want the civil population of the city to listen to such propaganda. Disregarding this appeal, Rabshakeh continues to address the civilians on the wall, advising them that they should not listen to Hezekiah (36:14–16a).

There is no reason to assume that this text contains accurate reports of actual speeches.[34] Nevertheless, it is evident that the biblical author was familiar with Assyrian propaganda. The main theme of Rabshakeh's first speech (Isa 36:4–10) is misplaced trust. Hezekiah and his people should not put their trust in words (v. 5), or in Egypt (v. 6), they should not even trust YHWH (v. 7). Rather, as emphasized in the second speech (36:13b–20), they should rely on the words of the Assyrian king (vv. 16–17). Interestingly, trust is a central topic in the royal inscriptions. According to Chaim Cohen, the "stereotypic phraseology describing the behaviour of Assyria's enemies and rebellious vassals almost invariably involves the usage of the verb *takālu*, 'to trust'."[35] Although Rabshakeh appears to be modeled on one or several real Assyrian officials, I think it is rewarding to treat him as a literary character, created by the biblical author(s) who composed this narrative. As an *embodiment* of Assyrian propaganda, he is portrayed as far from trustworthy. His claims are eventually disproved by the denouement of this legend (Isa 37:36–38).[36] But the attentive listener or reader may also detect some inconsistencies in his speeches.

To begin with, Rabshakeh speaks condescendingly of Hezekiah's empty words (Isa 36:5). However, this is apparently all that he himself can offer: words. Further, his references to the role of YHWH are mutually contradictory. In 36:7, he implies that YHWH is unwilling to help Hezekiah, since he dislikes his cultic reform (which involved the removal of altars dedicated to YHWH). He even asserts that YHWH actively supports Sennacherib in the current conflict (36:10). However, later on, in 36:20, he indicates that YHWH is just like the patron deities of the countries that had already been conquered by the Assyrian army: powerless, unable to defend his city and to save his own people. Clearly, Rabshakeh's purpose is to persuade the

---

[33] Grayson, "Assyrian Rule," 61. It should be noted, though, that Grayson's conclusions are based on rather scarce textual evidence. Possibly, this tactic was used only in a few exceptional cases.

[34] For a thorough analysis of this text, with references to previous research, which supports the conclusion that Rabshakeh's speeches were composed much later by a Judean author, see Ehud Ben Zvi, "Who Wrote the Speech of Rabshakeh and When?" *JBL* 109 (1990): 79–92.

[35] Chaim Cohen, "Neo-Assyrian Elements in the First Speech of the Biblical Rab-Šāqê," *IOS* 9 (1979): 32–48, quote on p. 39.

[36] This denouement should of course not be confused with the actual course of events. Cf. 2 Kgs 18:14–16.

inhabitants of Jerusalem that it is meaningless to rely on YHWH. But his rhetoric reveals the hypocrisy behind the high ideals celebrated by the official Assyrian ideology. Apparently relying on sheer numerical military strength (36:8–9), he fails to mention that faith in Assur would be the true key to success. Although professing to be the very opposite of such persons, the Assyrian official speaking in Isaiah 36 seems to fit the following description of Assyria's despicable enemies quite well: "Assyria's enemies trust in their own strength, their mighty walls, their numerous armies."[37]

Clearly, then, Rabshakeh is a *caricature*. Still, this character displays a certain complexity which goes beyond the simple stereotype. Reading the text from a postcolonial perspective, I am inclined to see him as an atypical example of cultural *hybridity*. He is a high Assyrian official, yet he speaks not only Aramaic, but Hebrew as well (Isa 36:11, 13). As might be expected, he is well informed concerning Assyria's victories in the past (36:18–19; cf. 10:9, which is strikingly similar). At the same time, however, he appears to possess inside knowledge about Judean controversies concerning the cult (36:7). Even more intriguing, and provocative, is his claim to know the will of YHWH. Indeed, he almost imitates a prophet like Isaiah, as he purportedly transmits the words spoken by YHWH to Sennacherib: "March against this land, and destroy it" (36:10).

More than one interpretation is possible. Is Rabshakeh pictured as a renegade, a Judean employed by the enemy?[38] Does he represent an inner foe of some kind? Should this character, as suggested by Christof Hardmeier, be understood as an oppositional YHWH prophet, a Jeremiah or Ezekiel, in disguise?[39] I find this hypothesis ingenious, but far-fetched and ultimately implausible.[40] The reader has no compelling reason to question Rabshakeh's Assyrian identity. However, on a closer look this identity turns out to be fuzzy and fluctuating. It contains elements of hybridity. Possibly coining a new phrase, I suggest that this can be seen as a case of *projected hybridization*. In the world of this narrative, Judean identity is construed as something stable (and seemingly untouched by all kinds of colonizing Assyrian influence), whereas the attacker's/colonizer's cultural identity is described (by means of a kind of projection) as being more fluid.

So far, the analysis of Isaiah 36–37 has mainly dealt with Rabshakeh's rhetoric, and his role in the drama. Something should also be said about other aspects of this narrative. King Hezekiah can be seen as an incarnation of certain ideals associated with resistance against the mighty empire(s). Firm in his belief in YHWH, he listens to his prophet, Isaiah, and he prays (37:1–20). As regards the concluding speech in this propaganda war, delivered by the prophet, a few comments may

---

[37] Cohen, "Neo-Assyrian," 41.

[38] Cf. Cohen, "Neo-Assyrian," 47, who maintains that his own investigation corroborates a theory put forward by Tadmor, "concerning the possible Aramean or perhaps even Israelite ultimate ethnic origin of this particular Rab-šāqê."

[39] See Christof Hardmeier, *Prophetie im Streit vor dem Untergang Judas: Erzählkommunikative Studien zur Entstehungssituation der Jesaja- und Jeremiaerzählungen in II Reg 18-20 und Jer 37-40* (BZAW 187; Berlin: de Gruyter, 1990), 321–99.

[40] See further Eidevall, *Prophecy*, 105.

suffice, since the analysis that was made of Isa 10:5-15 (see above) is largely applicable also here. This is another instance of *mockery*, or of the subgenre "divine mockery of a foreign king." However, there are several differences between Isa 10:5-15 and 37:21b-29. In the latter text, the foreign king is named (Sennacherib). We are told that the one who scorns him is "daughter Zion," a personification of the city and its inhabitants, but the derisive words are apparently uttered by the national deity via his mouthpiece. Moreover, this is explicitly described as a case of rhetorical retaliation, as *counter-mockery* (vv. 23-24). A different kind of imagery is deployed. Instead of the instrument metaphors used in chapter 10, the Assyrian king is now portrayed as an unruly beast of burden (37:29b). He is allowed to have a will of his own, but this is exactly what turns out to be the problem since he is disobedient to YHWH. Thus, the main accusation remains the same: arrogance (v. 29a). This allegation is exemplified by an inserted quotation (vv. 24-25), where Sennacherib brags about his achievements.

Interestingly, the biblical author demonstrates that s/he is (somehow) well informed concerning the contents of Assyrian royal inscriptions. Thus, one recognizes a central *topos* from that genre, the "journey to the west for wood," often taking the form of tree-felling expeditions in the mountain regions of Lebanon.[41] Sennacherib, on the other hand, is pictured as ignorant, at least when it comes to the achievements of YHWH (vv. 26-28). According to the pieces of Judean counter-propaganda which I have placed in my second group of texts (10:5-15; 36-37, and especially 37:21b-29), all Assyrian kings are, metaphorically speaking, unwitting instruments and/or unwilling animals, to be controlled by YHWH.

Third Stage: Propagandistic Pictures, Moving Away from Ambiguity

In the third group of texts, linked to what seems to be the final stage in the development of the image of Assyria, a new element is introduced: the downfall of the empire. These texts are less ambiguous than those discussed above, and more overtly propagandistic. While some of these passages (in the first place 10:16-19 and 14:24-27) may belong to an expansion and redaction of the Isaianic collection which took place during the reign of Josiah,[42] others could be even later. In Isa 10:16-19, Assyria's downfall is depicted with the help of two intertwined metaphors: an infectious disease and a devastating forest fire (cf. the tree-felling motif in 37:24). According to Isa 14:24-27 (esp. vv. 24-25), Assyria will be defeated by YHWH alone. At least, no other agents are mentioned, as it is declared that YHWH

---

[41] See Machinist, "Assyria," 723.

[42] Thus H. Barth, *Die Jesaja-Worte in der Josiazeit: Israel und Assur als Thema einer produktiven Neuinterpretation der Jesajaüberlieferung* (WMANT 48; Neukirchen-Vluyn: Neukirchener, 1977), esp. 34, 117-19, and Ronald E. Clements, *Isaiah 1-39* (NCBC; Grand Rapids: Eerdmans 1980), 5-6, 113, 146.

has resolved "to crush Assyria in my land, and trample it/him down on my mountain" (v. 25a). One may of course conjecture that this should be carried out by, say, the Babylonian army or the Medes. However, the place for the battle would seem to be Zion ("my mountain"). Thus, the scenery evoked has more in common with the legendary account in Isa 37:36–37 than with the events that actually led to the downfall of Nineveh. As a consequence of this decisive battle, it is stated that "his yoke" will be lifted from the shoulders of the people of Judah (v. 25b).

The yoke metaphor was probably conventional within Hebrew tradition already when this text was written. Still, it is *possible* (but not necessary) to interpret this as a subversive response to Assyrian propaganda. In the royal annals, the subordination of other peoples, including their obligation to pay tributes, is often described with the phrase "I imposed upon them my yoke."[43] A similar use of the yoke motif appears at the end of another text which celebrates the liberation from Assyrian oppression, viz. Isa 10:24–27a. In the opening line of this prophecy, the rod and staff metaphors from 10:5 recur. However, in 10:24, these tools are weapons in the hands of the Assyrians. Because of the rich intertextual ramifications, including allusions to the exodus tradition, I surmise that this prophecy was composed in retrospect, in the post-exilic period.

A late date is likely also in the case of Isa 30:27–33, the last text to be considered in the third group. The gruesome (but allegedly well-deserved) end of the Assyrians (or: of the Assyrian king, the text can be read in both ways) in the flames is accompanied by music and dance. The attitude in this text is perhaps best described as gloating. It almost transcends the limits of what could pass as political propaganda. Possibly, "Assyria" in 30:27–33 stands as a code name for a later empire (Persia or the Seleucid empire), or for some apocalyptic foe.[44]

EGYPTIAN INTERLUDE: THE HELPLESS HELPER

Several passages in the book of Isaiah contain images of Egypt. However, in most cases it is not possible to link the contents of the text to the short period (ca 609–605 BCE) during the first part of Jehoiakim's reign (and possibly at the end of Josiah's reign?), when Judah was an Egyptian vassal state.

In Isaiah 20, the reference is clearly to an earlier period, when Egypt was ruled by a dynasty from Cush (the 25th dynasty). This era came to an end as Assyria established control over Egypt in the 670s BCE. Whereas the oldest layer of chapter 19 (vv. 1–15) might be associated with this brief period of Assyrian domination (see v. 4), the five additions which constitute the latter half of chapter 19 (vv. 16–17 || 18 || 19–22 || 23 || 24–25) are commonly dated to the post-exilic period.[45] Only one oracle, 7:18–19, would seem to reflect a situation when Judah was actually threatened

---

[43] See Machinist, "Assyria," 86. Cf. CAD A/1, 65–66, s.v. *abšānu* as well as N/2, 260–64, s.v. *nīru* A.

[44] See further Eidevall, *Prophecy*, 62–63.

[45] In other words, these oracles should probably be dated to the Persian or, perhaps even more likely, the Hellenistic era. See Blenkinsopp, *Isaiah 1–39*, 317–19.

by Egypt. However, because this text speaks of two armies, the Egyptian and the Assyrian, invading the land of Judah from two sides (in collision or collusion?) this likely refers to the political situation that prevailed before 614 BCE.[46]

If one disregards the allusions to the exodus tradition that are scattered throughout the book, the remaining references to Egypt (Isa 30:1–5; 31:1–3; 36:6) are variations on a particular theme, viz. unreliability. According to the book of Isaiah, it is futile and foolish to rely on help from Egypt. The image of this formerly mighty empire as a helpless helper is most likely based on experience. In fact, this is a common denominator between the capture of Samaria in 722 BCE and the definitive defeat of Jerusalem in 586: Despite promises to assist their allies (Israel and Judah, respectively), the Egyptian army never arrived. At the same time, this portrayal of Egypt as weak and unreliable is reminiscent of Assyrian propaganda. Discussing the phrase "that broken reed (הקנה הרצוץ הזה)," which is used about Egypt in Rabshakeh's first speech (Isa 36:6), Cohen notes that Assyrian kings regularly used strikingly similar imagery when they referred to defeated enemies.[47] He concludes that "[t]here would hardly be a more appropriate way for a Neo-Assyrian official to denounce the worthlessness of trusting in an ally whom Assyria had defeated many times in the past."[48]

Especially if, as seems likely, the legend in chapters 36–37 was composed subsequent to Assyria's (temporary and partial) conquest of Egypt around 670 BCE, the broken reed metaphor can be seen as an authentic ingredient in Rabshakeh's speech. This observation, I suggest, attests further to the fundamental *hybridity* of the book of Isaiah, exemplified in its ambiguous attitude to Assyria. As the text ridicules one empire (Egypt), it virtually echoes the official rhetoric of another (Assyria).

BABYLON: ANTIPATHY AND AMBIVALENCE

From a strictly historical point of view, there is a risk of overstating the element of continuity between the Assyrian empire and its "successor," the Neo-Babylonian empire. It has been demonstrated by Vanderhooft that Nebuchadnezzar's policy toward subjugated regions differed considerably from the Assyrian mode of domination and exploitation.[49] Thus, the Babylonians did not build up an efficient local administration in order to integrate Judah (or the adjacent regions)

---

[46] See Eidevall, *Prophecy*, 31–32.
[47] Cohen, "Neo-Assyrian," 42.
[48] Cohen, "Neo-Assyrian," 43.
[49] See David S. Vanderhooft, "Babylonian Strategies of Imperial Control in the West: Royal Practice and Rhetoric," in *Judah and the Judeans in the Neo-Babylonian Period* (ed. O. Lipschits and J. Blenkinsopp; Winona Lake: Eisenbrauns, 2003), 235–62. Cf. also idem, *The Neo-Babylonian Empire and Babylon in the Latter Prophets* (HSM 59; Atlanta: Scholars Press, 1999).

into their empire, as the Assyrians had done. On the level of ideology and propaganda, it seems to be the case that Nebuchadnezzar "struggled . . . to distance himself from the rhetoric of the Neo-Assyrian kings."[50] However, the reader of the book of Isaiah gets another impression. The Babylonian empire seems to be quite similar to its Assyrian precursor, the main difference being that it is even more cruel and oppressive.

The taunt song in Isa 14:4b–21 is a case in point. As an instance of anti-imperial *mockery*, it can be compared to two passages in the book that are directed against an Assyrian ruler, namely, 10:5–15 and 37:21b–29 (see above). According to several scholars, the song in 14:4b–21 was indeed originally about an Assyrian king, most probably Sargon or Sennacherib.[51] This hypothesis is based on the following observations. Throughout the song, the tyrant remains anonymous. However, some features, such as the staff and rod (or scepter) metaphors in v. 5, would seem to indicate that he is Assyrian (cf. 10:5, 15). While the poem seems to allude to Canaanite mythology (vv. 12–14), the reader searches in vain for a reference to anything that would be typically Babylonian. In fact, the identification of the fallen tyrant as a *Babylonian* ruler is provided by the framework (which might be secondary): the introduction in vv. 3–4a (v. 4a, "then you shall take up this taunt song about the king of Babylon") and the ensuing oracle in vv. 22–23. It is thus possible that a poetic piece of anti-Assyrian propaganda was reapplied and directed against a Babylonian king (most probably Nebuchadnezzar) in the wake of the Babylonian capture of Jerusalem. Alternatively, the original composition referred to Babylonia. On either account, the *continuity* between these two Mesopotamian empires is foregrounded. This can perhaps be seen as a case of *projected mimicry*. In his high aspirations, the Babylonian king is pictured as trying hard to imitate Assyrian role models.

The main theme of Isa 14:4b–21 is the descent of the ruler, all the way from heaven to Sheol (vv. 9–15), a downfall foreboded by his hubris (vv. 9–15). In the remaining passages dealing with Babylonia (13:1–22; 21:1–10; 47:1–15), the theme is rather the downfall of the empire, or more specifically of the city of Babylon. Before discussing those texts, I would like to call attention to what is *missing*. There are no positive or neutral depictions of Babylon in the book of Isaiah. This empire, as opposed to Assyria (8:4; 10:5–6), is not endowed with a mission. Whereas the book of Jeremiah (at least the MT version) pictures Nebuchadnezzar as a servant of YHWH,[52] the book of Isaiah never speaks of Babylon acting as a servant or instrument of their own national deity. Why? I believe this has to do with the Zion-centered ideology entertained by the Isaianic authors and editors. Having de-

---

[50] Vanderhooft, "Babylonian Strategies," 248.

[51] Thus, e.g., Sweeney, *Isaiah 1–39*, 232–33. See also the discussion in Blenkinsopp, *Isaiah 1–39*, 286–87.

[52] Jer 21:1–10; 27:1–11. See further John Hill, *Friend or Foe? The Figure of Babylon in the Book of Jeremiah* (BibIntSup 40; Leiden: Brill 1999), 75–82, 106–11, 127–59. For an insightful discussion of Nebuchadnezzar's role according to the LXX and MT versions of Jeremiah, see also Newsom, "God's Other," 41–43. Cf. also Ezek 29:18–20.

stroyed and defiled the temple in Jerusalem, the Babylonians could not receive any honorary titles.

With regard to their uncompromising attitude, all texts dealing with Babylon would seem to correspond closely to the third group of texts dealing with Assyria. In *Prophecy and Propaganda* I stated that Babylonia is depicted as "the evil empire" *par excellence* and as the prototypical enemy of Judah and YHWH.[53] However, I also noted signs of *ambivalence* in some passages dealing with Babylon. As I set out to reread these passages in a perspective informed by Homi Bhabha's theories, such ambiguities seem to take on a new significance.

In Isaiah 13, the downfall of Babylon is pictured as the climax of a divine campaign against evil in the human world (13:11). However, some formulations recall the genre of city laments. In 13:19, Babylon is referred to as "the jewel among kingdoms (צבי ממלכות)." Read in isolation, this sounds like a piece of panegyric. Within context, though, it becomes ironical, since this glorious city will become destroyed and desolate like Sodom and Gomorrah. Nonetheless, the notion of beauty is evoked. The reader is reminded of the architectural masterpieces that made Babylon famous. Although the text describes the fate of Babylon as well-deserved, it cannot help deploring the destruction that it imagines. In a similar way, the description of acts of brutality against civilians, such as the rape of women and the murder of infants, performed by the (allegedly) ruthless Medes (vv. 16–18), might evoke feelings of sympathy for the population in Babylon. But this text appears to oscillate between empathy and *Schadenfreude*, between lament and desire for revenge. It is thus possible to interpret these horrifying features in the text also in a diametrically opposite way. Because the Babylonians ravished and killed women and children in Jerusalem, they will have to suffer exactly the same atrocities (cf. Ps 137:8-9).

In a way, I suggest, Babylon can be seen as a *mirror* of Judah. A basic equality is asserted, despite all appearances. Especially within parts of Isaiah 40–55, the capital cities of these two nations, Jerusalem and Babylon, can be regarded as a strange pair of twin sisters. They are dissimilar in many respects (exemplified in 47:11-15 by Babylonian interest and expertise in astronomy/astrology and various forms of divination), yet they are similar. In 47:1, the city of Babylon is addressed as "virgin daughter Babylon." This echoes the epithet "virgin daughter Zion" (Isa 37:21; cf. also 52:2). Somehow, the fates of these two metaphorical women are interrelated. The humiliation of the city of Babylon (who is pictured in 47:1-5 as a queen who ends up as an abused slave girl) is regarded as a precondition for the restoration of Zion.[54] When the mother of many children (Babylon) has become a bereaved

---

[53] Eidevall, *Prophecy*, 132.

[54] See C. Franke, "Reversals of Fortune in the Ancient Near East: A Study of the Babylon Oracles in the Book of Isaiah," in *New Visions of Isaiah* (ed. R. F. Melugin and M. A. Sweeney; JSOTSup 214; Sheffield: Sheffield Academic Press, 1996), 104-23, esp. 119.

widow (47:8–9), the other woman (Jerusalem) can be transformed from a childless divorcee/widow into a happy wife, blessed with children (50:1; 54:1–8).

As a whole, and especially in the part called Deutero-Isaiah, the book of Isaiah is uncompromisingly anti-Babylonian. Arguably, though, the images of Babylon are never completely free from ambivalence.

PERSIA: SILENT CONSENT OR SUPPRESSED OPPOSITION?

According to what I take to be the majority opinion among scholars, the final major edition of the book of Isaiah took place during the Persian era (this position does, however, not preclude the possibility that further additions were made throughout the Hellenistic era). Yet the Persian empire is not mentioned in this prophetic book. Arguably, this silence speaks volumes.[55] But whereof does it speak? I can see two main alternatives.

On the one hand, it is possible that the post-monarchic writers and editors supported Persia. They may even have been convinced that the Persian world dominion was authorized by their own deity, and that it was YHWH's will that Judah should end up as Yehud, a tiny little province within that vast empire. Just like the author of Ezra 7:26, they may have tended to regard "the law of your God" (YHWH) and "the law of the king" (of Persia) as more or less synonymous concepts. Members of the educated elite in Jerusalem, and in particular groups closely linked to the Second Temple, would have had their reasons to be loyal to their Persian over-lords, and it is likely that the editors of Isaiah belonged to such an elite group. After all, the Persian authorities had sponsored the building of the temple.

As a rule, prophecies are elicited by crises. If there was no crisis, why prophesy? If Persia did not pose any problem, why mention this empire in a prophetic book edited during the Persian era? That could be one way of explaining the conspicuous silence. The hypothesis that the editors were members of a *pro-Persian* group finds further support in the famous Cyrus oracle in Deutero-Isaiah (Isa 44:24–45:13).[56] According to this text, which may have originated shortly before or after Cyrus's triumphant entry into Babylon, this Persian general was elected by YHWH, and his mission was to rebuild Jerusalem: "He is my shepherd, and he shall carry out all my purpose" (Isa 44:28, NRSV). As if this was not enough, Cyrus is referred to as "his anointed/Messiah (מְשִׁיחוֹ)" in 45:1, although he himself is said to be unaware of his relation to YHWH (45:4).[57] This astonishing designation could have served as a hermeneutical key for post-monarchic readers of the book of Isaiah. As we have seen, the anonymous Assyrian king in Isa 10:5–15 could stand for all Assyrian rulers, just like Sennacherib in chapters 36–37. By the same token,

---

[55] For a discussion of the conspicuous silence regarding Persia in large parts of the Hebrew Bible, informed by postcolonial theory, see Berquist, "Postcolonialism," 22.

[56] For a more detailed, but in many ways different, discussion of the political implications of the Cyrus oracle, and several other related passages in Deutero-Isaiah, see Joseph Blenkinsopp's contribution to this volume.

[57] Cf. Newsom, "God's Other," 44–45.

Cyrus in 44:24–45:13 could stand for all Persian rulers. They would then all be regarded as appointed, and anointed, by YHWH. One may add the reflection that the palpable anti-Babylonian tendency of the book would be entirely consonant with a profoundly pro-Persian attitude.

On the other hand, the silence regarding Persia could indicate *ambivalence* toward this empire. To begin with, the Cyrus oracle can be regarded as applying to Cyrus personally, in his (alleged) capacity as liberator and temple-founder. He was the one who put an end to the Neo-Babylonian empire in 528 BCE, and this could be seen as a kind of revenge for what happened in 586. Hence, he could be given the honorary title "Messiah." However, Cyrus is not referred to as a *Persian* general, or king, in Isa 44:24–45:13. There is thus no reason to extend the notion of divine election to his successors on the throne. Such a reading of the Cyrus oracle opens up for an alternative explanation of the book's silence concerning Persia, in terms of *suppressed opposition*.

There has never existed such a thing as an entirely benevolent and non-oppressive empire. Persia was by no means an exception. The imperial order had to be maintained. The tributes had to be paid. In Nehemiah 9, toward the end of a lengthy prayer uttered by Ezra, it seems that we get a rare glimpse of a voice that is otherwise suppressed in large parts of the Hebrew Bible, a voice speaking of Persian domination experienced as oppression: "Here we are, slaves to this day—slaves in the land that you gave to our ancestors to enjoy its fruit and its good gifts. Its rich yield goes to the kings whom you have set over us because of our sins" (Neh 9:36–37a, NRSV).[58] This critique against the Persians is, at most, indirect. It is part of a prayer, the immediate context speaks of repentance, the foreign rulers are seen as appointed by YHWH, and Persia is not explicitly mentioned. Still, this complaint must be understood as referring to hardships suffered under Persian dominion.

Arguably, fear of retaliation may have stopped the Jewish intellectuals, including the prophets and scribes editing prophetic books, from speaking up openly against the foreign oppressors of their own day. In such a situation, it is likely that parts of the population will seek to express their opinion by means of what Scott has called *hidden transcripts*, that is, "disguised forms of public dissent."[59] One of the strategies adopted by the dissenters would be *anonymity* (including the use of pseudonyms).[60] Clearly, the editors of the book of Isaiah chose to remain anonymous. But the principle of anonymity/pseudonymity can be applied to the object of opposition, in this case the Persian empire, as well. For instance, the utterance in Isa 33:1 may have been composed in the 5th or 4th century, as an accusation

---

[58] On the implications of this quotation, cf. Daniel L. Smith-Christopher, "Abolitionist Exegesis: A Quaker Proposal for White Liberals," in *Still at the Margins* (ed. R. S. Sugirtharajah; London: T & T Clark, 2008), 137.

[59] Scott, *Domination*, 20.

[60] Scott, *Domination*, 140–54.

against Persia:[61] "Ah, you destroyer, who yourself have not been destroyed; you treacherous one, with whom no one has dealt treacherously! When you have ceased to destroy, you will be destroyed; and when you have stopped dealing treacherously, you will be dealt with treacherously" (NRSV). Moreover, several oracles addressing Assyria or Babylon could easily have been applied to Persia. In at least one case, Isa 30:27-33, an ostentatiously "anti-Assyrian" prophecy may even have originated in the Persian era, employing "Assyria" as a code name for the actual oppressor: Persia.[62]

Summing up so far, the book of Isaiah expresses a whole range of attitudes to empires, from loyalty to opposition, from mimicry to mockery. The reader comes across several divergent (and hardly reconcilable) images and perspectives. Apparently, the reader is free to choose between these perspectives, as s/he seeks a strategy in a specific situation: Is this particular empire elected by YHWH? Can it be seen as an instrument in his hand, or should it rather be denounced as an arrogant enemy deserving to be punished for his hubris? Is this an utterly evil empire doomed to destruction?

Although the book of Isaiah contains a variety of different perspectives on empires, it is perhaps possible to say something more definite about the opinion of the final editors on this topic. In the concluding section of this paper, I examine the macrostructure of Isaiah 1-66, with special attention to the compositional framework, in order to elucidate the perspective of the redactors.

A MACROSTRUCTURAL VIEW: EMPIRE REJECTED AND REAFFIRMED

Composed and edited during centuries characterized by imperialist domination, the book of Isaiah is itself to a large extent dominated by empires—or, to be more precise, by discourse related to empires. However, the book begins and ends on a different note, focusing on Jerusalem and Judah. While the first references to named empires are found in chapter 7 (vv. 17, 18-20: Assyria and Egypt), the last one occurs in 48:20 (Babylon). In other words, the entire section preceding the pivotal chapter 6, with its report of a vision and a calling experience, is completely void of such references.[63] The same holds for the last eighteen chapters.

---

[61] See Wildberger, *Jesaja 3: Jesaja 28-39* (BKAT 10/3; Neukirchen-Vluyn: Neukirchener, 1982), 1287-88.

[62] Alternatively, "Assyria" is here a code name for the Seleucid empire. Cf. Eidevall, *Prophecy*, 63. Arguments for a post-exilic dating have been adduced by Blenkinsopp, *Isaiah 1-39*, 423-24. See further the brief analysis of Isa 30:27-33 above, in the section dealing with the "third stage" in the development of the image of Assyria.

[63] Cf. Christopher Begg, "Babylon in the Book of Isaiah," in *The Book of Isaiah / Le livre d'Isaïe: Les oracles et leurs relectures, unité et complexité de l'ouvrage* (ed. J. Vermeylen; BETL 81; Leuven: Leuven University Press, 1989), 121-25, esp. 124. It is commonly assumed that Isa 5:26-29 originated as a depiction of an Assyrian army. Quite possibly, the anonymity which characterizes this passage is due to its position within the overall structure of the book. See further Eidevall, *Prophecy*, 26-28, 175.

If chapters 7 through 48 relate Judah's history under the empires, the enlarged editorial framework of this prophetic book, comprising the introductory section (chs. 1–5) and the concluding chapters (49–66), tells quite another story. Even though Judah is constantly threatened by other nations, the identity of the attackers and colonizers seems to be of minor importance (cf. Isa 1:7–8; 3:1–4:1; 5:13, 26–29). Sooner or later they are bound to fall, all of them. Judah and YHWH will take revenge on their enemies, symbolized by Edom (63:1–6). In the end, the motif of foreign armies surrounding Jerusalem (7:1; 29:1–8; 31:4–5; 36–37) will be transformed into a picture of peaceful pilgrimage. From all parts of the world people will travel to Zion, seeking wisdom and bringing material goods (2:2–5; 60:1–14). That seems to be the message of the editorial framework of the book of Isaiah.

One might also attempt to deduce a message, transmitted through a kind of *hidden transcript*, from the macrostructure of Isaiah 1–66. The overall arrangement, I suggest, indicates a certain worldview which we might call "proto-apocalyptic." According to this view, the history of the world is thought to follow a divine plan. No political powers last forever. *Empires rise, but ultimately they are destined to fall.* This applies to Assyria (cf. the three stages in the Isaianic depiction of Assyria outlined above) and Babylonia—and by implication, also to Persia! They will be forgotten, and their names will be erased. As history reaches its ultimate goal, YHWH will create a new world, "the new heavens and the new earth, which I will make" (Isa 66:22, NRSV).

It is important to notice the "nationalist" and partisan character of this seemingly "universalist" vision. After centuries of vassalage, the reader is told, freedom will prevail. Free at last, free from all empires! But those passages that seem to undermine all empires are not free from imperialist ideology. This can, I suggest, be seen as a consequence of the cultural hybridity of the final editors. The fundamental tenets of imperial propaganda were inscribed in their own worldview. Instead of denouncing the very rhetoric of domination and subjugation, of center and periphery, the editors reproduced it, but for their own purposes. In their brave new world, Jerusalem is the self-evident center. There will be a steady influx of tributes to the city (60:1–14), and all enemies will be defeated, in a perpetual repetition of the legendary account of the defeat of the Assyrians in 701 BCE (Isa 66:24; cf. 37:36).

SUMMARY

Does the book of Isaiah uphold or undermine empire? As adumbrated in the introduction, it is not possible to give a short and simple answer to that question. Reading the relevant texts from a perspective informed by postcolonial theory, I have demonstrated that this prophetic book contains a variety of attitudes towards empires, ranging from loyalty to fierce opposition or outright mockery. In the case of Assyria, it seems possible to trace several stages of diachronic development, related to shifting political situations. Sometimes the texts show signs of mimicry. On the whole, the book of Isaiah is characterized by a high degree of ambivalence towards the great empires.

On the macrostructural level, however, the message of the book of Isaiah can be seen as far from ambiguous. According to this "vision" (cf. 1:1) in its entirety, Judah/Yehud, that petty nation/province downtrodden by a series of mighty over-lords, will eventually, and with the help of the divine overlord YHWH, become an empire (cf. 66:6–24): the empire that strikes back.

7

The Theological Politics of Deutero-Isaiah[1]

Joseph Blenkinsopp

COPING WITH CATASTROPHE

Those of us who have never had to live through a catastrophic situation will find it hard to imagine what life was like for the survivors in Judah in the autumn and winter of 586 BCE. The murder and mayhem, destruction of property, loss of the public institutions which sustained communal living, the monarchy in the first place, created a situation of extreme deprivation, disorientation, numbness and anomie. People had to fall back for survival on whatever resources were still available in the household and kinship network to which they belonged. Sooner or later questions about why it happened and who was responsible would be raised, and sooner or later such questions would be directed at their ancestral deity who "neither slumbered nor slept" in protecting his people, his city Jerusalem, and the house of David, and yet had singly failed to do so. Something like this happens in all comparable situations, but in this instance the questioning would have been rendered more insistent by the religious reforms carried out a few years earlier during Josiah's reign with their heavy concentration on political and religious centralization.

Such questioning is implicit in practically all the biblical texts from the exilic period. Our concern is with the fate of the dynasty on which the whole apparatus of public life depended, and with whatever options were available after it had been extinguished. But before addressing that issue directly, it will be useful to take in

---

[1] This paper corresponds to chapter four of *David Remembered: Kingship and National Identity in Ancient Israel* (Grand Rapids: Eerdmans, 2013), 54–70, reprinted by kind permission of the publisher; all rights reserved.

the larger picture by presenting a rough sketch of the range of response to the disaster reflected in texts from that time.

One option was to simply reject the official "Yahweh alone" orthodoxy. Following on the assassination of Gedaliah about four years after the fall of Jerusalem, some of the surviving military leaders and many of the ordinary people sought refuge in Egypt from the anticipated Babylonian reprisals, taking a protesting Jeremiah with them (2 Kgs 25:25-26; Jer 41:1-43:7). After settling in the garrison town of Tahpanhes (Daphne, today Tell Defneh), they were once again reminded by Jeremiah in a typical jeremiad that the disaster recently visited on them had come about on account of their addiction to cults other than that of Yahweh (Jer 44:1-14). This time, however, the prophet's listeners, both men and women, rejected Jeremiah's explanation of the disaster in the most peremptory manner. On the contrary, they insisted, responsibility lay with those, including Jeremiah himself, who had tried to persuade them to abandon the cult of "the Queen of Heaven." The veneration of this goddess, they claimed, had been an essential element in public and private religious practice in Judah at all times and with all categories of the population since the beginning.[2] The abandonment of her cult is the real reason, they told him, why we find ourselves in this miserable situation. The women concluded by stating their determination to continue making offerings and libations to the Queen of Heaven and venerating her image.[3] What we have here, then, is an alternative explanation for the disaster of 586 BCE.

So much for the religious reforms of Josiah and his supporters! But what happened in Egypt was not an isolated incident. Even before the final catastrophe, the image of the goddess, ejected from the temple precincts by Josiah's reform party (2 Kgs 23:4, 6-7), found its way back there about three decades later as we read in Ezekiel's visionary tour of the temple (Ezek 8:5-6). A post-disaster literary stratum of Isaiah also testifies to the impact of disaster on the revival in Judah of chthonic cults together with the veneration of the goddess (Isa 1:29; 57:3-13; 66:17). There is even a denunciation of the cult of deities presiding over fate, fortune, or chance (Isa 65:11), an anticipation of the Greek *moira*. This is a by no means unfamiliar reaction to disaster and the loss of a sense of control and meaning which major disasters tend to induce.[4]

---

[2] The identity of this *malkat haššāmayim* (the original vocalization, cf. LXX, Jer 51:17, ἡ βασιλίσσα τοῦ οὐρανοῦ) is uncertain. Similar titles are borne by the Assyrian Ištar (*malkat šamāmī*; e.g. VAS 10 213: 8) and the West Semitic Anat (*b'lt šmm*; KTU 1.108:7), but the goddess Ašerah, so prominent throughout Israelite and Judean history, cannot be excluded. See Cornelis Houtman, "Queen of Heaven," DDD: 678-80.

[3] This is one of the very rare occasions in the Hebrew Bible where women are heard speaking on the subject of religion.

[4] The deities Gad and Měnî are rendered in LXX by δαίμων and τύχη, respectively; Vulg. has only one name: *Fortuna*. On these deities see S. David Sperling, "Meni מני 'Fortune'," DDD: 566-68; Joseph Blenkinsopp, *Isaiah 56-66: A New Translation with Introduction and Commentary* (AB 19B; New York: Doubleday, 2003), 278-79. A parallel instance is the "deal with death" contracted by the Judean leadership faced with terminal danger from Assyria towards the end of the eighth century BCE, and denounced in Isa 28:14-22. Recourse to necromancy and

Those who chose not to follow the example of their fellow Judeans in Egypt, and who in their grief and perplexity remained faithful to Yahweh and the ancestral traditions, would sooner or later have felt obliged to justify their choice to themselves as well as to those, within and outside of their own community, who were asking "Where now is your god?" (Ps 42:4; 115:2). Much of the writing which has survived from the post-disaster period addresses this question in one way or another. It is especially in evidence in the re-reading and re-editing of the sayings of prophets, especially those who passed judgment on the religious infidelity of their contemporaries. An example from the Assyrian period may be mentioned. Among the diverse kinds of material in the book named for Amos, active in the middle decades of the eighth century BCE, is a brief gnomic poem about the necessity and ineluctability of prophecy:

> Do two walk together unless they have made an appointment?
> Does a lion roar in the forest when it has no prey?
> Does a young lion cry out from its den when it has caught nothing?
> Does a bird fall into a snare on the earth when there is no trap for it?
> Does a snare spring up from the ground when it has taken nothing?
> Is a trumpet blown in a city and the people are not afraid?
> Does disaster befall a city unless Yahweh has brought it about?
> [Surely Yahweh God does nothing without revealing his secret to his servants the
>   prophets]
> The lion has roared, who will not fear?
> Yahweh God has spoken, who will not prophesy? (Amos 3:3–8)

The seventh in the list of rhetorical questions which make up the poem has provoked an interpretative scribal comment in the following verse (in brackets) which, while assuming the required affirmative answer, goes on to observe that, if that is so, Yahweh God always warns of impending and avoidable disaster, and therefore is free of blame. Since "his servants the prophets" is the standard post-disaster Deuteronomistic term for the prophetic succession,[5] the stricken city is Jerusalem, and on account of the fact that the disaster awaiting it was announced in advance by Yahweh's prophetic servants, places the blame where it belongs: with the people and their rulers. It therefore at the same time absolves Yahweh from the charge of injustice and caprice.[6]

The same conclusion is reached by a more direct route in the concluding paragraph of Hosea addressed to the reader of the book. The language and idiom

---

the occult is a well-attested phenomenon at times of catastrophe. See my "Judah's Covenant with Death (Isaiah xviii 14–22)," *VT* 50 (2000): 472–83.

    [5] 2 Kgs 9:7; 17:13, 23; 21:10; 24:2; also in passages in Jeremiah attributable to a Deuteronomistic editor: Jer 7:25; 25:4; 26:5; 29:19; 35:15; 44:4.

    [6] This solution to the problem of theodicy arising from the disaster of 586 BCE is already apparent in Dtr's comment on the extinction of the Kingdom of Samaria in 722 BCE: "Yahweh warned Israel and Judah by every prophet and every seer . . . but they would not listen; they acted stubbornly like their ancestors . . . therefore Yahweh was angry with Israel and removed them out of his sight" (2 Kgs 17:13–20).

have persuaded practically all commentators that it was appended to the book during the time of the Second Temple:[7]

> Let the wise understand these matters, and let the judicious acknowledge them. The ways of Yahweh are straight, and the righteous walk in them, while sinners stumble in them. (14:10)

The message is addressed especially to those troubled by Hosea's repeated affirmation about the responsibility of Yahweh for putting an end to the Kingdom of Samaria. Rather than setting out to prove that this decision of Yahweh was morally justified, the scribe who added the injunction simply asserts that while the justice and wisdom of divine action will be self-evident to the wise and upright, the acceptance of this self-evident truth is obscured and hindered by an immoral way of life. Ezekiel appears to make a similar point in replying to the complaint that "the way (i.e., conduct) of Yahweh is not right and just" (Ezek 18:25).[8] Ezekiel rejects this charge only after refuting the idea of intergenerational moral responsibility implicit in the complaint that his contemporaries were being punished for the sins of their forebears. He does this by means of the case history of a three-generational family: a righteous grandfather, a violent and immoral son, a grandson who does not follow his father's example—concluding with a statement of individual moral accountability: whether you are righteous or wicked depends on you alone, not on your parents and antecedents. Only the one who sins dies; moral accountability is not intergenerational (Ezek 18:1-24). More directly relevant to the debate about the morality of divine action, however, is Ezekiel's case history of a land—Judah, for example—devastated by the disasters of famine, wild animals, the sword, and pestilence (Ezek 14:12-23). He concludes that even if Noah, Daniel and Job, those three models of wisdom and righteousness from ancient times, were living in that land, they would save no one but themselves, not even their immediate family members, by virtue of their righteousness (Ezek 14:12-23).[9]

---

[7] On the language of Hos 14:10—"the ways of Yahweh" (דרכי יהוה), the stumbling of the wicked and rebellious (verbal stem כשל), and the frequent contrast between the righteous (צדיקים) and the wicked (רשעים)—cf. Prov 10:29; 24:16. A. A. Macintosh (*A Critical and Exegetical Commentary on Hosea* [ICC; Edinburgh: T & T Clark, 1997], 583) draws the conclusion that by the time of its composition in the post-exilic period the book of Hosea had become to all intents and purposes Scripture.

[8] "Not right and just" is an attempt to translate לֹא יִתָּכֵן. "The way of the Lord is unfair" (NRSV) seems to be too weak, as if the Lord is not playing according to the rules; "The Lord acts without principle" (REB) is stronger but perhaps not strong enough; "unprincipled" is not the same as "unjust."

[9] In this respect Ezekiel appears to differ from the author of the dialogue between Abraham and Yahweh about Yahweh's decision to destroy Sodom in Gen 18:22-33. That this dialogue is a late addition to the narrative from a time after the fall of Jerusalem has often been argued since Julius Wellhausen, *Die Composition des Hexateuchs und der historischen Bücher des Alten Testaments* (4th ed.; Berlin: de Gruyter, 1963), 25-36. See, for example, Claus Westermann (*Genesis* [Neukirchen: Neukirchener Verlag, 1979], 347-48, 352), who attributes

As to what extent these debates among the *literati* reflected discussion and self-questioning among the Judean public we can only guess. At any rate, life had to go on even in the aftermath of tragedy and disaster. The survivors would have put their lives back together as best they could, as their forebears did after the ravages of the Assyrian army under Sennacherib a little more than a century earlier. We have no information on how Judah was governed during the remaining forty-three years of Babylonian rule. Mindful of the recent history of rebellion, the imperial overlord would probably have given up any further attempt at proxy rule through local officials, and would therefore have appointed a Babylonian governor. During that short half-century, however, fundamental changes were taking place on the international scene. In 550 BCE the Median empire was overrun by the Iranian Cyrus II, and in the next two years it was the turn of Elam, Parthia, Hyrcania, and Armenia. By the end of the decade Cyrus was the master of the Lydian empire that had been ruled by the fabled Croesus, together with the rest of Asia Minor, Eastern Iran, and much of Central Asia. By the beginning of 539 BCE Cyrus was ready to advance against Babylon, and in October of that year he entered the city in triumph. Since Judah was a province in the empire ruled from Babylon, these shape-changing events were calculated to have a direct impact on Jewish communities in Judah and elsewhere. The question then arises: did the change from Babylonian to Persian rule elicit a corresponding change in attitude to life under imperial control and the loss of native institutions, including the native dynasty? About that time, the mid-sixth century BCE we begin to hear a prophetic voice with a new and controversial answer to that question.

TOKENS OF FAITHFUL LOVE TO DAVID (ISA 55:1-5)

The only mention of David in Deutero-Isaiah (chs. 40–55) or for that matter Deutero- and Trito-Isaiah together (chs. 40–66), occurs towards the conclusion of Deutero-Isaiah, at the beginning of the last chapter (55:1–5) in which many of the themes which recur throughout the section are recapitulated. This one reference to the Davidic dynasty provides a point of departure for a discussion of the author's proposed solution to the loss of the dynasty and his theological politics in general.

After the invitation to accept the free gift of food that nourishes (vv. 1-2), the address continues as follows (vv. 3-5):

---

it to a post-exilic theologian. This kind of dialogue is without parallel in Genesis but is reminiscent of disputations in Ezekiel and Malachi. There are two issues here: the first, the fate of the righteous caught up in divine judgment on an immoral city; the second, whether the righteous can influence the fate of the unrighteous and, if so, under what conditions, and at what critical mass. See my articles "Abraham and the Righteous of Sodom," *JJS* 33 (1982): 119–32 and "The Judge of All the Earth: Theodicy in the Midrash on Genesis 18:22-33," *JJS* 41 (1990): 1–12.

Come to me and listen carefully,
Hear me, and your spirit will revive.
I shall make a perpetual covenant with you,
the tokens of faithful love I showed to David
As I appointed him a witness to peoples,

a prince who ruled over nations,
so you will summon a nation you do not know,
and a nation that does not know you will come in haste to you,
for the sake of your God,
for the Holy One of Israel who has made you glorious.

The most natural interpretation of this appeal is that God will show you, the prophet's fellow-Judeans, the same favor he showed David in the past.[10] These "tokens of faithful love" imply a guarantee of perpetuity for the Davidic dynasty, as stated in Nathan's oracular pronouncement (2 Sam 7:8–17) and elsewhere (2 Sam 23:1–7; Ps 89:27–37); in effect, a perpetual covenant (ברית עולם), as is explicit in 2 Sam 23:5 and implicit in our text. But the point is that now the commitment concerning the dynasty has been reinterpreted, reformulated, and transferred to the people as a whole, those addressed by the author who had survived the disaster which swept the dynasty away.

The passage continues by applying this insight to international relations, always of decisive significance for small nations, then as now, whose fate was to live in the shadow of oppressive empires. David's relations with foreign nations as overlord and source of the blessings of justice and peace are now reformulated in terms of a new relationship of the people as a whole to the outside world which will bring the author's fellow-Judeans recognition and honor. Use of the singular, גוי, ("nation") in v. 5 (twice) would, in the circumstances, hint at Persia under the rule of Cyrus, a figure overwhelmingly present throughout the first section of Deutero-Isaiah (chs. 40–48). Moreover, the statement "you will summon a nation you do not know, and a nation that does not know you will come in haste to you" echoes the frequent summons addressed to Cyrus in the same text (Isa 41:25; 42:6; 45:3, 4), even though he does not know Israel's God (45:4–5). In 55:3–5, read in the light of Deutero-Isaiah as a whole, the summons would refer to Cyrus as

---

[10] חַסְדֵי דָּוִד, only here and 2 Chr 6:42, is parsed as objective genitive in keeping with the context, by Hugh G. M. Williamson, "'The Sure Mercies of David': Subjective or Objective Genitive?," *JSS* 23 (1978): 31–49, rather than subjective genitive, referring to deeds performed by David, as A. Caquot, "Les 'grâces de David': à propos d'Isaïe 55,3b," *Sem* 15 (1965): 45–59; W. A. M. Beuken, "Isa. 55.3-5 The Restoration of David," *Bijdragen* 35 (1974): 49–64; Pierre Bordreuil, "Les 'grâces de David' et I Maccabee ii 57," *VT* 31 (1981): 73–76. That David is the recipient rather than the origin of the tokens of faithful love is the view of most recent commentators; among English-language exegetes see R. Norman Whybray, *Isaiah 40-66* (NCB; London: Oliphants, 1975), 191; Brevard S. Childs, *Isaiah* (Louisville: Westminster John Knox Press, 2001), 434–45; Joseph Blenkinsopp, *Isaiah 40-55: A New Translation with Introduction and Commentary* (AB 19A; New York: Doubleday, 2002), 370–71; John Goldingay and David Payne, *Isaiah 40-55. Volume II* (ICC; London: T & T Clark, 2006), 371–75.

representative of the nation summoned to act as agent of the God of Israel in the conquest of Babylon anticipated for the near future.

The need to rethink the established dogma of the perpetuity of the Davidic dynasty arose from the intractable data of historical experience. The eclipse of the Davidic dynasty, signaled by the public slaughter of the sons of Zedekiah, last of the line, and the dragging of the blinded king into exile (2 Kgs 25:7), had happened within the lifetime of many of the prophet's audience, and perhaps also that of the prophet himself writing during the last years of Babylonian rule in the mid-sixth century BCE. Ps 89 contains one of the most poignant expressions of bewilderment and anguish at the apparently definitive annulment of the covenant by which the permanence of the national dynasty was thought to have been guaranteed. This lament has enough in common with the theme and even the language of Isa 55:3-5 to suggest that the author of our text, and of Isaiah 40-55 as a whole, was familiar with it and had it in mind. Covenant language occurs in both Isa 55:3-5 and Ps 89 where the key term ברית appears four times and חסד seven times.[11] It is clear nevertheless that the Isaian author goes well beyond the psalmist who can still plead with Yahweh to bear in mind his promises, and can still utter the age-old complaint עד מתי? ("how long?" v. 47 emended text). For the Isaian author, on the contrary, the dynastic promise has undergone a fundamental reinterpretation. Hence the complete absence of allusion to David and the Davidic dynasty in Deutero-Isaiah either as a historical reality, or the object of hope for the future, or a feature of eschatological scenarios, a situation unparalleled in prophetic texts dated to the exilic period.[12] But this situation, remarkable in itself, leaves unaddressed the issue of an acceptable alternative form of governance once the break with the native dynasty is accepted as inevitable. We must now ask whether the author of Isaiah 40-55 had his own answer to that question.

---

[11] Childs, *Isaiah*, 434-37; Goldingay and Payne, *Isaiah 40-55*, 372. Otto Eissfeldt ("The Promises of Grace to David in Isaiah 55:1-5," in *Israel's Prophetic Heritage: Essays in Honor of James Muilenberg* [ed. B. W. Anderson and W. Harrelson; New York: Harper & Row, 1962], 196–207) points out the parallels in detail but also a fundamental difference in the psalm vis-à-vis Isa 55:3-5, in that the psalmist is addressing more directly the disconfirmation of the promise to David. Nahum M. Sarna ("Psalm 89: A Study in Inner Biblical Exegesis," in *Biblical and Other Studies* [ed. A. Altmann; Cambridge; Harvard University Press, 1963], 29–46) dates the psalm, a composite of hymn, oracle and lament, to the reign of Ahaz during the Syro-Ephramite attack on Judah in the eighth century BCE. The psalm does not seem to match this situation: the attack of Syria and Samaria on Jerusalem did not succeed (see v. 41) and Ahaz was not dethroned (see vv. 40, 45). Scott R. A. Starbuck ("Theological Anthropology at a Fulcrum: Isaiah 55:1-5, Psalm 89, and Second Stage Traditio in the Royal Psalms," in *David and Zion: Biblical Studies in Honor of J. J. M. Roberts* [ed. B. F. Batto and K. L. Roberts; Winona Lake: Eisenbrauns, 2004], 247–65) suggests a date for the psalm in its final form after the death of Josiah and deposition of Jehoahaz, therefore when the dynasty was in terminal crisis.

[12] Cf. Jer 17:24-25; 22:1-4; 23:5-6; 30:8-9; 33:14-26; Ezek 34:23-24; 37:24-28; Amos 9:11-12; Mic 5:1-4, and frequently in Isaiah 1-39 (9:1-6; 11:1-9; 16:5). Taking in this broader view of Deutero-Isaiah makes it difficult to accept the more benign alternative that the promise to David is now to be shared with all the people rather than transferred to them, as noted by W. C. Kaiser, "The Unfailing Kindnesses promised to David: Isaiah 55:3," *JSOT* 45 (1989): 41–98.

THE HISTORICAL CONTEXT: PROSPECTS AND OPTIONS

Any attempt to address this issue must take account of the historical context in which the author of Deutero-Isaiah[13] was active, a context which takes in the period from the extinction of the dynasty to the time of writing, by broad agreement the last decade of Babylonian rule (ca. 550–539 BCE). To recapitulate: The final eclipse of the Davidic dynasty occupied the quarter century following the death of Josiah during which four of his descendants hastened the end by their ineptitude. The public execution of the male children of Zedekiah, last of the four (2 Kgs 25:6–7), was a deliberate act aimed at finally extinguishing the dynasty and, with it, any hope of independence for "the rebellious city harmful to kings and provinces" (Ezra 4:15). But there remained one surviving representative of the dynasty, the exiled Jehoiachin. An appendix to the Deuteronomistic History records that in the first year of his reign, therefore 562/561 BCE, Amel-Marduk granted amnesty to Jehoiachin, giving him a pre-eminent position among other exiled rulers at the Babylonian court (2 Kgs 25:27–30). If this implies that Jehoiachin was being groomed to return to Jerusalem as a client ruler the plan came to nothing since Amel-Marduk was assassinated a few months later by his brother-in-law Neriglissar. Jehoiachin therefore died in Babylon after all, as predicted by Jeremiah (Jer 22:26).

At the time of the composition of Deutero-Isaiah this was very recent history. In retrospect, it must have seemed to many of this prophetic author's contemporaries who had survived the terrible half-century since the death of Josiah as if that tragic event marked, in effect, the end of the line for the dynasty. This would have made it easier to accept the transfer of the promises to David from the dynasty to the people as a whole. The same view is expressed in a more subtle way in the Chronicler's rewritten version of Josiah's death and obsequies (2 Chr 35:20–

---

[13] Use of the term "author" calls for explanation. Without attempting to argue the case in detail, I am assuming a basic thematic unity throughout chs. 40–55 and must confess to some hesitation with regard to recent attempts to section the work into layers, assigning dates to each. This seems to me to be especially the case with passages which ostensibly, in the context, refer to Cyrus II and have been generally so understood, but are re-dated to the reign of Darius I. I have in mind the dividing up of Isa 45:1–7, the primary Cyrus text, in the redactional *tour de force* of Reinhard G. Kratz, *Kyros im Deuterojesaja-Buch: Redaktionsgeschichtliche Untersuchungen zu Entstehung und Theologie von Jes 40–55* (FAT 1; Tübingen: Mohr Siebeck, 1991), but also of the older study of Jean Marcel Vincent, *Studien zur literarische Eigenart und zur geistigen Heimat von Jesaja, Kap. 40–55* (BET 5; Frankfurt am Main: Peter Lang, 1977) and, more recently, Odil Hannes Steck, "'Israel und Zion': Zum Problem konzeptioneller Einheit und literarischer Schichtung in Deuterojesaja," in *Gottesknecht und Zion: Gesammelte Aufsätze zu Deuterojesaja* (FAT 4; Tübingen: Mohr Siebeck, 1992), 173–207; also Ulrich Berges, *Das Buch Jesaja: Komposition und Endgestalt* (Herder's Biblische Studien 16; Freiburg: Herder, 1998), 322–413. On the need for a less drastic approach to *Redaktionsgeschichte* see the remarks of Hans-Jürgen Hermisson, "Einheit und Komplexität Deuterojesajas: Probleme der Redaktionsgeschichte von Jes 40–55," in *The Book of Isaiah: Le Livre d'Isaïe: Les oracles et leurs relectures unité et complexité de l'ouvrage* (BETL 81; ed. J. Vermeylen; Leuven: Leuven University Press/Peeters, 1989), 286–312.

27). The latter concludes, uniquely, with a memorial lament which reads like a lament for the Davidic house as a whole and all that it stood for.

In surveying this half-century of turmoil we note the emergence of different points of view on what kind of future was possible and tolerable in the absence of the native dynasty and faced with the overwhelming imperial power represented by the Babylonians and, in prospect, the Persians. To these points of view corresponded parties with conflicting opinions on the fundamental issue of acquiescence in or active opposition to imperial rule in its different forms. The appointment of Gedaliah over the province sharpened the issue and raised the stakes on the conflicts about a future without the dynasty (2 Kgs 25:22-26; Jer 40:1-41:18); and this would be especially the case if Gedaliah was appointed as client king, since he was certainly not of Davidic descent. It would also render more contextually intelligible the assassination of Gedaliah by Ishmael who was, or claimed to be, of Davidic descent (Jer 41:1).

The biblical account of the situation is obviously incomplete, but the texts have much to say about Jeremiah and the Shaphanids in opposition to policies pursued by those advising Zedekiah and their allies. Party conflict in the last phase of the kingdom of Judah may be reflected in the final chapter of the History. It seems likely that its original conclusion was the definitive statement that "Judah went into exile out of its land" (2 Kgs 25:21) rather than the inconsequential bit of information with which it concludes in its present form (25:30).[14] If this is so, two appendices must have been added. The first is the account of the appointment of Gedaliah, his assassination, and an exodus en masse to Egypt to avoid the anticipated Babylonian reprisal (2 Kgs 25:22-26). The second, which holds out a sliver of hope for a future restoration, records the rehabilitation of Jehoiachin by Amel-Marduk (written disphemistically "Evil-Merodach" in the biblical text) and therefore must have been added before the assassination of the latter in 560 BCE.[15] All of this is in sharp contrast to the conclusion of Chronicles where the focus is no longer on the national dynasty but on Cyrus as the divinely inspired agent of Yahweh (2 Chr 36:22-23). And with Cyrus we return to Deutero-Isaiah and its author's response to the issues of his own day.

---

[14] Recent discussion in Thomas C. Römer, *The So-Called Deuteronomistic History* (London/New York: T & T Clark, 2005), 140.

[15] The situation is more complex for those who argue for a Josian edition of the History concluding with the statement about the incomparability of Josiah in 2 Kgs 23:25: "Before him there was no king like him who turned to Yahweh with all his heart and soul and strength, according to all the law of Moses." After experiencing the four, or maybe five rulers who followed him, a later scribe has added: "nor did any like him arise after him," followed by a statement in which Yahweh rejects Judah, Jerusalem, and its temple (23:25b-27). The general sense seems to be that the dynasty ended, in effect, with Josiah. For a summary account of the double redaction theory, together with competing views of the "Cross school" and the "Göttingen school," see Albert de Pury, Thomas Römer, and Jean-Daniel Macchi (eds.), *Israël construit son histoire: L'historiographie deutéronomiste à la lumière des recherches récentes* (Le Monde de la Bible 34; Geneva: Labor et Fides, 1996), 46-58; Römer, *The So-Called Deuteronomistic History*, 27-35.

CYRUS, DIVINELY-INSPIRED AND DIVINELY-APPOINTED SUCCESSOR
TO THE DAVIDIC LINE

According to Isaiah 40–48 Cyrus is destined to be the principal agent of national rehabilitation and restoration for Judean communities in Judah and the diaspora. Karl Budde stated this very clearly many years ago: "Cyrus stands at the very center of the prophet's world view."[16] He is the one who will defeat Judah's enemies, Babylon in the first place,[17] impose an international order based on justice and peace (42:1–4),[18] allow, even facilitate, the repatriation of those forcibly deported (42:7; 45:13), and make possible the rebuilding of Jerusalem and its temple (44:28; 45:13). These tasks are to be discharged under the direct inspiration and aegis of Yahweh, Israel's king.[19] Such expectations would not have seemed unreasonable in view of propaganda of the kind disseminated in the Cyrus Cylinder text published within a year of the fall of Babylon. In the second half of this manifesto Cyrus, speaking in his own name, claimed to have restored the gods of subject peoples to their original sanctuaries and permitted their devotees to return to their native lands.[20] Most commentators conclude that Deutero-Isaiah, or the greater part of it, was composed before the promulgation of this text, some time between 550 and 538. Pro-Persian propaganda would, however, have been in circulation during the last years of the reign of Nabonidus, probably disseminated by Marduk priests offended by Nabonidus' neglect of the *akītu* festival and his

---

[16] Cited in Max Haller, "Die Kyros-Lieder Deuterojesajas," in *EYXAPIΣTHPION: Studien zur Religion und Literatur des Alten und Neuen Testaments: Hermann Gunkel zum 60. Geburtstage, dem 23. Mai 1922 dargebracht von seinen Schülern und Freunden, und in ihrem Namen* (FRLANT 36; ed. H. Schmidt; Göttingen: Vandenhoeck & Ruprecht, 1923), 261.

[17] Isa 41:1–5, 25–29; 43:14; 45:1–7, 13; 46:11; 48:14–16.

[18] The nature of the commission mandated in 42:1–4, that of imposing an international order based on justice (משפט occurring three times in this short passage), is the function of a ruler not of a prophet or priest. It has several of the features of a royal installation ritual, cf. Ps 2; 72; 110. The identification of the עבד in 42:1–4 with Cyrus has often been argued or assumed, e.g., Haller, "Die Kyroslieder des Deuterojesaja," 262–63; Sydney Smith, *Isaiah Chapters XL–LV: Literary Criticism and History* (Schweich Lectures 1940; London: Published for the British Academy by Oxford University Press, 1944), 54–57; Sigmund Mowinckel, *He That Cometh* (Oxford: Blackwell, 1956), 189–91. It should be added that since the book of Isaiah has been the object of a continuous and cumulative process of reinterpretation, this first of Duhm's servant passages could have been reapplied to other figures at a later time. See my *Isaiah 40-55*, 209–12.

[19] Isa 41:21; 43:15; 44:6. With the verb העיר ("stir up," "inspire") in Isa 41:2, 25; 45:13; cf. 2 Chr 36:22; Ezra 1:1.

[20] The relevant statements correspond to lines 32–33 of the Cylinder, see the translation in *ANET*, 315–16. It is acknowledged, however, that this is propaganda probably emanating from Babylonian priests hostile to Nabonidus, and that Persian policy vis-à-vis subject peoples was not significantly different from that of their imperial predecessors. See, inter alios, R. J. van der Spek, "Did Cyrus the Great Introduce a New Policy Towards Subdued Nations?," *Persica* 10 (1982): 278–83; Amélie Kuhrt, "The Cyrus Cylinder and Achaemenid Imperial Policy," *JSOT* 25 (1983): 83–97.

other alleged impieties, and the prophet could have become acquainted with it at that time.

On the assumption that the author of Isaiah 40–55 had a particular form of governance in mind for the immediate future, we must go on to ask in what capacity Cyrus was to fulfill this commission assigned to him by Yahweh. I will argue that Deutero-Isaiah is attempting to persuade his public that Yahweh is now bringing about a new dispensation in which Cyrus, as Yahweh's agent, will take over the succession to the now defunct Davidic dynasty, warranted by an authority which transcends by far descent through the male line, namely, direct divine inspiration not only of the prophetic author but of Cyrus himself.[21] Since this solution called for abandoning beliefs long cherished together with aspirations for political autonomy, we can appreciate that many of the hearers would be predisposed to reject the message. An earlier commentator put this is even stronger terms: "If Cyrus was the anointed of Yahweh, he had taken the place of the line of David, and had become the true king of Judah . . . The consequence, equally inevitable, of this proclamation of Cyrus must have been that the prophet would seem to some of his own people a traitor, worthy of death."[22] Hence the weight attached to prophetic authority in these chapters, validated by the Deuteronomistic verification-falsification theory (Deut 18:21–22), in other words, the fulfillment of earlier predictions.[23] Hence also the repeated emphasis on the cosmic power of the deity who sponsors and guarantees the truth of the prophet's message.[24] These recurring themes testify to the earnestness of the prophet's claim to a hearing while at the same time betraying an implicit acknowledgment of the likelihood of rejection. One indication of the latter may be detected in the gradually increasing exasperation at the failure of those addressed to accept the message.[25]

That this is the author's political solution to the current crisis is supported by the complete silence of Deutero-Isaiah on David, the Davidic dynasty, and its destiny, with the exception of Isa 55:3–5. It can also be deduced more directly from the titles assigned to Cyrus. These include such familiar designations as "servant" (עֶבֶד) and "shepherd" (רֹעֶה) which encapsulate the age-old Mesopotamian ideal of the just ruler and are likewise part of the Davidic titulature.[26] If the first of the four

---

[21] The verb (עוּר > הֵעִיר) can have a meaning analogous to prophetic inspiration, with reference to the Servant of the Lord (Isa 50:4), Zerubbabel and Joshua (Hag 1:14), and diaspora Jews (Ezra 1:5). I take it that this is the sense in which Cyrus is said to be inspired (Isa 41:2, 25; 45:13; also 2 Chr 36:22; Ezra 1:1).

[22] Smith, *Isaiah Chapters XL–LV*, 74.

[23] Isa 41:22–23, 25–29; 44:7–8, 26–28; 48:3–5, 16b.

[24] Isa 40:12–14, 21, 26, 28; 42:5; 45:7, 12, 18; 48:13. See my article "The Cosmological and Protological Language of Deutero-Isaiah," *CBQ* 73 (2011): 493–510.

[25] Isa 42:18–25; 43:22–28; 45:9–13; 46:8–13; 48:1–11.

[26] David as the servant of Yahweh in 2 Sam 3:18; 1 Kgs 8:24–26; 2 Kgs 19:34; Jer 33:21–22, 26. In Ezek 34:23 and 37:24 David is both servant and shepherd. David, who is presented as literally a shepherd, is reminded by the Israelite tribal elders that he was designed by Yahweh as shepherd and ruler (נגיד, 2 Sam 5:2 = 1 Chr 11:2; also Ps 78:71–72).

Duhmian *Ebedlieder* (42:1–4), with the following comment (42:5–9), was *at that time* referred to Cyrus, as proposed earlier, it would imply a commissioning of the Persian ruler as Yahweh's royal servant and a presentation of him in that capacity to the people. Isa 42:1–4 reads, in fact, like a solemn verbatim report of a ceremony of installation in office. The idea behind the ruler as servant is not, or at least not primarily, that he is to serve his people, but that he is to function in the service of the deity who commissioned him and whose will he is to implement. Whereas in the Cylinder text Cyrus is commissioned by and acts in the name of Marduk, in Isaiah he is the servant of Yahweh. An inscription from the Abu-Habba (ancient Sippar) collection in the British Museum, from the reign of Nabonidus, refers to Marduk who "aroused Cyrus, king of Anshan, his young servant," who then went on to defeat the Medes.[27] The metaphor of shepherding, on the other hand, tempers the image of absolute royal power with a concern for justice and care for society's losers and outcasts (Isa 40:11–12). As a metaphor for just and equitable rule, it features in royal annals throughout Mesopotamian history, for example, with reference to Hammurapi and Assurbanipal.[28] As shepherd, therefore, Cyrus will see to the well-being of the prophet's defeated and dispirited fellow— Judaeans, the rebuilding of Jerusalem, and the restoration of the ruined cities of Judah (Isa 44:28).

The most striking of these titles attached to the native dynast in several texts,[29] and to Cyrus in Deutero-Isaiah, is מָשִׁיחַ, "anointed one":

> This is what Yahweh says about his anointed one, about Cyrus:
> "I have grasped him by his right hand
> to beat down nations before him,
> depriving kings of their strength;
> to open doors before him,
> with no gates closed to him" (45:1)

Commentators have experienced problems with the text and syntax of this verse, quite apart from the question whether לְכוֹרֶשׁ ("about Cyrus") should be elided as an interpolation.[30] There is certainly more than one way of translating the verse,

---

[27] Text in Paul-Alain Beaulieu, *The Reign of Nabonidus, King of Babylon, 556–539 B.C.* (Yale Near Eastern Researches 10; New Haven & London: Yale University Press, 1989), 108. Several scholars have noted parallels between this text and Deutero-Isaiah.

[28] See G. Wallis, "רָעָה *rāʿâ*; רֹעֶה *rōʿeh*," *TDOT* 13: 544–553.

[29] E.g. 1 Sam 2:10, 35; 2 Sam 19:22; 22:51; 23:1 and often in Psalms; Lam 4:20 is particularly poignant and relevant to the situation addressed by Deutero-Isaiah: "Yahweh's anointed, the breath of our life, was taken in their traps, although we had thought to live among the nations, secure under his shadow."

[30] On these issues see Karl Elliger, *Deuterojesaja 40,1–45,7* (BKAT 11/2/1–6; Neukirchen-Vluyn: Neukirchener Verlag, 1978), 481–503; Klaus Westermann, *Isaiah 40–66: A Commentary* (OTL; Philadelphia: Westminster, 1969), 152–55, 162; Blenkinsopp, *Isaiah 40–55*, 243–45; Goldingay and Payne, *Isaiah 40–55*, 2:17–22. Few have followed Charles C. Torrey, *The Second Isaiah: A New Interpretation* (Edinburgh: T & T Clark, 1928), 42, 357 and James D. Smart, *History and Theology in Second Isaiah: A Commentary on Isaiah 35, 40–66* (London: Epworth, 1967), 115–34

but the translation offered above is defensible. Anointing is an important element in ceremonies of installation in the office of kingship, in Judah as elsewhere in the Near East, and such a ceremony may be alluded to in the passage which the statement cited above introduces (Isa 45:1–7). In this ceremony the deity addresses the king-designate directly, as here and in Ps 2:7–9, and presents him to the assembly, as in Isa 42:1–4. Other features—holding him by the hand (Isa 45:1, also 42:6), calling him by name (Isa 45:3, 4), giving him a title or throne name (v. 4), ending, perhaps, with an allusion to investiture (v. 5 verb *'āzar*, "bind," "gird")— are familiar features of the practice and ideology of royalty in the ancient Near East. Several of them appear on the Cyrus Cylinder with reference to Cyrus as appointee of the imperial Babylonian deity Marduk, and all are familiar from the language of the Babylonian court.[31]

THE INTERNATIONAL CONTEXT OF DEUTERO-ISAIAH'S ENDORSEMENT OF CYRUS

This prophetic endorsement of Cyrus is rendered more intelligible by what happened in the aftermath of the fall of Babylon in 539 BCE. The Cylinder text states the claim of Cyrus to be king of Babylon as legitimate successor of Nabonidus, a claim justified by sponsorship on the part of Marduk, imperial god of Babylon. This text records how Marduk was angry with Nabonidus, looked for a replacement, chose Cyrus, and commanded him to take the city and restore the traditional cult.[32] Cyrus was therefore given religious legitimation as successor to the last Babylonian king. Towards the end of the Cylinder text, Cyrus reports the discovery of an inscription of Assurbanipal whom he describes as "a king who preceded me," that is, as king of Babylon.[33] One of the titles of Cyrus which appears on contemporary inscriptions is therefore "king of Babylon, king of the lands" (*šar Bābili šar mātāti*).[34] His succession to the discredited Nabonidus, and therefore also

---

who, for quite different reasons, deleted לכורש as an interpolation. Klaus Baltzer, *Deutero-Isaiah: A Commentary on Isaiah 40–55* (Hermeneia; Minneapolis: Fortress, 2001), 223, agrees that it is interpolated but adds rather mysteriously that Deutero-Isaiah was the interpolator.

[31] Discussion of parallels in Isaiah 40–55 with Babylonian *Hofstil* go back all the way to the much-cited article of Rudolph Kittel, "Cyrus und Deuterojesaja," *ZAW* 18 (1898): 149–62. Kittel argued that the close parallels, even in wording, between Marduk's relation to Cyrus in the Cylinder and Yahweh's relation to the same monarch in Deutero-Isaiah cannot be explained by direct dependence either way but only by familiarity on the part of Deutero-Isaiah with the traditional and stereotypical language of the Babylonian court. In the almost equally-cited article, "II Isaiah and the Persians," *JAOS* 83 (1963): 415–21, Morton Smith, while not questioning the parallels, proposed that the biblical author could have drawn on pro-Persian propaganda disseminated among Jewish expatriates in Babylon before the fall of the city.

[32] *ANET*, 315.

[33] Kuhrt, "The Cyrus Cylinder and Achaemenid Imperial Policy," 88; *The Persian Empire: A Corpus of Sources from the Achaemenid Period* (London/New York: Routledge, 2007), 72.

[34] M. A. Dandamaev, *Persien unter den ersten Achämeniden (6. Jh. v. Chr.)* (Beiträge zur Iranistik 8; Wiesbaden: Reichert, 1976), 96–100; *A Political History of the Achaemenid Empire*

to the illustrious Nebuchadnezzar II, was thus accepted as legitimate, at least by the Marduk priesthood, on the theological grounds of their god's sponsorship. After the conquest, Cyrus restored the spring *akītu* (new year) festival in Marduk's Esagila sanctuary, neglected by Nabonidus, and confirmed the legitimacy of his claim to the throne by presiding over the festival, a circumstance which could lead to reflection on the Persian attitude to the Jerusalem temple as emblematic of and instrumental in imperial control of Judah. (One indication of the new function of the Jerusalem temple, viewed from the Persian perspective, is the requirement that prayers for the royal family in Susa be incorporated into the temple liturgy, Ezra 6:9–10.) It was the rejection of this *religious* legitimation of Persian succession to the Babylonian throne which led to the dynastic revolt of Nidintu-Bēl, who claimed, perhaps truthfully, to be the son of Nabonidus and heir to the great Nebuchadnezzar II. A second Babylonian revolt followed shortly afterwards led by a certain Arakha, referred to as an Armenian but of obscure antecedents, who was crowned in Babylon as Nebuchadnezzar IV, and whose revolt was suppressed towards the end of 521 BCE.[35] Both were essentially dynastic revolts.

A similar pattern emerged after the conquest of Egypt by Cambyses in 525 BCE. Cambyses assumed the throne as legitimate successor to the last of the Saitic Pharaohs, Psammeticus III or, since the latter's reign was short and insignificant, that of his predecessor Amasis II (570–526 BCE). As such, he was accepted as the founder of the twenty-seventh dynasty, and is addressed in these terms in the autobiographical inscription of the Egyptian notable Udjahorresnet.[36]

Jerusalem, however, was not Babylon, one of the nodal points in the Achaemenid empire, nor was it Memphis. Deutero-Isaiah's argument for legitimation was along the same lines, but it was evident that Cyrus would rule over Judah neither in his own person nor through a native appointed as a client king, but through a provincial governor who would answer to the satrap of Babylon-Transeuphrates. Perhaps the memory of the convulsive events following on the death of Josiah excluded the more accommodating option of relative autonomy under a native ruling as client king, even if a suitable candidate had been available.

A final note. Deutero-Isaiah's acceptance of the legitimacy of empire was not unconditional. It was contingent in the first place on leaving Jewish communities under Persian rule free to worship their own deity in their own place of worship and to conduct undisturbed their own religious practices. Fortunately, tolerance and even support of local cults was a characteristic of Persian imperial policy. In

---

(Leiden: Brill, 1989), 54–56.

[35] The primary source is the Bisitun inscription (columns I 77–II 5; IV 28–29). Cuneiform texts dated to the autumn of 521, during the brief reign of Arakha / Nebuchadnezzar IV, have come to light in southern Mesopotamia; see Amélie Kuhrt, "Babylonia from Cyrus to Xerxes," in *Persia, Greece and the Western Mediterranean c. 525 to 479 B.C.* (ed. J. Boardman et al; vol. 4 of *The Cambridge Ancient History;* 2nd ed.; Cambridge: Cambridge University Press, 1988), 112–38 (129–30). See also Herodotus, *Hist.* III.150–160 who, however, is not well informed on the reign of Darius I.

[36] Dandamaev, *A Political History of the Achaemenid Empire*, 76–78; Joseph Blenkinsopp, "The Mission of Udjahorresnet and Those of Ezra and Nehemiah," *JBL* 106 (1987): 409–21.

this respect the Deutero-Isaian solution anticipates the situation described in the opening chapters of the book of Daniel in which Daniel and his companions profit by the educational opportunities available in the Babylonian empire, serve at the imperial court, and can even rise to high office. They do so, however, while observing strictly the dietary laws and the customary prayers and refusing to worship other deities. Deutero-Isaiah's theological position must have been experienced as radical when it was first enunciated. It is even more so in its implications, since it opened up the way to the severing of religious ties with nationality and territory and to contemplating, perhaps for the first time, the possibility of a future without the apparatus of an independent state system.

8

The Yehudite Collection of Prophetic Books and Imperial Contexts: Some Observations

Ehud Ben Zvi

I. INTRODUCTION

The proper starting point for advancing any observations on a topic such as "the Yehudite Collection of Prophetic Books and Imperial Contexts" is an explicit statement of what is meant by the relevant key terms. By "the Yehudite Collection of Prophetic Books" I do *not* refer to a collection consisting only of Haggai, Zechariah (or some proposed Haggai-Zechariah corpus, or Zechariah 1–8) and Malachi; *nor* do I refer to a collection including these books and sections from Isaiah (esp. Isaiah 14–27 and 56–66), some "additions" to other prophetic books (esp. Jeremiah and Ezekiel) and perhaps Jonah and Joel.[1] Instead I refer to the collection of prophetic books that likely existed and was read and reread in the Late Persian (or the early Hellenistic) period. This collection, as well as *most* of the ancient Israelite books that eventually ended up in the Hebrew Bible, emerged, at least in something close to their present form, among the *literati* of a small community in a small and marginal province within a large empire.[2] It is reasonable to assume that the compositional versions of the present fifteen prophetic books (Isaiah-Malachi)

---

[1] As commonly done; cf., among many others, Lester L. Grabbe, *A History of the Jews and Judaism in the Second Temple Period, Volume 1 Yehud: A History of the Persian Province of Judah* (LSTS 47; London / New York: T & T Clark, 2004), 85–97.

[2] On the marginal importance of Yehud for the Achaemenid empire, see, for instance, Pierre Briant, "Histoire impériale et histoire régionale: À propos de l'histoire de Juda dans l'Empire achéménide," in *Congress Volume: Oslo 1998* (ed. A. Lemaire and M. Sæbø; VTSup 80; Leiden: Brill, 2000), 235–45 (238 and passim). The lack of substantial growth in terms of settlements and population within the province throughout the Persian period also supports the marginality of Yehud in the Persian imperial eco-system.

constitute a corpus that is representative of the contents of that collection and may be used as such.[3]

The choice to focus on the entire collection of prophetic books read and reread by the community, rather than on a relatively small set or potential subsection thereof, which are construed all on the basis of possible dates of authorship, is of crucial importance for the reconstruction of the social mindscape and intellectual history of the community in the relevant period.[4] Communities shape and express their discursive world through their repertoire of texts as they are *read* by

---

[3] I would like to stress that I am dealing with the collection of prophetic books as they were likely read and reread in this social context. This implies looking at them within their *Sitz im Diskurs* at the time. Moreover, I am looking at this collection of books as texts that reflected and shaped memory of past and future events. (Readers could remember events from the future as well as from the past; they vicariously experienced them through their readings and rereadings.) Since the collection is, among other things, one of past and future construing texts, it is reasonable to use approaches informed by memory studies as heuristic tools. The latter can help us to understand generative grammars that make certain memories more likely to be remembered than others. In other words, they help us understand systemic tendencies that influenced what was remembered and the reasons that certain memories were shaped in the ways in which they were. It will be shown that imperial contexts played numerous roles in these processes. All these matters are critical for any historical reconstruction of the intellectual discourse of Yehud in the late Persian (or early Hellenistic) period.

(It goes without saying that historians of the intellectual discourse of Yehud, as historians of any discourse for that matter or historians in general can only construct their own scholarly reconstruction of the relevant readers and their readings and rereadings. Of course, some reconstructions are better than others, according to historical standards. On my own take on historical methodology in general and in particular in relation to historical studies of ancient Israel see my "Clio Today and Ancient Israelite History: Some Thoughts and Observations at the Closing Session of the European Seminar for Historical Methodology," presented, as evident from the title, at the closing session of the seminar [2012] and forthcoming in the collected essays volume emerging from that meeting that is currently being edited by L. L. Grabbe, the convener of the seminar. See also the bibliography on historical methodology cited there.)

[4] On "social mindscapes" see E. Zerubavel, *Social Mindscapes. An Invitation to Cognitive Sociology* (Cambridge: Harvard University Press, 1997); E. Zerubavel, *Time Maps: Collective Memory and the Social Shape of the Past* (Chicago: University of Chicago Press, 2003). The concept of "mindscape" precedes, of course, Zerubavel and goes back to M. Maruyama who used "the term 'mindscape' to mean a structure of reasoning, cognition, perception, conceptualization, design, planning, and decision making that may vary from one individual, profession, culture, or social group to another," M. Maruyama, "Mindscapes and Science Theories," *Current Anthropology* 21 (1980): 589–99 (591).

The study of social mindscapes involve, *inter alia*, that of accepted and shared ways of thinking in a group of generating ideas, questions and ways of addressing them, of providing meaning to 'data' and actually construing 'data' by focusing on particular matters and not others, of assigning significance to memories, stories, and actually shaping the production of memories according to particular patterns. Moreover, involves the study of how all these are deeply interconnected.

the community and as they shape and evoke social memories in the group.[5] Texts are not read in a way un-informed by other texts within the repertoire of the community (thus, the importance of the *Sitz im Diskurs* for understanding how a text was actually read within it) nor according to exclusive and exclusivist subsets constructed on the basis of their chronological claims or (supposed) dates of authorship.[6] To use a metaphor, the various texts that exist within the repertoire of a community are comparable to "words" or "sentences" within a general language. To understand the language and its underlying "grammar," one cannot limit oneself to "new words." Significantly, even most of these "new words" were presented to and read by Yehudite *literati* as "old words" (e.g., Isaiah 14–27 and 56–66). In any case, as they reread their texts, they kept construing the (implied) authors of these texts and its main characters.

The meaning of the other crucial term/concept, namely "empire," also demands some clarification. Certainly not all empires are the same but first, and most important, there is no agreement on what an empire is or was.[7] Second, in

---

[5] The stress on "historical authors" and "historical redactors" rather than on "community" and "communally read texts" is probably a remnant of a "great men," traditionally modernist historiographic tendency. Significantly, the "real" authors and characters with which the community interacted as they read and reread these books were those they construed to be as such, that is, a communal, implied author of the text. It is worth noting that it is very unlikely that they ever construed a lengthy series of implied redactors.

[6] If comparison with historical work on contemporary social groups, despite all its obvious problems and limitations, may still have an element of relevance, one may note that historians today would not attempt to reconstruct the general social mindscape of Canadians (or a particular subset of Canadians) in any region of the country in 2013, or in the last decade for that matter, by looking only at texts (in its most comprehensive meaning) "published" only in the relevant group and only in that region. The reason is simple: Canadians in any region are informed by, construe the meaning of, and "consume" (and thus construct) far more texts than those published in a single year or decade or only those in their region. Yehud is different and certainly did not participate in a world similar to ours, but still, it is very unlikely and contradicted by their very texts that they would construe their ideological world on the basis of texts that they read (and were asked to read) as written in the Persian period (e.g., Haggai, Zechariah, and Malachi) or on a set of sections that they would have to extract out of books that presented themselves from earlier periods (i.e., texts that *we today* tend to identify as "additions" and "supplements").

[7] There is, indeed, a significant debate on how to define "empire." One of the most cited or referenced observation concerning the plethora of definitions is:

They [numerous definitions of empire] share in common a view of empire as a territorially expansive and incorporative kind of state, involving relationships in which one state exercises control over other sociopolitical entities (e.g. states, chiefdoms, nonstratified societies), and of imperialism as the process of creating and maintaining empires. The diverse polities and communities that constitute an empire typically retain some degree of autonomy—in self- and centrally-defined cultural identity . . . , and in some dimensions of political and economic decision making. Most authors also share a conception of various kinds of empires distinguished by differing degrees of political and/or economic control, viewed either as discrete types or as variations along a con-the last decades there has been a considerable debate about models of ancient empires and perhaps even an interpretive shift in terms of which models are more appropriate for historical reconstructions of actual, historical empires (as opposed to its representation in some of the literature emanating from the center). To illustrate, there is considerable debate about how these empires actually worked and in particular on how they, once these became well-established, (tended to) administer their territories in particular. Did they (tend to) rule *over* a plethora of various local societies or also and perhaps even in the main *through* these societies, or more precisely, their elites. To what extent were ancient imperial polities run, in practical terms, by and according to "universal," "rational," royal policies and general "laws" enacted to fulfill particular imperial aims and alternatively, to what extent did ancient empires represent a polity based on processes of ongoing "negotiations" with a plethora of different local leaderships leading to outcomes that may or may not be similar to one another, even if always involving unequal partners?[8] Unsurprisingly, there is considerable debate about how to understand the referent of "the Achaemenid Empire" among contemporary historians.[9]

---

tinuum from weakly integrated to more highly centralized polities (Carla M. Sinopoli, "The Archaeology of Empires," *Annual Review of Anthropology* 23 [1994]: 159–80 [160]).

For citations of or explicit references to this observation, see, for instance, Elspeth R. M. Dusinberre, *Aspects of Empire in Achaemenid Sardis* (Cambridge: Cambridge University Press, 2003), 196; Anselm C. Hagedorn, "Local Law in an Imperial Context: The Role of Torah in the (Imagined) Persian Period," in *The Pentateuch as Torah: New Models for Understanding its Promulgation and Acceptance* (ed. G. N. Knoppers and B. M. Levinson; Winona Lake: Eisenbrauns, 2007), 57–76 (59–60). Sinopoli, "Archaeology of Empires," summarizes and discusses also the large variation among empires. Cf. Mark Chavalas, "The Age of Empires: 3100–900 BCE," in *A Companion to the Ancient Near East* (ed. D. C. Snell; Malden/Oxford: Blackwell, 2005), 34–47.

[8] This chapter is clearly not the place to discuss at any length these general matters, even if the results of these discussions have an impact on reconstructions of how ancient empires, once established, were likely experienced by local populations and particularly local elites outside the main center of power. On these issues and with examples, see, for instance, M. M. Austin, "Hellenistic Kings, War and the Economy," *Classical Quarterly* 36 (1986): 450–66; J. G. Manning, *The Last Pharaohs: Egypt under the Ptolemies, 305–30 BC* (Princeton: Princeton University Press, 2010), 1–19; and John Ma, *Antiochos III and the Cities of Western Asia Minor* (Oxford: Oxford University Press, 2000). A common critique to the "legalistic" model of ancient empire is that it is anachronistic. I thank Sylvie Honigman for her comments on these matters (personal note). Matters, of course, do not change in any significant way if instead of using the abstract term "empire" one uses terms such as the kingdom/household of "the great king, king of kings, king of countries containing all kinds of men [and women], king in this great earth far and wide," "one king for many, one lord for all" (see DE; i.e., Darius Inscription on Mount Elvend, and the "parallel" inscription of Xerxes [XE] on the same place, one next to the other; for an English translation of the text see A. Kuhrt, *The Persian Empire: A Corpus of Sources from the Achaemenid Period* [2 vols.; London: Routledge, 2007], 1:301, 304).

[9] See, for instance, Pierre Briant, *From Cyrus to Alexander: A History of the Persian Empire* (Winona Lake: Eisenbrauns, 2002), 1.

Moreover, just as "nations" are imagined communities, so were empires. Being part of the "Persian Empire"[10] was above all an act of social imagination on the part of the community of Yehud.[11] As all acts of social imagination, this is an act of imagination of a particular historical community, and thus contingent on, for instance, the social mindscape of the community, its memories, its self-understanding, etc. Different groups in the Persian Empire likely imagined their being part of the Persian Empire in substantially different ways. Different groups developed different imperial experiences, even if they include some undisputable overlaps.

This said, references to "imperial context" and its importance for reconstructions of the historical matrix within which prophetic books—and other books within the authoritative repertoire of Yehud—emerged can be extremely helpful, provided that it is clear what, even if only heuristically, is meant by "imperial context." Here, and for pragmatic reasons only, I refer to (willing or unwilling) participation in *an unequal network of multiple ethnocultural groups that includes numerous contact areas* (e.g., cultural, economic, political, social), and *various dynamic processes affecting different aspects of the life of these groups* (e.g., acculturation and perceived resistance to acculturation, economic flows of goods and material—including taxes and trade, complex processes involving the build-up, maintenance and projection of permanent, seemingly overwhelming military power, etc.), which is *sustained by the presence of a central authority and its main socio-political and symbolic structures.*

To be sure, "imperial context" in that sense, and even "universal" imperial context, was nothing new to communities in the ancient southern Levant, but a long standing reality in the area.[12] No one alive in Persian-period Yehud would have had anyone in his or her family, for generations, who lived outside some sort of "universal" imperial context. To imagine a world in this social context was, by default, to imagine one characterized by "imperial contexts," even if these contexts could be imagined in different ways.

As suggested above, living in an imperial context impacted multiple aspects of the life of the community. This contribution, however, is an attempt to explore *some* of the ways in which the imperial context of the community was intertwined with processes of social memory formation and re-formation, concerning past and future events that were evoked through the reading and rereading of the prophetic books. In other words, and from a slightly different but closely related perspective, it is about (discursive) "generative grammars" that created systems of preferences and dis-preferences that contributed much to the shaping of images and texts within the collection of prophetic books.

---

[10] As opposed to simply paying (forced) taxes and the like.

[11] The same applies, of course, to any other community that existed "within" such an empire.

[12] I am using the adjective "universal" here to distinguish "world hegemony" empires such as Assyria, Babylon (even if its center *formally* refused to imagine/present itself as a "universal" empire until the reign of Nabonidus), Persia, Alexander, Rome and the like from non-world hegemony empires (e.g., the Ptolemaic or Seleucid empires, or the socially remembered, imagined regional empire of David and Solomon).

Certainly, the imperial experience of the Yehudite *literati* could not but strongly affect, directly and indirectly, in ways known or unbeknownst to them, their literary activities. The importance of this seemingly trivial observation for the social and intellectual history of Yehud becomes apparent once one takes into consideration that these activities were central to processes of identity formation and negotiation within the community, and that, at least from the *literati*'s perspective, this community was construed as centered around divine teachings contained in the very authoritative literature of the community that represents the outcome of their literary activities (both as writers/composers/editors and as readers and re-readers).

It is also hardly surprising that cultural trends, images and conceptual frames, some of which had a *longue durée* and which may be identified with "empire," were internalized and, through this process, re-signified by Yehudites; just as later Judahites certainly did so in the late Second-Temple period and most certainly earlier Judahites did as well, each according to their own imperial context. As historical cross-cultural studies indicate, ethnocultural groups that participate, willingly or unwillingly, in a "world" cultural and socio-political system tend, over time, to appropriate and internalize discourses, images, and concepts present in their "world" socio-cultural system, but that originated outside the inner group. As they do so, they re-signify the images and concepts so as to enhance their ability for social reproduction. In other words, what we may call hybridity regularly emerges in such cases.[13] It is worth noting, however, that these groups would rarely see and most rarely internalize their discourses as some form of "hybrid"; for them, it is their very own culture, and as such it serves to shape their sense of identity. Moreover, they would tend to see trajectories of continuity linking their present with their past. To be sure, issues of legitimization are involved in the matter, but also of self-identity.[14]

---

[13] One may note that hybridity, in this sense, is not only a matter of Yehudite Israel. It is the hallmark of social discourses within later Jewish communities through time. A few examples suffice: the Hasmonean state and its discourse, Alexandrian Hellenistic Jewish intellectual discourses, medieval thinkers such as Ibn Ezra and Rambam, the emergence of Reform Judaism and neo-orthodox Judaism in the 19th century, discourses such as the neo-Kantian philosopher Hermann Cohen in late 19th- and early 20th-century Germany, the emergence of Jewish (political) nationalism in Eastern and Central Europe and Zionism in particular, Lubavitcher Messianism of the 20th century, and present-day American Jewish discourses (e.g., signs such as "Occupy Oakland not Palestine" that embody and communicate the [religious] discourse of groups such as those around the bi-monthly Tikkun and rabbi Michael Lerner, or the phenomenon of Orthodox Jewish rock [or folk] music). From this perspective, one might say that a history of Jewish thought or Judaic systems/discourses is or even can only be a history of multiple forms of hybridity through time and geographical and social space. But Jews were/are certainly not alone in this respect. In fact, cultural interactions, appropriations and re-significations are the norm, not the exception.

[14] One example, among the myriad of possible examples, is the Hasmonean presentation of their rule as in continuity with a "biblical" past; see 1 Macc 9:22; 16:23 and very extensively in 1 Macc 14:4–14.

Of course, imperial centers are also influenced by, appropriate, and resignify substantial cultural aspects of ethnocultural groups outside the original imperial center and thus create their own forms of hybridity, which dynamically shape the center through intercultural interactions at the interface between different ethnocultural groups.[15]

As per its title, the point of this contribution is not to discuss hybridity in general, but particular manifestations in a very particular community. To do so, it has to deal with particular "generative grammars" that caused certain social memories of past and future empires to be preferred or dis-preferred within Persian Yehud, or at least among its *literati*.[16] This said, a final, general, cross-cultural consideration is in order. Social memories tend to be preferred or dis-preferred in a community according to the degree to which they are consistent, evoke or even serve to embody central meta-narratives or sections thereof that stand at the core of the collective memory, and that serve important roles in processes of formation of social identity within and for the community.

Turning now to the collection of prophetic books, even the most cursory analysis of the memory-scape shaped and evoked by the prophetic books shows that: (a) one city, Jerusalem, stands at the very center of this "memory-scape"; and (b) two imperial powers, Assyria and Babylon, dominate the mindshare of the community that read and reread these books and in the process shaped its memories of the community's *past*.[17] Observation (a) is the starting point for the next section of this essay and observation (b), for section three.

---

[15] Cultural influences of the type mentioned above are all too present in the Achaemenid, Roman, Parthian and Mughal empires, to mention a few. Leaving aside "global" empires, Syrian/Levantine influence on New Kingdom Egypt is well known and so is Egyptian influence in the Ptolemaic empire, and, of course, there is Kassite Babylon. Although, since the first Aramean migration to Northern Mesopotamia, there was a process of Arameanization of Neo-Assyrian culture and language, which obviously preceded the expansion of the empire to control the Aramean heartland, there was strong Aramean influence in Assyria; the Assyrian empire became so influenced by the Arameans that it could be characterized as an Assyrian-Aramean empire.

Similar tendencies are at work in recent empires. It is probably not perchance that current Indian historians are emphasizing not only how much the UK influenced India, but how much India has influenced the UK. To be sure, this is not necessarily the case in other (formerly) colonized groups, but still shows that cultural influences may go in multiple directions even today.

[16] To use a metaphor suggested to me by a colleague, who is an archaeologist and historian, my approach here is to focus on patterns that emerge from a view from above the surface, that is, from a helicopter overview of a site and its region, rather than focusing on a detailed (ground-perspective) study of each building or room at a particular site. Both approaches are necessary to advance knowledge on the site/issue, but they require different methodological approaches and raise different questions.

[17] A word about mindshare in the context of studies of the intellectual world of the early second temple period is in order. The concept of mindshare is important in memory studies, because obviously not all memories show the same level of mindshare in a community. Some carry much weight and are activated much more than others. For instance, and close to our area, much more mindshare was allocated to the monarchic Temple than to any other

II. ON JERUSALEM, EMPIRES, AND KINGS IN THE CONSTRUCTED AND REMEMBERED (MAINLY) PRESENT AND FUTURE OF THE YEHUDITE LITERATI

A comprehensive analysis of the multiple aspects associated with remembering Jerusalem in the Achaemenid period is well beyond the scope of this or any essay.[18] Given that this contribution is about "imperial contexts" and prophetic books, a more helpful starting point is to note that Jerusalem and its temple were, among many other things, local manifestations of Achaemenid imperial will and control. The re-building of the temple and of Jerusalem and their rise to prominence in Yehud (over the previous Benjaminite center, which had been prominent during Neo-Babylonian times) were deeply involved in and associated with imperial power, allocations, and even with taxation, since temples served directly or indirectly also as tax centers and "sanctuaries" for goods.[19] Certainly, the shift of the

---

building in Jerusalem within the social memory about the monarchic period that existed at least among the Jerusalem-centered *literati* of the late Persian period in Yehud; similarly, the mindshare of a site of memory like Moses, the lawgiver and the greatest prophet was far larger than Joshua, even if the latter conquered the land, within the world of knowledge of the community. Both observations teach us a lot about the discourse and the social mindscape of the *literati* in Yehud. In general, one may say that usually there is a degree of correlation between social mindscape and social mindshare. Social memories with relative large mindshare in a particular group, are most often those that fit well with the general social mindscape of the mnemonic community. I discussed the importance of the concept of social mindshare for studies of social memory in ancient Israel in my "Remembering the Prophets through the Reading and Rereading of a Collection of Written Prophetic Books in Yehud: Methodological Considerations and Explorations," in *Remembering and Forgetting in Judah's Early Second Temple Period* (eds. E. Ben Zvi and C. Levin; FAT 85; Tübingen: Mohr-Siebeck, 2012), 17–44.

[18] I explored *some* of these aspects in three separate essays: Ehud Ben Zvi, "Exploring Jerusalem as a Site of Memory in the Late Persian and Early Hellenistic Period," in *Memory and the City in Ancient Israel* (ed. D. Edelman and E. Ben Zvi; Winona Lake: Eisenbrauns, forthcoming); idem, "Shaping and Balancing Memories of pre-David and pre-Israelite Jerusalem in late Persian Yehud," in *Urban Dreams and Realities: The City in Ancient Cultures* (ed. A. Kemezis; Leiden: Brill, forthcoming); and idem, "Jerusalem as a Mnemonic System and the Social Mindscape of Late Persian/Early Hellenistic Yehud/Judah," in a forthcoming volume (in French), edited by Frederic Amsler and Christophe Nihan. A full exploration of these aspects would require several monographs.

[19] Of course, this is not to deny that Ramat Raḥel did serve as an imperial taxation center, which is evident from the recent excavations led by O. Lipschits. On the Jerusalemite temple and taxation, see also J. Schaper, "The Jerusalem Temple as an Instrument of the Achaemenid Fiscal Administration," *VT* 45 (1995): 528–39; idem, "The Temple Treasury Committee in the Times of Nehemiah and Ezra," *VT* 47 (1997): 200–206. For an argument against the position that the Jerusalem Temple played a role in imperial taxation; see P. R. Bedford, "The Economic Role of the Jerusalem Temple in Achaemenid Judah: Comparative Perspectives," in *Shai le-Sara Japhet: Studies in the Bible, its Exegesis and its Language* (ed. M. Bar-Asher et al; Jerusalem: Bialik Institute; 2007), 3*–20* (14*–20*). A serious discussion of Bedford's argument is beyond the scope of this contribution. It may be noticed that during Hellenistic times, the temple played, in one way or another, an important role in taxation see,

capital of the province of Yehud to Jerusalem, and the likely construction of some type of wall around it,[20] required imperial decisions.[21] The situation that results stands then, among others, as a marker of Achaemenid power.

Leaving aside the highly debated proposal of a "Persian imperial authorization" of the Pentateuch,[22] the entire authoritative literature—including the collection of prophetic books—adopted by the Jerusalem-centered *literati*, was to some extent the outcome (and representation) of locations and institutions directly associated and representing, among other things, imperial power.

The association of Torah, proper cult, the welfare and centrality of Jerusalem with imperial power (and control) is, as is well known, most explicit in Ezra-Nehemiah. The book is later than the Persian period, but it is difficult to assume that the underlying discursive "grammar" of the book evolved only and *ex nihilo* after the fall of the Persian empire. In addition, the book of Isaiah puts such a position to rest with the glorification of Cyrus for the sake of Israel and Jerusalem (see below). Also, one has to take into consideration that the Achaemenid empire was remembered as the worldly power that commanded the rebuilding of temple, enabled the restoration of the settlement in the land (see memories of "the return")[23] and of the city, and thus, indirectly, what emerged from them.[24]

---

for instance, "the tribute and taxation demanded by the Seleukid kings from Judaea are often expressed in the sources as a lump sum of silver, to be provided by the high priest acting as tax collector" (G. G. Aperghis, "Jewish Subjects and Seleukid Kings: A Case Study of Economic Interaction," in *The Economies of Hellenistic Societies, Third to First Centuries BC* [ed. Z. H. Archibald, J. K. Davies, and V. Garielsen; Oxford/New York: Oxford University Press, 2011], 19–41, here 35).

In any event, even if for the sake of the argument one were to accept Bedford's position concerning Achaemenid Yehud, there can be no doubt that ("rebuilt") Jerusalem would still be remembered as *also* an Achaemenid project.

[20] On the (highly debated) matter of the walls of Jerusalem, see Israel Finkelstein, Ido Koch, and Oded Lipschits, "The Mound on the Mount: A Possible Solution to the 'Problem with Jerusalem'," *JHebS* 11 (2011): article 12 (which is freely available online at http://www.jhsonline.org/Articles/article_159.pdf) and the bibliography mentioned there. The essay appears under the same title in *Perspectives on Hebrew Scriptures VIII* (ed. Ehud Ben Zvi; Piscataway: Gorgias Press, 2012), 317–39.

[21] Even if taken at the level of satrapy. Not everything in an empire has to go to the highest level of central administration.

[22] On the matter, see, in particular, Konrad Schmid, "Persian Imperial Authorization as a Historical Problem and as a Biblical Construct: A Plea for Distinctions in the Current Debate," in *The Pentateuch as Torah: New Models for Understanding its Promulgation and Acceptance* (ed. G. N. Knoppers and B. M. Levinson; Winona Lake: Eisenbrauns, 2007), 23–38 and bibliography there. Cf. James W. Watts, ed., *Persia and Torah: The Theory of Imperial Authorization of the Pentateuch* (SBLSymS 17; Atlanta: Society of Biblical Literature, 2001).

[23] For the present purposes it is irrelevant that the land was historically not completely "empty" or that the "return" could not have involved massive migration to the "empty land." What is relevant is that the Persian empire was construed and remembered as the power that allowed the "return," and thus, "the return" was construed and remembered as (*inter alia*) a manifestation of the worldly power of Persia; even if the latter was construed, as expected, as ultimately stemming from YHWH's power).

Out of this background, a "generative grammar" of images and memories emerges, with a strong preference for constructing and remembering the Persian empire (in contradistinction to other universal empires of the past) in a very positive light. This "grammar" generates both active acts of imagination and substantial discursive omissions. This was, however, not the only "generative grammar" at work. Processes of formation of self-identity conducive to social reproduction required that Israel be imagined as the (adopted) "son" of its own deity, that Jerusalem and its temple be construed as the cosmic center and the place from which the divine instruction will come, and that Israel itself be (self-)imagined as a primary worldly agent, not a secondary (or lower) one. These considerations led to preferences to remember a future that goes well beyond the Persian empire and to the allocation of far more mindshare to these memories of the future than to those of re-foundation under the Persian empire.

All these general observations require further elaboration. To begin with, the lack of explicit criticism and above all lack of memories about any announcements of punishment/judgment against Persia by YHWH in prophetic literature is, no doubt, a salient feature of the collection of prophetic books. It stands in sharp contrast with the treatment allocated to Assyria and Babylon (see section III) and to any country or people of any significance known to the remembering community, temporally located within the time-frame portrayed in the collection of prophetic books, *including* Israel and Judah.

At times, it has been suggested that little can be learned from this observation, beyond the perils for the community that arise from criticizing the ruling power, and the actual impossibility of such criticism. But several considerations argue against this position. First, although one should not disregard concrete per-

---

I discussed the matter of the *memory* of the return to the "empty land" elsewhere. See Ehud Ben Zvi, "Total Exile, Empty Land and the General Intellectual Discourse in Yehud," in *The Concept of Exile in Ancient Israel and its Historical Contexts* (ed. E. Ben Zvi and Ch. Levin; BZAW 404; Berlin: de Gruyter, 2010), 155–68.

[24] I want to stress that I am not maintaining that the community in Yehud was a colonial institution that forcefully colonized Judahites who remained in the land after the destruction of Jerusalem. In fact, elsewhere I argued against historical reconstructions of the Persian period based on claimed long-term conflict between returnees and remainees. See, for instance, Ben Zvi "Total Exile"; and idem, "Inclusion in and Exclusion from Israel as Conveyed by the Use of the Term 'Israel' in Postmonarchic Biblical Texts," in *The Pitcher is Broken: Memorial Essays for Gösta W. Ahlström* (ed. S. W. Holloway and L. K. Handy; JSOTSup 190; Sheffield: JSOT Press, 1995), 95–149.

Similarly, I am *not* maintaining that ancient Israel (as understood in Yehud) was a (colonial) Persian invention. Persian activities may have facilitated the development of certain (theological, text-centered) ideas of Israel, but this is a far cry from invention. This (theological, text-centered) Israel was the "invention" of Jerusalem-centered Yehud, a province that existed, as any other, within an imperial system. Its discourse and the social/political conditions in which it evolved could not but reflect "imperial circumstances." To say that Israel was an invention of the Persian center is as absurd as stating that because the persecutions of Antiochus IV facilitated the development of late Second Temple discourses, Antiochus IV invented the latter.

ils that historical agents might have faced if they criticized the empire, from a systemic perspective, any strong emphasis on the *impossibility* of criticism is problematic. There are numerous cross-cultural examples of explicit and implicit acts of cultural resistance.[25] Moreover, the existence of a "public transcript" does not negate the possibility of a "hidden transcript/s." In addition, even if, during Achaemenid days, one were to grant that it was impossible for Yehudites to criticize in any way or form or to construe divine pronouncements that would involve the fall of the Persian Empire, even if in the far future, why would that be impossible during the early (or for that matter later) Hellenistic times?[26] These considerations indicate that the lack of memories of announcements of doom against Persia or negative characterizations of it was not only the result of imperial coercion. There existed in Yehud a strong preference to set the Persian empire aside from those of other nations (e.g., Babylon, Assyria) and glorify it, because by doing so the community was, within their own discourse, indirectly legitimizing and enhancing positive self-constructions of Jerusalem, its temple, Israel, and its Jerusalem-centered divine instruction along with the authoritative literature that encoded it.

To be sure, a salient positive character is not created only through the lack of negative characterization, as remarkable as this may be in this particular context. To begin with, as I discussed elsewhere,[27] studies on social memory show that there exists a cross-cultural tendency to organize memory so as to coalesce around a few main symbolic figures/sites of memory; these are the "great heroes" of the past who draw the attention of the remembering community to their own (construed) personal figures and to what they had done, including institutions that they had established.[28] Since Cyrus served as the greatest and the most positive site of

---

[25] Historians of Judaism/s cannot but bring to mind the extreme case of *Toldot Yeshu*. This very polemical text was kept for centuries. For recent discussion, see Peter Schäfer, Michael Meerson, and Yaacov Deutsch, eds., *Toledot Yeshu ("The Life Story of Jesus") Revisited: A Princeton Conference* (TSAJ 143; Tübingen: Mohr Siebeck, 2011). Of course, *Toldot Yeshu* itself was an excellent case of (polemical) hybridity, as it appropriated Christian narratives and in polemical ways turned them upside-down. The same holds true for *Sefer Zerubavel*. See David Biale, "Counter-History and Jewish Polemics Against Christianity: The *Sefer Toldot Yeshu* and the *Sefer Zerubavel*," *Jewish Social Studies* 6 (1999): 130–45.

[26] One may add further: Should we imagine that the Persian center would consistently care about Yehudite prophecies about a distant future, or even care enough to read and reread prophetic books that existed only in Hebrew and could be read only by Yehudite *literati*? One has to keep in mind that Yehud was a marginal, poor province which in reality could not revolt against Persian rule and that the Achaemenid empire was not a 20th-century totalitarian state.

[27] Ehud Ben Zvi, "Exploring the Memory of Moses 'The Prophet' In Late Persian/Early Hellenistic Period Yehud/Judah," in *Remembering Biblical Figures in the Late Persian and Early Hellenistic Periods: Social Memory and Imagination* (ed. D. V. Edelman and E. Ben Zvi; Oxford: Oxford University Press, 2013), 335–64.

[28] Although social memory is historically contingent, the mentioned processes tend to be comparable (though not identical) across different cultures and societies (though certainly not all). This is so because they relate to the ways in which social memory and social mindscapes are likely to be shaped. For comparative purposes, with processes in a very dif-

memory of a Persian in Yehud (and in Greece as well,[29] and perhaps in other ethno-cultural groups at around this time), it is only expected that his figure would symbolically embody all Persians[30] and that he would be associated in Yehud's social memory with the beginning of the rebuilding process.[31] The re-builder of the Temple could not but be construed as a very positive character.[32] He was not of Israel, since he had to be Persian, but a mnemonic tendency to *partially* Davidize him is to be expected.[33] It is thus not the result of random chance that Cyrus is presented and remembered as Yhwh's shepherd and anointed,[34] or that both David and Cyrus (the "founder" and the "re-founder" of the temple, respectively) serve as sites of memory that embody their respective peoples.[35] One may add also explicit refer-

ferent society and time, but still focused on the importance of main figures for social memory, one may look at Christopher Kaplonski, *Truth, History and Politics in Mongolia: The Memory of Heroes* (London: Routledge, 2004), esp. 182–86.

[29] See Lynette Mitchell, "Remembering Cyrus the Persian: Exploring Monarchy and Freedom in Classical Greece," in *Remembering Biblical Figures in the Late Persian and Early Hellenistic Periods: Social Memory and Imagination* (ed. D. V. Edelman and E. Ben Zvi; Oxford: Oxford University Press, 2013), 283–92.

[30] See the contribution by Joseph Blenkinsopp to this volume and particularly his analysis of Isa 55:3–5 (cf. J. Goldingay, *The Message of Isaiah 40–55: A Literary-Theological Commentary* [London: T & T Clark, 2005], 549–50).

[31] See Isa 44:28; 45:1–7, 12–13; 2 Chr 36:22; cf. Ezra 1; 4:3. Note also "[t]he expectation that the city devastated by the Babylonians will be restored by Cyrus is frequently expressed (45:13; 49:14–18; 51:3)," as stated by Joseph Blenkinsopp, *Isaiah 40–55: A New Translation with Introduction and Commentary* (AB 19A; New York: Doubleday, 2002), 247.

If, for the sake of the argument, one were to grant Albertz's position that originally the Persian king in Isa 40:1–52:12 was Darius not Cyrus, that Cyrus eventually became "the king" would be most meaningful and, needless to say, consistent with the systemic preference for a memory that has Cyrus in that role. See Rainer Albertz, "Darius in Place of Cyrus: The First Edition of Deutero-Isaiah (Isaiah 40.1–52.12)," *JSOT* 27 (2003): 371–83.

[32] Central institutions in antiquity tended to develop social memories within which they were founded by great personages of the past, not by "nobodies" or "evil characters." It is not by chance that the temple in Jerusalem was associated with the figures of David and Solomon and that on the whole these characters tended to be lionized.

[33] Note that Zerubbabel, the Israelite/Yehudite associated with building the temple, ends up being evoked as a Davidide in 1 Chr 3:19 and is elevated in Haggai 2:21–22. Centuries later, other central figures were partially Davidized: Jesus, Hillel, and Rabbi Yehuda HaNasi. In all these cases, the construction and the remembering of these figures as Davidides served important discursive and ideological functions in the relevant social groups. On general matters of social memory, mindscape, and socially construed genealogies, see Eviatar Zerubavel, *Ancestors and Relatives: Genealogy, Identity, and Community* (Oxford: Oxford University Press, 2012).

[34] See, for instance, Isa 44:28; 45:1; cf. 2 Sam 5: 2 (|| 1Chr 11:2); 7:7 (|| 2Chr 17:6); Ps 78:71–72; 2 Sam 19:22; 23:1; 2 Chr 6:42.

[35] David is the real "founder" of the temple in Chronicles. In Kings, the story is different as Solomon has a more important role. Given general, transcultural mnemonic tendencies, one would have expected a preference for a memory of David as both founder of the dynasty and founder of the temple, and particularly so since he is the "founder" of Israel's Jerusalem (i.e., his conqueror). The existence of a truncated expectation in Samuel-Kings went hand in

ences to the elevated character of Cyrus[36] and the implied central mnemonic narrative conveyed by the trajectory from Isaiah chapters 36–39 to chapters 40–48, i.e., from Hezekiah to Cyrus. All these contribute much to the construction of an important site of memory, namely, the foreign king who was worthy of being selected by YHWH to initiate the rebuilding of city and temple.[37]

Against this background of the lionization of Cyrus, the most heuristically helpful question seems to be (at least to me) not whether one may find somewhere some underlying or implied criticism of Cyrus or the Persians in the prophetic or other books, or in general in the discourse of the period.[38] It is also not whether one may argue that Cyrus's image could have been somewhat downgraded because he was remembered among Yehudite *literati* as one whose mission was just for the sake of Israel, or whose success reflects the power of YHWH, a deity whom he does not know (Isa 45:4). In fact, that is difficult to argue. His characterization as one who does not know YHWH is basically a way to keep him Persian and, in fact, as a kind of embodiment of Persia.[39] None of the other observations about his charac-

---

hand with the need of a memorable story explaining why the expectation was truncated and, of course, removing any possible stain on David, at least concerning this matter. Chronicles goes further as it characterizes David as the "founder" (though not the actual "builder") of the temple and by communicating a close association of the temple with both David and Solomon, but there is already a strong echo of this in 2 Kgs 21:7. Moreover, one has to keep in mind that Chronicles and Samuel-Kings shaped together a single general mnemonic system in the late Persian/early Hellenistic period. The social memory of the community at the time was influenced by both, and its readings of one corpora could not but inform and be informed by readings of the other. I am currently completing an essay for a collected essays volume on this topic. In the meantime and on converging lines between Chronicles and some voices in Samuel-Kings see my previous, "Are There Any Bridges Out There? How Wide Was the Conceptual Gap between the Deuteronomistic History and Chronicles?," in *Community Identity in Judean Historiography: Biblical and Comparative Perspectives* (ed. G. N. Knoppers and K. A. Ristau; Winona Lake: Eisenbrauns, 2009), 59–86.

[36] See, for instance, Isa 44:(24–)28; 45:1–8, 12–13. Goldingay, *Message of Isaiah*, 253–300, describes all of Isa 44:24–45:25 as "the triumph of Cyrus." See also Cyrus's background presence in Isaiah 40–48, which is correctly stressed by Blenkinsopp (see his essay in this volume); cf. esp. Isa 48:12–15.

[37] It is worth noting that I am focusing neither on the putative words of a prophet called Deutero-Isaiah nor on the world portrayed in these sections of the book of Isaiah, but on memories evoked by reading this book in late Persian (or early Hellenistic) Judah. The readership most likely imagined Cyrus as the beginning of the "reconstruction." That Cyrus was imagined in Judah as having a "warm spot" in his heart for Jerusalem and as YHWH's victor, was not categorically different, from a social memory perspective, from the case of a later community imagining and remembering something very similar in relation to Alexander (see *Ant.* 11.325–39).

[38] See the thoughtful contribution of Erich S. Gruen, "Persia Through the Jewish Looking-Glass," in *Cultural Borrowings and Ethnic Appropriations in Antiquity* (ed. E. S. Gruen; Oriens et Occidens 8; Stuttgart: Franz Steiner, 2005), 90–104; and in an extended version, under the same title, in *Jewish Perspectives on Hellenistic Rulers* (ed. T. Rajak et al; Hellenistic Culture and Society 50; Berkeley: University of California Press, 2007), 53–75.

[39] Both in Greece's and Yehud's memory, Cyrus is always a *Persian* king. This said, Cyrus may be "elevated" within this discourse by texts that evoke a memory of him as similar to

terization portray Cyrus in a negative light. The statement that he was chosen by
YHWH for the sake of Israel is not only to be expected, given that the text is written
for and by Israel, but also would have been appreciated by the empire itself and its
propaganda.[40] It is also an excellent example of appropriation and reshaping of
imperial memories. Cyrus's success was turned, discursively, into YHWH's and Israel's success. Such appropriations, needless to say, facilitated both adaptation to
and participation in the imperial world and the kind of resistance to "foreign" ideology and even mindscape that allowed for inner group self-valorization and social
reproduction.

From a heuristic perspective, it seems to me that the most helpful question for
the purpose of understanding the discourse of the period is of a different kind:
namely, given that he was so great, why is there relatively little about Cyrus in the
prophetic literature (and in the general repertoire of authoritative texts in Yehud)?

To be sure, part of the answer is that the collection of prophetic books drew
much of the attention and mindshare of the reading community to: (a) the catastrophe of 586 BCE (and thus also to its forerunners [the fall of Samaria] and coun-
terparts [the deliverance of Jerusalem in 701 BCE]); and (b) the utopian future. Cyrus and the entire process of rebuilding the city and temple were thus sandwiched
between the two and, according to the system of preferences governing social
memory in Yehud, they were left with less social mindshare and textual space.

This answer, as correct as it is, raises an even more important underlying issue. Just as the existing second temple of the Persian period was construed as far
less important in the broad scheme of things, and thus far less worthy of being
"remembered" than the one of the past and the future utopian one that would
replace it, so Cyrus was far less important than the future utopian king who would
replace him (YHWH, or in some versions, a highly elevated, more-than-human Davidide).[41] And so the future empire that would replace the Persian empire was
much more important and worthy of being remembered than the Persian empire
itself.

The last observation is particularly important for any study of the impact of
"world" imperial circumstances in the production of the prophetic books collec-

---

Israel/Jacob; see the image envelope in Isa 48:12–15 created by the use of forms from the
root קרא, but notice also the presence of a difference as well. Note also the similarities and
differences evoked by קְרָאתִיו in the book: Isa 48:15 (the caller is YHWH, and the called is Cyrus) and Isa 51:2 (the caller is YHWH, and the called is Abraham); and see also Isa 41:9; 42:6;
49:1 (the caller is YHWH, and the called is the Servant/Israel).

[40] Cf. the Cyrus Cylinder or the Verse Account of Nabonidus.

[41] For memories of a future in which Davidides are absent see, for instance, those
evoked by Isaiah 40–66; Jer 50:4–5, 19–20; Hos 2:18–22; 14:6–9; Obadiah; Zephaniah 3. For
memories of a future with a Davidide, see, for instance, those evoked by Isa 9:5–6; 11:1–9; Jer
23:5–6; 30:8–11; 33:14–26; Ezek 34: 23–30; 37:15–28; Hos 3:5; Amos 9:11–15; Mic 5:1. It is worth
noting that this Davidide was already imagined as highly elevated and very different from
any image of a monarchic David or Solomon that existed in the social memory of the community (see Isa 9:5–7; 11:1–9; Hos 3:5).

tion. A future world without a world-empire was probably beyond the imagination of the community and its ability to experience (virtually, of course) the future through their readings of (authoritative) future-constructing texts. This being so, the logic of the situation and of the discourse in Yehud led to a clear outcome: the "good" empire must be superseded by a utopian empire, YHWH's empire, with its capital in Jerusalem.

Within the logic of the discourse of Yehud, a world permanently run by YHWH through kings and empires other than Israel or its king, with a marginal Jerusalem, was inherently unstable, even if these kings (and, indirectly, YHWH) ran it for the sake of Israel (Isa 45:5). An orderly and stable world was conceived as one that could only be grounded on "true" not illusory knowledge. But in the Achaemenid imperial world, even the great Cyrus, YHWH's anointed, does not know YHWH, does not know the reason for his successes or the "real" purpose of his endeavors. Cyrus's own knowledge is illusory and, in fact, mis-knowledge. He is certainly not alone, however. YHWH is the creator and ruler of the world, but this deity is mostly unknown throughout the earthly world. Jerusalem is the city truly at the center of the world, but it is a very small village unknown to most inhabitants of the "world," and thus it cannot fully fulfill its cosmic roles. This Jerusalem of the Persian empire is not, in the earthly world, a universal source of wisdom/torah (e.g., Isa 2:3; Mic 4:2). It is not light or the place of light to the world (Isa 60:1–3, 19–20). Thus, the Persian imperial world is one in which the "truth" was a "secret" known only to those in Yehud who are able to read the authoritative books or have others who read these books to them. This secret is not manifested in the world, and is hidden by a world that actually looks like a book of mis-knowledge. Such a world cannot stand forever, even if Cyrus is its earthly king.

Such a world is explicitly contrary to YHWH's wishes (see, for instance, Isa 45:5–7). Even when this world was imagined as peaceful and seemingly stable, it was remembered as one doomed to fall (see Zech 1:8–17) and to be replaced.

The alternative, future, yet continuously remembered empire of Israel/YHWH (see below) was, of course, not a minor site of memory with marginal social mindshare. Not only was it evoked by numerous texts in prophetic literature (e.g., Isa 2:2–4; 42:1, 6; 45:14; 49:7, 23; 51:4–5; 56:6–7; 60:9; Mic 4:1–3; Zeph 2:11; Hag 2:7–8; Zech 8:20–22; 9:10), but also it was indispensable for developing the concept of what a prophetic book was supposed to be. It was the ultimate end-point of the plot in the main ("historical") meta-narrative of ancient Israel, and a source of hope for the community.

These memories of the future facilitated accommodation to present imperial circumstances, in practical terms, by resisting hegemonic claims on what the community considered of most importance from their own perspective. It rejected any aspect of imperial hegemonic narratives and world constructions that contradicted the self-understanding of the Yehudite community. These memories of the future, so commonly evoked by prophetic books, produced alternative narratives that allowed the community to hold fast to its sense of self and thus its social reproduction over time.

Since these memories of the future empire were such core features of Yehud's social mindscape (or at least that of its *literati* and likely its elite), their explicit presence could not have been restricted to prophetic texts. One would anticipate that they would appear in other types of texts, within which memories of the future could be encoded, and this is actually the case (e.g., Ps 22:30; 68:30; 72:8–10; 96:7–10; 97:6–7).

The *literati* in Yehud, and those who were influenced by them, imagined a future empire, but how did they imagine it?[42] Certainly, and despite reference to "David," it was not in terms of their (social) memories of the Davidic/Solomonic empire, despite the general tendency in the ancient Near East towards restoration-ist images. For Yehud, the imagined future would not be like the imagined (glorious) past. Several reasons account for this choice: for one, within their main historical narrative, this "glorious" past led to catastrophe. Moreover, the Davidic/Solomonic empire was not construed as a "world" or universal empire.[43] Yet, YHWH was a universal "king" and thus his kingdom had to be construed as "universal."

Many of the basic imperial topoi that were used to imagine and remember this future empire resembled the image of the actual empire of the time, and through it, those of previous empires.[44] A few examples will suffice to make the point.

Images such as those of peoples flowing to the new imperial center (Zion) and bringing their gifts to Zion and to the king, gifts of treasures from various peoples or human resources gathered to and for the sake of the new imperial city,[45] do involve adaptations and reversals of the common imperial image of the nations paying homage to the king of kings, despite the substantial variety among them.[46] The construction of Jerusalem/Zion as the imperial city at the center of the world, is

---

[42] I have previously discussed some features of this ideal future or sets of related futures. In the following paragraphs I will revisit and further develop some highlights of my previous discussion that are particularly relevant to the discussion here. See Ehud Ben Zvi, "On Social Memory and Identity Formation in Late Persian Yehud: A Historian's Viewpoint with a Focus on Prophetic Literature, Chronicles, and the Dtr. Historical Collection," in *Texts, Contexts and Readings in Postexilic Literature: Explorations into Historiography and Identity Negotiation in Hebrew Bible and Related Texts* (ed. L. Jonker; FAT II/53; Tübingen: Mohr-Siebeck, 2011), 95–148 (135–41).

[43] Texts such as 1 Kgs 5:9–14 and 1 Kings 10 shape a larger horizon to Solomon's fame and cultural influence, but his empire was not imagined/construed as a world/universal-empire.

[44] As is well-known, the Achaemenid empire used and reshaped ideological motifs that go back to the Neo-Assyrian empire.

[45] See, for instance, Isa 2:2–4; 45:14; 55:3–5; 60:10–16; Jer 3:17; Mic 4:1–4; Hag 2:7–8; Zech 10:20–22.

[46] See, e.g., DNa, DE, DZc. For an English translation of DNa, the inscription in the upper registrar in his tomb in Naqš-i Rustam, see A. Kuhrt, *The Persian Empire*, 2:502–3; for one of DZc, the inscription of Darius I on a stela set up at Kabret in Egypt, see A. Kuhrt, *The Persian Empire*, 2:486; for DE, the inscription of Darius on Mt. Elvend; see A. Kuhrt, *The Persian Empire*, 1:301, 304. The latter is almost identical to the inscription of Xerxes (XE) that stands next to it.

another case of appropriation and reversal of common imperial images, with a very *longue durée*. The royal garden in which the king is supposed to spend time is now in future Jerusalem (and the Temple) and evokes Eden.[47] Certainly, YHWH was imagined as "the great king, king of kings, king of countries containing all kinds of men, king of this earth far and wide."[48] It is Israel, not the Assyrian king, who is remembered as "a light to the nations" (Isa 42:6). The empire, once it is established, is orderly and without conflict; in fact, it is one in which "history" reaches its end, as the world becomes intrinsically stable (and peaceful). This is again a (modified) version of the image that the Achaemenid empire tried to project.

From a heuristic perspective, it is perhaps more interesting to note the ways in which this new empire might have been imagined as structurally different from existing empires or empires of the past. One obvious difference is that, at the center of the Persian empire, there were the separate figures of the king and of Ahura Mazdā.[49] There was, however, a very strong current in Yehudite discourse (and in its prophetic books) that remembered a future empire at whose center the traditional kingly and divine figures would collapse into one; YHWH alone is king, in that future empire.

Significantly, often Israel as a whole is also imagined with royal attributes.[50] In which way might this "royal" role for Israel as a whole be implemented in the new Empire, since it could not be, in the traditional sense, "king"? And what does it say about how "kingly-ness" is construed in the discourse of the *literati* in Yehud? I will return to this question, but at this point it is worth noting that, at times when non-YHWH royal figures are imagined, they are imagined in terms quite opposite to those associated with worldly kings (e.g., the servant of YHWH in Isaiah 40–55; the king of Zech 9:9–10). There is here a clear tendency to imagine an imperial world different from any present or even elevated form of the present imperial world.

For instance, at times, the community imagined and remembered dramatic military confrontations in the period leading to the establishment of the empire,[51] but unlike the cases of present and past empires, no human hero/king took a central role as the successful warrior (and most masculine male) who established the

[47] See Xenophon, *Oec.* 4.13 (cited in A. Kuhrt, *The Persian Empire*, 2:510); and on Jerusalem, see Terje Stordalen, "Heaven on Earth – Or Not? Jerusalem as Eden in Biblical Literature," in *Beyond Eden: The Biblical Story of Paradise (Genesis 2-3) and Its Reception History* (ed. K. Schmid and Ch. Riedweg; FAT II/34; Tübingen: Mohr Siebeck, 2008), 28–57, (36–40); and Ben Zvi, "Exploring Jerusalem as a Site of Memory."

[48] On this motif, see M. Liverani, "Memorandum on the Approach to Historiographic Texts," *Or* 42 (1973): 178–94 (189–91).

[49] And those of the king and of Assur and of Marduk, in the Neo-Assyrian and Neo-Babylonian empires, respectively.

[50] See, for instance Isa 55:3–5; note the characterization of Israel as the "son" of the deity, e.g. Hos 11:1. Israel may take the traditional slot of a king (e.g., Isa 45:14; and outside prophetic literature, see, for instance, social memories of Israel's covenant with YHWH) and see the attributes of Israel in Hos 2:21.

[51] See, among many others, Ezek 39; Joel 4:9–21; Zeph 3:8–20; Hag 2:6–7; Zech 14.

empire through his military might (with the help of the gods, of course). Instead the successful warrior is YHWH.

Significantly, most great kings set their path to establishing their empire by waging offensive wars, not by defending their capital,[52] yet YHWH is often imagined in these terms. This is not an empire based on any heroic actions by humans, but by YHWH and his actions. The social memories associated with the foundation of YHWH's empire were very different from those associated with the foundation of the Persian empire (or any other empire).

At the center of YHWH's (future) empire stands Jerusalem, not as the city of a human king, but as YHWH's city, and as the city of the temple. People will flow to Jerusalem to receive torah (in the sense of true divine teachings) and wisdom from Zion, not from a new Solomon (contrast Isa 2:2–4 and Mic 4:1–4 with 1 Kgs 5:9–14 and 1 Kings 10). It is a wisdom that is institutionalized (temple and *literati*, representing Israel) not personalized (a human king). The temple/Zion is the source of blessing in this imperial world. To be sure, this future empire was YHWH's but within the discourse of the community, this meant that it had to be construed as a Zion/Temple/torah-centered (world) empire.

Of course, it was also Israel's empire, but Israel was also construed as Zion/Temple- and torah-centered, and to a large extent as encapsulating the very nature of the empire. This means, of course, that in practical terms, this is an empire in which at its center are priests and *literati*. To imagine that Israel was kingly in this context meant that, from a discursive and ideological perspective, a torah-centered community[53] was kingly. Of course, it also meant, from a different perspective, that the *literati* themselves, indirectly, were kingly, too.

Since this is an empire at whose center stood Temple and torah, the community in Yehud had to deal with the issue of the partial acculturation of the nations other than Israel. It is worth noting that in this regard, the empire of YHWH was imagined as somewhat different from the Achaemenid empire. In the latter, ethnocultural groups were not *required* to partially (but significantly) Persianize themselves, nor were they required to acculturate themselves by following a single path that leads to a common end-stage for all non-Persian groups.

---

[52] Or, even failing initially to successfully defend it. See Zech 14:1. For YHWH's defeating the enemy in Israel's/YHWH's land, see also Ezek 39:1–20 and Isa 14:24–27.

[53] One may say that sociologically, the Jerusalemite temple had an important hand in legitimizing the community's Torah, but discursively and ideologically, torah legitimized the temple. For the present purposes, the latter is the crucial observation. On these matters, see Ehud Ben Zvi, "Imagining Josiah's Book and the Implications of Imagining it in Early Persian Yehud," in *Berührungspunkte: Studien zur Sozial- und Religionsgeschichte Israels und seiner Umwelt: Festschrift für Rainer Albertz zu seinem 65. Geburtstag* (ed. R. Schmitt, I. Kottsieper, and J. Wöhrle; AOAT 250; Münster: Ugarit Verlag, 2008), 193–212. Cf. Thomas C. Römer, "Transformations in Deuteronomistic and Biblical Historiography: On 'Book-Finding' and other Literary Strategies," *ZAW* 109 (1997): 1–11; idem, "Du Temple au Livre: L'idéologie de la centralization dans l'historiographie deutéronomiste," in *Rethinking the Foundations: Historiography in the Ancient World and in the Bible: Essays in Honour of John Van Seters* (ed. T. C. Römer and S. L. McKenzie; BZAW 294; Berlin: de Gruyter, 2000), 207–25; idem, *The So-Called Deuteronomistic History: A Sociological, Historical and Literary Introduction* (London: T & T Clark, 2005), 55, 175–83.

In the future world empire imagined in Yehud, however, the many "others" (and the Other) had to be partially Israelitized. In this future world, the main features that were associated with nations other than Israel were replaced by those typical of Israel, and thus in this universal empire the very identity of these nations is re-formulated.

This is an imperial world that reflects a dream of cultural conquest and assimilation of the Other to the center of the discourse of the future empire, and of the community that dreams such dreams.[54]

It is worth noting that in the universal empire of YHWH, the king (YHWH) was imagined as actively desiring and acting towards the acculturation/partial Israelitization of the Other. Kings in historical world empires, be they Assyrian, Babylonian, or Persian, did not champion cultural and identity shifts that would turn entire "peripheral" populations into partially "inner groups." Kings did not have world-wide cultural missions.[55] To be sure, processes of acculturation did happen, but they were for the most part the outcome of processes of "intergroupal" exchanges. Although they were likely influenced by matters of prestige, "social capital" and the like, they were not the result of central, monarchic planning.[56]

---

[54] See, among many examples, Isa 56:1–8.

[55] As shown, concerning Assyria, in Angelika Berlejung, "The Assyrians in the West: Assyrianization, Colonialism, Indifference, or Development Policy?," in *Congress Volume Helsinki 2010* (ed. M. Nissinen; VTSup 148, Leiden: Brill, 2012), 21–60. Of course, the same is true of the Hellenistic kingdoms. Neither Alexander nor any of the later Hellenistic kings engaged themselves in a world mission of "Hellenization." In fact, Hellenistic kings often showed an ability to adapt and appropriate local ideologies and cultures; see, for instance, the famous Borsippa Cylinder of Antiochos I (268 BCE). On these issues and the problematic historical character and background of once common claims about Hellenistic kingdoms as promoters of forced, institutional Hellenization and related positions about the nature of these kingdoms/empires, see, among others, Amélie Kuhrt and Susan M. Sherwin-White, *From Samarkhand to Sardis: A New Approach to the Seleucid Empire* (London: Duckworth, 1993), 141–87; Manning, *The Last Pharaohs*, esp. ch. 2 (29–54). See also J. Ma, "Kings," in *A Companion to the Hellenistic World* (ed. A. Erskine; Oxford: Blackwell, 2003), 177–195. It must be kept in mind that empires were based on negotiation, not negotiation among equals to be sure, but still negotiation with local groups and particularly their elites. This is certainly true of the Hellenistic empires, see, for instance, Manning, *The Last Pharaohs*, J. K. Davies, "The Interpenetration of Hellenistic Sovereignties," in *The Hellenistic World: New Perspectives* (ed. D. Ogden; London: Duckworth and The Classical Press of Wales, 2002), 1-21; R. Strootman, "Kings and Cities in the Hellenistic Age," in *Political Culture in the Greek City After the Classical Age* (ed. R. Alston, O. van Nijf, C. Williamson; Groningen-Royal Holloway Studies on the Greek City After the Classical Age 2; Leuven: Peeters, 2011), 141-53. Through these processes of negotiations, kings tended to appropriate and partially resignify local cultural traditions and locals tended to appropriate and resignify some Hellenistic traditions; both groups thus tended to create a kind of ever shifting "third-space" in which both could interact each for their one benefit. Similar considerations apply not only to ancient empires, but modern as well.

[56] This explains, for instance, why the initiative to become a polis most often originated within local groups, not Hellenistic kings. Concerning the general cultural processes see note above.

YHWH's/Israel's future empire was remembered in this respect as having at its center priorities that were not those of past or future kings of universal empires. This again says much about the way in which Israel conceived its future "kingly-ness" (see above).

The construction of YHWH's/Israel's empire discussed here represents under-dog dreams of empire. They are proof positive of an internalization (and adapta-tion) of the imperial discourses. They represent a clear case of resistance through the creation of meta-narratives and the act of remembering and experiencing (vir-tually) what they tell. It may also be some form of social (over?)response (even if not necessarily self-conscious) to the partial "Arameanization" of Yehud during the Persian period,[57] now turned into a memory of a future partial (but far more substantial) Israelitization of the entire world.

The question of the partial Israelitization of the Other was bound to raise the question of whether the Other may change enough to be able to join the center of the future empire. Although foreigners loyal to the Persian king served in periph-eral roles in the court of the Persian king, could be awarded honors and rewards and even invited to the King's table, they could not become members of the impe-rial inner circle. Not incidentally, intermarriage at the level of the Persian king was not allowed, whether involving foreign women or even Persian women who were not from the nobility.[58] What about future Israel? Would they be able to live in the imperial court (i.e., Jerusalem) and receive royal rewards? What about joining the King's table? Would they be able to become full members of the inner circle (i.e., priests) and intermarry with members of this circle? These questions require a

---

[57] Note both the use of Aramaic in Yehud and the introduction of the Aramaic lapidary script. On the latter, see Oded Lipschits and David S. Vanderhoft, *The Yehud Stamp Impressions: A Corpus of Inscribed Impressions from the Persian and Hellenistic Periods in Judah* (Winona Lake: Eisenbrauns, 2011), 63–73; but note also that discontinuity in script is balanced with continu-ity in design. Note also that despite the introduction and prevalence of Aramaic, the authori-tative texts of the community continued to be written in Hebrew. Cf. Ehud Ben Zvi, "The Communicative Message of Some Linguistic Choices," in *A Palimpsest: Rhetoric, Ideology, Stylis-tics and Language Relating to Persian Israel* (ed. E. Ben Zvi, D. V. Edelman, and F. Polak; Pisca-taway: Gorgias Press, 2009), 269–90. The question of the partial "Arameanization" of Yehud requires a separate in-depth study.

It is worth stressing that the Aramaic language was only one of the important lan-guages of the empire. A simple example suffices: the vast majority of the Persepolis Fortifica-tion Texts were not in Aramaic. Processes of partial "Arameanization" varied among the different groups constituting the Persian empire in both contents and extent. On Aramaic in the eastern part of the Achaemenid empire, see Josef Wiesehöfer, *Ancient Persia: From 550 BC to 650 AD* (London: Tauris, 1996), 118, in which the matter is approached from the perspective of our knowledge of the situation in the later Parthian empire.

[58] See, for instance, Maria Brosius, "Greeks at the Persian Court," in *Ktesias' Welt = Ctesias' World* (ed. J. Wiesehöfer, R. Rollinger, and G. B. Lanfranchi; Classica et orientalia 1; Wiesba-den: Harrassowitz, 2011), 69–80.

separate analysis, but suffice it to say that multiple answers co-existed and balanced each other in the discourse of late Persian/early Hellenistic Yehud/Judah.[59]

Another aspect of the memories of the future world empire of YHWH/Israel as construed in late Persian Yehud: It is clear that dreams of the Yehudites did not focus on the basic structures of worldly world empires (e.g., central administration, regional administrations, army, communications, regular collection of taxes), and as mentioned above, they did not focus on human military heroes. When people in Yehud imagined and remembered the future empire of YHWH and Israel, their mindshare was not occupied by the usual functions and personages of any historical polity (or state). Instead their attention focused on torah, temple, priests, teachers of torah and the like. They were at the center of the new empire. Their imagination and memories drew them away from the known "political-wordly" realm and towards a world in which the latter does not necessarily constrain social imagination and the generative power of their ideological discourse. As I mentioned elsewhere, it is precisely in that world that the *literati* of Yehud could "compete and beat" the actual empire, while at the same time, and partially because of their success in that endeavor, be able to adapt well to it in their regular, but ideological and discursively, "less significant" life.[60] Yet, at the same time, their very ability to do so, to think in this way, was dependent on the very imperial circumstances in which they lived. The existence of the community neither required nor depended on the kind of "state" structures and institutions (including a standing and thus, costly army) that were vital for even a vassal kingdom such as monarchic Judah. They were a province in a larger Persian empire.[61]

---

[59] To be sure, there are texts such as Isa 66:21 and Isa 14:1 or Isa 56:1–8, but on the other hand also like Ezek 44:7; and there are, of course, Pentateuchal texts (e.g., Lev 17:8–9; Num 15:14), but there are many different types of non-Israelites and all these texts require careful exegesis. Moreover, there is also the traditional concept of a hereditary priesthood, but at the same time, the line may be expanded to include "adopted sons" into the lineage, as in the case of Samuel, implied by the fact that he is an Ephramite in Samuel but a Levite in Chronicles. I discuss further this particular case and its implications in Ehud Ben Zvi, "A Balancing Act: Settling and Unsettling Issues Concerning Past Divine Promises in Historiographical Texts Shaping Social Memory in the Late Persian Period," in *Covenant in the Persian Period: From Genesis to Chronicles* (ed. R. J. Bautch and G. N. Knoppers; Winona Lake: Eisenbrauns, forthcoming).

[60] Ben Zvi, "Social Identity and Formation."

[61] The basic critique and even rejection of "state" structures appears too in historiographical books (e.g., 1 Sam 8:11–18 may reflect a similar imperial context). But this is also an issue that demands a separate discussion. It suffices for the present purposes to note that an ideal future reminiscent of the non-state period of Judges is projected into the ideal future not only in relation to Judah (see Obad 20), but also and paradigmatically in relation to Egypt (see Isa 19:20). These two images, however, demand a separate discussion as well.

III. ON THE REMEMBERED MAIN EMPIRES OF THE PAST

Turning from the "universal" remembered empire of the future to those of the past, as mentioned above (end of section I), two imperial powers grabbed most of the mindshare of the community in the set of social memories encoded and evoked by the collection of prophetic books: Assyria and Babylon. Assyria was a universal empire which was associated in the main narrative of Israel's past with the fall of the northern kingdom and its failure to conquer (and destroy) Jerusalem during the time of Hezekiah. Both Assyria's success against the northern kingdom and its (remembered) failure before Jerusalem contributed much to its negative characterization. In the case of the former, this held true for obvious reasons. The latter held true because military failure was associated with moral failure. The salience of the deliverance of Jerusalem before the Assyrian army in social memory shaped a strong mnemonic (and narrative) preference for the presence of great heroes (YHWH, Hezekiah, Isaiah) and their counterpart, great villains (Sennacherib), confronting each other at the central world place at a crucial time. Thus, the story of the deliverance of Jerusalem evolved so as to evoke in the community in Persian Yehud not only the pious behavior of Hezekiah and the successful role of the prophet Isaiah (contrast with the pair Zedekiah/Jeremiah)—and a sense that Israel has agency and its actions influence history—but also the figure of a hubristic enemy bent on fighting and mocking YHWH, who was thus surely to fall.[62]

To be sure, there was a strong "generative grammar" within the discourse of Yehud that generated an association between universal empire and hubristic behavior. Clearly the king of such an empire occupied the structural/mnemonic slot of YHWH, the real universal king; moreover, there was the discursive and ideological expectation that the king of a universal empire be constructed/imagined in Yehudite social memory as one who boasted of his power and trusted those elements (divine, natural, social) upon which he relied (his gods, terrain, fortifications, army and the like)—the worst of them went to the extreme of thinking themselves as para-gods.[63] Needless to say, this would constitute hubristic behavior, from the perspective of the *literati* in Yehud. In fact, the same holds true even for less than "traditional" universal empires within their social memory, as the case of Tyre in Ezekiel 27 and 28 shows.[64] But as the case of the Persian empire (see above) demonstrates beyond any doubt, a strong "generative grammar" may exist, but it produces no substantial outcome if other "generative grammars" hinder or

---

[62] See, for instance, Isa 10:10–11; Isa 37:23–29 // 1 Kgs 19:22–28.

[63] See, for instance, Isa 14:3–23; Ezek 31; 32. This motif is also part and parcel of imperial discourses. See Mario Liverani, "Kitru, kataru," *Mesopotamia* 17 (1982): 43–66.

[64] On Ezekiel 27, see John B. Geyer, "Ezekiel 27 and the Cosmic Ship," in *Among the Prophets: Language, Image and Structure in the Prophetic Writings* (ed. P. R. Davies and D. J. A. Clines; JSOTSup 144; Sheffield: JSOT Press, 1993), 105–26. Tyre trusts its wealth and the sea; Jerusalem has the Temple. See Ian D. Wilson, "Tyre, a Ship: The Metaphorical World of Ezekiel 27 in Ancient Judah," *ZAW* 125 (2013): 249–62.

pre-empt such an outcome.[65] Conversely, in the case of the negative characterization of Assyria, tendencies to cast it as hubristic are reinforced by strong preferences to cast it in the most negative terms, due to the social memory dynamics of remembering the events in the 14th year of Hezekiah and by social memories of catastrophes suffered by Israel at Assyrian hands, which in turn create a preference for more mindshare for and high descriptions of its fall.[66]

The Babylonian empire was mnemonically associated for the most part with the catastrophe of 586 BCE. This association, along with the very fact that Babylon was a world "empire" and that it was defeated by Cyrus, generated a strong preference for negative memories and constructions of Babylon.[67]

To be sure, memories of Egypt are also evoked in the collection of prophetic books, but not so much as a successful universal empire, but rather as the unsuccessful foil to the winning world empires, Assyria and Babylonia. Of course, if we include Deuteronomy as the "prophetic book of Moses" among the prophetic books—in addition to being part of the pentateuchal, hexateucal, deuteronomistic historical, and primary history collections[68]—Egypt becomes the prototypical house of bondage, the place out of which YHWH had to extricate Israel, so Israel could come into being. Leaving Egypt was thus imagined as leaving the (Egyptian) empire, as leaving Babylon was imagined as leaving the Babylonian empire. This set of memories and sites of memories shaped a strong preference for the development of negative characterizations of Egypt, as the archetypal "evil empire," and liberation from it, as the archetypal case of deliverance from this type of "imperial" subjugation.

An aspect of the imperial construction of Egypt, Assyria, and Babylon is, of course, their transformation into geographical/spatial sites of memory associated with Israel's exile. Significantly, one can observe a significant shift in the basic narrative about leaving exile. In two cases, leaving physically the territorial heart of the empire was remembered as a crucial step towards the establishment of a torah/temple-centered community. In the first and foundational instance, it was Egypt, but its slot is taken in the re-foundation part of the main meta-narrative by Babylon. The plot that the community remembers is thus helical, not cyclical.

To be sure, there are references to other empires. But they were assigned less textual space in the collection of prophetic books and in the social mindshare of the community (e.g., Tyre).[69] Far more important for historical reconstructions of

---

[65] It is worthwhile to stress that the contrast between images of Assyria and Babylonia as cruel, pitiless powers, on the one hand, and Persia as a kind and generous one, on the other, is the product of particular social memory processes in Yehud. They are not a reflection of essentially divergent attitudes towards rebellions; see the way in which Darius I put down the rebellions against him at the beginning of his reign (DB 32–33).

[66] See above all Nahum 2; for other examples, see Isa 14:21–24; 30:27–33; Zeph 2:13–15 (and note the placement and relative extent of the reference to Assyria in Zeph 2:4–15).

[67] E.g., Isa 13; 14:3–24; Jer 50; 51:24–28.

[68] See Ehud Ben Zvi, "Exploring the Memory of Moses 'The Prophet'."

[69] Tyre was imagined and remembered in prophetic literature as the center of what we may call today a commercial empire and Tyre, the city, and its king as at the center of a

the full scope of the intellectual discourse of late Persian Yehud are the substantial memories encoded in and evoked by the prophetic book collection that balance the thrust of the memories of empires mentioned before. To illustrate, and focusing again on the two main universal empires of the past, there are texts that asked the community to construe and remember the Babylonian empire (and characters that represented and symbolized it) in extremely positive light, not when Babylon is fallen or when it is about to be replaced as the center of the world by Jerusalem, but at the height of its power, just when it destroyed Jerusalem, the Temple, and sent Israel into "exile."

Babylonia at its zenith, the very universal empire that destroyed Jerusalem, was also generally imagined containing at its heart the very territory most suitable for Israel's exile.[70] Although a somewhat elevated figure of Nebuchadnezzar,[71] particularly as YHWH's servant, is to be expected (see Jer 25:9; 27:6—cf. Isa 10:5—and in Jer 25:1–14, note also vv. 11–12), and particularly since he successfully destroyed Jerusalem, which in the discourse of Yehud could have only been understood as having been selected by YHWH to do so, the same cannot be said of Nebuzaradan, who is explicitly characterized as a pious foreign leader, who not only acknowledges YHWH's power and justice, but also thinks and talks like a pious Israelite/Judahite/Yehudite. In fact, Jer 40:2–3 asks the community to remember a Nebuzaradan, the very same person who burned the temple and Jerusalem and deported Israel and the temple vessels (2 Kgs 25:8–11; Jer 39:9; 52:12–27), as a person who thought and talked as a godly disciple of the prophet, as Jeremiah would have thought and talked.[72]

Turning to Assyria, although there is Nahum, there is also Jonah. Significantly, the "king of Nineveh" is not to be imagined as the king of a falling polity, but of one at the height of its power (see Jonah 3:2–3). Clearly, the book of Jonah, among

---

world, like imperial kings and cities. Of course from the perspective of the remembering community this is a kind of "anti-world" and Tyre is a kind of "anti-Jerusalem." See, for instance, Ezekiel 27–28 and also cf. Ezek 26:16–18 and note 64 above.

Given Aram's importance in the historical process that led to the fall of Samaria, the tendency to "bracket" it, particularly in Hosea, is worth noting. On this matter, see Ehud Ben Zvi, "The Study of Forgetting and the Forgotten in Ancient Israelite Discourse/s: Observations and Test Cases," in *Cultural Memory in Biblical Exegesis* (ed. P. Carstens, T. Hasselbach, and N. P. Lemche; Perspectives on Hebrew Scriptures and its Contexts 17; Piscataway: Gorgias Press, 2012), 155–74.

[70] See, for instance, Jer 29; Ezek 33:21–29; and contrast with how Egypt, which did not destroy Jerusalem, was imagined in this regard: see Jer 40:7–41:18; 42:1–22; 43:1–13; 44:1–30.

[71] See John Hill, "'Your Exile Will Be Long': The Book of Jeremiah and the Unended Exile," in *Reading the Book of Jeremiah: A Search for Coherence* (ed. M. Kessler; Winona Lake: Eisenbrauns, 2004), 149–61 (152–56); idem, *Friend or Foe? The Figure of Babylon in the Book of Jeremiah MT* (BibIntSup 40; Leiden: Brill, 1999), 103–10, 130–39, 198–99, 203–5.

[72] "The author wants to persuade us that Nebuzaradan was a pupil of Jeremiah (40:2–3)," writes Klaas A. D. Smelik in "The Function of Jeremiah 50 and 51 in the Book of Jeremiah," in *Reading the Book of Jeremiah: A Search for Coherence* (ed. M. Kessler; Winona Lake: Eisenbrauns, 2004), 87–98 (97). Compare also Jer 40:2 with Jer 32:23.

many other things, serves to balance, to the best of its potential within the community, the memories associated with Nineveh.

These are not some odd cases one can "safely ignore" in reconstructions of the intellectual discourse of the period, nor are the perspectives that they raise restricted to texts in the prophetic book collection.[73] These memories served to balance the mindshare of extremely negative constructions of past, universal empires. While positive constructions of their present "universal" empire may have contributed to the images of past empires,[74] these texts shaped an image of the past empires and their populations[75] as containing the seed of their transformation into loyal members of the future empire of YHWH/Israel, as (discursively necessary) pre-figurations of that future. At the same time, Babylon and Assyria are past empires and as such they have to pass. Even Jonah, as read and reread in Yehud, has two endings.[76]

IV. FINAL OBSERVATION

These observations do not and cannot address within the boundaries of a single essay the gamut of issues associated with "empire" and "imperial conditions," the prophetic collection of books, and matters of social memory and mindscape in late Persian/early Hellenistic Yehud. It is hoped, however, that they provide a fruitful and somewhat distinctive springboard for multiple, future conversations on these matters.

---

[73] Chronicles (and books in the deuteronomistic historical collection, and the book of Genesis) shaped memories of several virtuous, powerful foreign kings. See Ehud Ben Zvi, *History, Literature and Theology in the Book of Chronicles*, 270–88; previously published as "When a Foreign Monarch Speaks," in *The Chronicler as Author: Studies in Text and Texture* (ed. M. P. Graham and S. L. McKenzie; JSOTSup 263; Sheffield: Sheffield Academic Press, 1999), 209–28.

[74] Note, for instance, the case of the positive characterization of the Other in the land, before Israel could take possession of it, that is, during the patriarchal period. One may also compare these positive others with those populating constructions of the Persian empire in Yehud. On these matters, see Ehud Ben Zvi, "The Memory of Abraham in the Late Persian/ Early Hellenistic Yehud/Judah," in *Remembering Biblical Figures in the Late Persian and Early Hellenistic Periods: Social Memory and Imagination* (ed. D. V. Edelman and E. Ben Zvi; Oxford: Oxford University Press, 2013), 3–37 (18–21). A Persian-period connoted flavor might be at work also in the portrayal of the sailors in Jonah's ship. Note the multiplicity of gods/cultural backgrounds associated with them, which is balanced by their shared behavior, which provides a pre-figuration of the behavior of "the Others" at the time of the future empire of YHWH/Israel.

[75] In Jonah, see the partial Israelitization of not only the king of Nineveh, but also the entire population of the city and earlier within the book's story that of the sailors in the ship.

[76] As I maintained in Ehud Ben Zvi, *Signs of Jonah: Reading and Rereading in Ancient Yehud* (JSOTSup 367; London: Sheffield Academic Press, 2003). I discussed there also the motif of *partial* Israelitization of "the Other" in Jonah at some length.

9

Power, Politics, and Prophecy in the Dead Sea Scrolls and Second Temple Judaism

Alex P. Jassen[1]

The constellation of sectarian communities associated with the Dead Sea Scrolls was overmatched in power and prestige by other contemporary Jewish groups.[2] The sectarian Dead Sea Scrolls condemn the priests in Jerusalem as impure stewards of a defiled temple, denounce the Hasmoneans as illegitimate rulers,

---

[1] Earlier versions of this article were presented at the University of Chicago (February 2013) and the Yeshiva University Symposium on the Dead Sea Scrolls (March 2013). I thank all those in attendance for their helpful feedback. I am especially grateful to Dr. Shalom Holtz, who served as a respondent for the presentation at Yeshiva University and offered many helpful suggestions.

[2] My use of the term "constellation of sectarian communities" reflects the assumption that the Dead Sea Scrolls contain a collection of writings that represent a shared ideology and set of practices that are distinctive in the broader landscape of Second Temple period Jewish groups. At the same time, these writings do not represent a singular community and thus attempts to outline the sectarian beliefs and practices must account for diversity within the sectarian documents. Two primary models have been proposed: (1) The diversity reflects the historical progression of related sectarian communities; (2) The sectarian documents reflect the literary output of a broad network of communities spread throughout the land of Israel. On these issues, see especially, Alison Schofield, *From Qumran to the Yaḥad: A New Paradigm of Textual Development for The Community Rule* (STDJ 77; Leiden: Brill, 2009); John J. Collins, *Beyond the Qumran Community: The Sectarian Movement of the Dead Sea Scrolls* (Grand Rapids: Eerdmans, 2010). As with most aspects of sectarian ideology, approaches to violence and power are not uniform. For an attempt to situate this diversity within the first model (historical progression), see Alex P. Jassen, "Violence and the Dead Sea Scrolls: Sectarian Formation and Eschatological Imagination," in *Violence, Scripture, and Textual Practice in Early Judaism and Christianity* (ed. R. S. Boustan, A. P. Jassen, and C. J. Roetzel; Leiden: Brill, 2010), 13–45.

and craft a portrait of the Pharisees as misguided interpreters of the law. The sectarians viewed themselves as God's chosen people and believed that only their priestly leaders could restore the temple to its pristine state; only their teachers properly understood the divine law. Yet, the sectarians recognized the ever-present reality that they were far from these positions of power in Jewish society. In the face of this reality, the sectarians constructed an identity of themselves and other Jews that explained their disempowered status and delegitimized the prestige of these other groups. At the same time, the sectarian writings imagine an imminent end of days in which the present imbalance of power would be remedied through the annihilation of all the enemies of the sectarians.

The present study examines the role that views of prophecy and competing claims to contemporary prophecy played in this identity formation. As in many late biblical and Second Temple texts, several texts in the Dead Sea Scrolls reflect a suspicious attitude toward prophets. The condemnation of false prophets is commonly found in the context of competing claims to authority with sectarian enemies, most notably the Hasmoneans and Pharisees. This study explores the ways the charge of false prophecy serves as a means to delegitimize the social and political authority of the targets of these accusations. In the context of the Dead Sea Scrolls, the disempowered sectarians deploy the accusation of false prophecy as a tool for their imagined resistance against the empowered Pharisees and Hasmoneans.[3]

POWER AND POLITICS IN THE DEAD SEA SCROLLS

Portraits of Hasmonean Power in the Dead Sea Scrolls

Throughout the Dead Sea Scrolls, the Hasmoneans are portrayed as powerful enemies determined to bring destruction to the sectarians. Most accounts of the Dead Sea Scrolls sectarian communities highlight the strong antagonism between the sectarians and the Hasmonean priests/kings.[4] For example, while scholars de-

---

[3] The present study limits itself to intra-Jewish conflict. The power dynamic described here for the sectarians and their Jewish opponents is equally applicable to the relationship with Rome. Yet, the attempt to reverse this power dynamic is considerably different for intra-Jewish opponents versus foreign opponents such as Rome. In particular, views of prophecy and competing claims to present-time prophecy play no role in the sectarians' attempts to reverse Roman power. On portraits of Roman power and the sectarian response, see the discussion in Alex P. Jassen, "War and Violence," in *T & T Clark Companion to the Dead Sea Scrolls* (ed. G. J. Brooke and C. Hempel; London: T & T Clark Bloomsbury, forthcoming).

[4] See, e.g., Lawrence H. Schiffman, "Community Without Temple: The Qumran Community's Withdrawal from the Jerusalem Temple," in *Qumran and Jerusalem: Studies in the Dead Sea Scrolls and the History of Judaism* (Grand Rapids: Eerdmans, 2010), 81–97; Edward Dąbrowa, "The Hasmoneans in Light of the Dead Sea Scrolls," in *The Dead Sea Scrolls in Context: Integrating the Dead Sea Scrolls in the Study of Ancient Texts, Languages, and Cultures* (ed. A. Lange, E. Tov, and M. Weigold; VTSup 140; Leiden: Brill, 2011), 1:501–10.

bate the precise identity of the Wicked Priest, it is almost certainly one of the Hasmonean high priests.[5] The sectarian scrolls describe a range of brutality perpetrated by the Hasmoneans, both against other Jews and toward the sectarians. Similar to the descriptions of the Romans in *Pesher Habakkuk* (1QpHab), several texts outline the violent tendencies of the Hasmoneans. *Pesher Nahum* (4Q169), for example, condemns the "Lion of Wrath"—a sobriquet for Alexander Jannaeus (103–75 BCE)—for killing his Jewish opponents.[6] Similarly, *4QTestimonia* (4Q175) identifies Jericho as rebuilt by the "Man of Belial"—generally understood as John Hyrcanus (134–104 BCE)—to be a flashpoint for violence and the spilling of innocent blood.[7]

The most prominent portrait of Hasmonean tyranny in the scrolls, however, is directed at the sectarians and their leaders. *Pesher Psalms* describes the oppression of God's "holy people" at the hands of the "wicked princes," almost certainly a reference to the Hasmonean dynasty (4Q171 1–10 iii 7–8). *Pesher Habakkuk* personalizes the dominance of the Hasmoneans by outlining the struggle between the Teacher of Righteousness and the Wicked Priest. 1QpHab 9:8–12 interprets the "violence and bloodshed" in Hab 2:8 as referring to crimes of the Wicked Priest against the Teacher and his community. 1QpHab 11:4–8 describes the pursuit of the Teacher at his place of exile by the Wicked Priest in order "to swallow him up with his poisonous vexation." *Pesher Psalms* goes so far as to accuse the Wicked Priest of attempting to murder the Teacher of Righteousness (4Q171 1–10 iv 8–10). The *Pesharim* and the *Thanksgiving Hymns* (e.g., 1QH^a 10:20–29; 12:9–11; 13:9–18) provide further examples of oppression suffered by the Teacher and his followers. Although the perpetrators of this oppression are never fully identified, it is likely that many of these further examples are similarly intended as part of the broader portrait of Hasmonean cruelty toward the sectarians.[8]

Scholars have long mined these passages for clues regarding the origins of the sectarians and the identities of the Teacher of Righteousness and the Wicked Priest. This approach, however, assumes that the descriptions of the Hasmonean persecution of the sectarians should in fact be constructed in purely historical terms. It is possible that some of the examples of outsider oppression found in the scrolls did in fact transpire. It is more likely, however, that these portraits of persecution are part of a larger narrative of victimhood crafted within the various

---

[5] See James C. VanderKam, "The Wicked Priest Revisited," in *The "Other" in Second Temple Judaism: Essays in Honor of John J. Collins* (ed. D. C. Harlow et al.; Grand Rapids: Eerdmans, 2011), 350–67.

[6] On this passage and the identification of the "Lion of Wrath" as Alexander Janneaus, see Josephus, *B.J.* 1.92–98; *Ant.* 13.376–83, and the discussion in David Flusser, "Pharisees, Sadduccees, and Essenes in Pesher Nahum," in *Judaism of the Second Temple Period: Volume 1: Qumran and Apocalypticism* (trans. Azzan Yadin; Grand Rapids: Eerdmans; Jerusalem: Magnes and Jerusalem Perspective, 2007), 214–57 (220); Lawrence H. Schiffman, "Pharisees and Sadducees in Pesher Nahum," in *Qumran and Jerusalem*, 337–52 (340–43) (see note 4).

[7] See Hanan Eshel, "The Succession of High Priests: John Hyrcanus and His Sons in the Pesher to Joshua 6:26," in *The Dead Sea Scrolls and the Hasmonean State* (Grand Rapids: Eerdmans, 2008), 63–90, and fuller discussion below.

[8] See my discussion of these additional texts in Jassen, "War and Violence."

sectarian communities. The rejection of the sectarians by the rest of Jewish society was likely a result of indifference rather than persecution. Persecution, however, is a much more powerful internal rhetorical tool than indifference.[9] The Hasmoneans are constantly painted as the aggressors in contrast to the victimized sectarians—the true followers of God. In creating this narrative of victimhood, the sectarians presume that the Hasmonean authorities care deeply about this group of detractors, some of whom have withdrawn to the desert. In so doing, the sectarians increase their own prestige while simultaneously making very clear that they are no match for the dominant Hasmonean forces.

Portraits of Pharisaic Power in the Dead Sea Scrolls

The Pharisees represent a second intra-Jewish opponent of the community. Treatments of the Pharisees must distinguish between the Pharisees of history—about whom precious little can be verified—and the portrait of the Pharisees found in the writings of their detractors.[10] Although the Dead Sea Scrolls do seem to contain some information about the historical Pharisees, the description of the Pharisees in the sectarian writing is undoubtedly a tendentious portrait written by a group deeply opposed to the Pharisees.[11] The sectarian Dead Sea Scrolls portray the Pharisees as expositors of Jewish law—generally with a tendency toward leniency—who seemingly command a wide group of followers. The historical elements in this portrait, however, are obscured by the caricature of the Pharisees in these texts as ill-informed interpreters of the law who lead their followers astray. The sectarians view themselves as the only true expositors of Jewish law and therefore the only ones who can properly provide instruction in Jewish society. The portrait of the dual empowerment of the Pharisees and the marginalization of the sectarians therefore further reinforces the sectarians' narrative of victimhood.

The Pharisees are repeatedly condemned for their misguided leadership and erroneous interpretations of the law. Though the Pharisees themselves are never presented as oppressive or hostile, their faulty leadership at times leads to violence and bloodshed perpetrated by others against fellow Jews. This portrait is especially prominent in the presentation of the Pharisees in column two of *Pesher Nahum*.[12]

---

[9] See Carol A. Newsom, *The Self as Symbolic Space: Constructing Identity and Community at Qumran* (STDJ 52; Leiden: Brill, 2004), 318.

[10] On this issue, see David Goodblatt, "The Place of Pharisees in First Century Judaism: The State of the Debate," *JSJ* 20 (1989): 12–30; Martin Goodman, "Josephus and Variety in First Century Judaism," in *Judaism in the Roman World: Collected Essays* (AJEC 66; Leiden: Brill, 2006), 33–46.

[11] See bibliography below cited in nn. 14, 17 for a range of approaches to the contribution of the Dead Sea Scrolls to understanding the Pharisees.

[12] On the Pharisees in this text, see Flusser, "Pharisees, Sadduccees, and Essenes," 214–57; Schiffman, "Pharisees and Sadducees," 337–52.

Pesher Nahum interprets the "city of crime" in Nah 3:1a as referring to "city of Ephraim, the Seekers after Smooth Things, at the end of days, that the[y will] conduct themselves in deception and falsehoo[d]" (4Q169 3-4 ii 2).[13] "Ephraim" and "Seekers after Smooth Things" are two code words for Pharisees in *Pesher Nahum*.[14] This invective is expanded in the interpretation of the next lemma from Nah 3:1b-3, in which the Pharisees are censured for their collusion with the foreign empire and the resultant bloodshed:

> Its interpretation concerns the domain (ממשלת) of the Seekers after Smooth Things that there shall not cease from the midst of whose congregation the sword of the nations, captivity, and plunder, fever, and exile from fear of the enemy and a multitude of guilty corpses will fall in their days, and there shall be no end to the sum of their slain, and even over their fleshly bodies they shall stumble by their guilty counsel. (4Q169 3-4 ii 3-6)

This passage is no doubt related to *Pesher Nahum*'s earlier report that the "Seekers after Smooth Things" collaborated with the Seleucid king Demetrius to overthrow the "Lion of Wrath" (Alexander Jannaeus) (4Q169 3-4 i 2). In particular, *Pesher Nahum* interprets the "sword" from the scriptural lemma to refer to the "sword of nations," thereby heightening the censure of the Pharisees for their collusion with the foreign empire.

Pesher Nahum continues its attack on Pharisaic authority in its interpretation of Nah 3:4:

> [Its] interpretation [con]cerns those who lead Ephraim astray, in whose teaching is their falsehood, and whose lying tongue and dishonest lip(s) lead many astray, [their] kings, officers, priests, and people, with the proselyte who converts. They shall destroy cities and clans with their plot; nob[l]es and rul[ers] shall fall because of the [insol]ence of their speech. (4Q169 3-4 ii 8-10)

As scholars have noted, this passage seems to create a distinction between the Pharisaic leaders of Ephraim and their followers.[15] This distinction allows *Pesher Nahum* to reinforce further its denouncement of the Pharisees for their misguided leadership and false interpretation of the law. As in earlier passages, disastrous consequences ensue.

---

[13] Translations follow Shani L. Berrin, *The Pesher Nahum Scroll from Qumran: An Exegetical Study of 4Q169* (STDJ 53; Leiden: Brill, 2004).

[14] See Flusser, "Pharisees, Sadducees, and Essenes," 218-24; Schiffman, "Pharisees and Sadducees," 339-48; Berrin, *Pesher Nahum*, 92-99, 109-18. See also James C. VanderKam, "Those Who Look for Smooth Things, Pharisees, and Oral Law," in *Emanuel: Studies in the Hebrew Bible, Septuagint and Dead Sea Scrolls in Honor of Emanuel Tov* (ed. S. M. Paul et al.; VTSup 94; Leiden: Brill, 2003), 465-77; idem, "The Pharisees and the Dead Sea Scrolls," in *In Quest of the Historical Pharisees* (ed. J. Neusner and B. D. Chilton; Waco: Baylor University Press, 2007), 222-36 (225-28).

[15] See Schiffman, "Pharisees and Sadducees," 346-47; Berrin, *Pesher Nahum*, 109-18.

Scholars debate the precise historical framework presumed by *Pesher Nahum*. Much of this debate is framed by the reference to the "domain" (ממשלת) of the Pharisees in 4Q169 3–4 ii 4. Most scholars understand this term to refer to some degree of Pharisaic political authority. The historical setting of this passage is therefore located during points in time when Josephus describes the Pharisees as possessing such power: either during the reign of Salome Alexandra (76–67 BCE) or during the period of the conflict between her sons Hyrcanus II and Aristobulus II (67–63 BCE).[16] While this debate may be important for understanding the contribution of *Pesher Nahum* to the reconstruction of the history of the Pharisees in Hasmonean times, it misses the rhetorical point of *Pesher Nahum*'s portrait of the Pharisees.

The sectarian community envisions the Pharisees as one of its primary competitors with regard to interpretation of the law and positions of leadership in Jewish society. This rivalry is especially present in the *Damascus Document* and stands behind the legal disagreements in *Miqṣat Ma'ase Ha-Torah*.[17] The community always asserts the correctness of its position and the misguided nature of Pharisaic teachings. At the same time, these condemnations of Pharisaic teachings acknowledge the realities of Pharisaic political and religious power. The reference to the "domain" (ממשלת) of the Pharisees is far too general to refer to any specific point in time during the Hasmonean period. More likely, it has in view all points in time when the the sectarians imagined the Pharisees wielding influence.[18] In so doing, *Pesher Nahum* reinforces the rhetorical point that there is little distinction between Pharisaic power during the period of Salome Alexandra or her sons. To the spurned community, the most troubling issue is the mere fact that the Pharisees possess any degree of control over local Judean politics and religious practice.

Even as it acknowledges political realities, *Pesher Nahum* turns on its head the primary claim of the Pharisees for this position of authority. Their claim to be expert interpreters of the law is exposed as a fraud. For *Pesher Nahum*, the Pharisees' teachings are based on falsehood and as such their religious and political counsel only leads to disastrous results. The portrait of the Pharisees in *Pesher Nahum* only further contributes to the community's sense of disempowerment. The utter disdain for Pharisaic political and religious leadership and its consequences reinforce

---

[16] For the earlier period, see J. D. Amoussine, "Éphraïm et Manassé dans le Péshèr de Nahum," *RevQ* 4 (1963): 389–96 (392–93); Flusser, "Pharisees, Sadducees, and Essenes," 232–33. For the later period, see A. Dupont-Sommer, "Le commentaire de Nahum découvert près de la mer Morte (4Qp Nah): Traduction et Notes," *Semitica* 13 (1963): 55–88 (73–74). For fuller discussion, see Berrin, *Pesher Nahum*, 217–30.

[17] On debates with the Pharisees in the *Damascus Document*, see especially Lawrence H. Schiffman, "The Pharisees and Their Legal Traditions According to the Dead Sea Scrolls," in *Qumran and Jerusalem: Studies in the Dead Sea Scrolls and the History of Judaism* (Grand Rapids: Eerdmans, 2010), 321–36 (327–31); VanderKam, "Pharisees," 226–27. On *Miqṣat Ma'ase Ha-Torah*, see Schiffman, "The New Halakhic Letter and the Origins of the Dead Sea Sect," in *Qumran and Jerusalem: Studies in the Dead Sea Scrolls and the History of Judaism* (Grand Rapids: Eerdmans, 2010), 112–22.

[18] See Berrin, *Pesher Nahum*, 219.

the sectarian belief that the community rightfully should hold these levers of power in Judean society.

Empowering a Disempowered Community

The world that the Dead Sea Scrolls sectarians inhabited generated a profound disconnect for the sectarians as they forged their self-identity. On the one hand, the sectarians viewed themselves as the elect of God and their priestly leaders as the only ones knowledgeable of the true application of the divine law.[19] In this sense, the sectarians regarded the reigning local power structure as a temporary aberration. Yet, they simultaneously recognized that they were a disempowered minority relative to the overpowering might of the Hasmoneans. It made no difference whether the portrait of Hasmonean power was real or imagined. Indeed, the narrative of victimhood crafted by the sectarians only served to reinforce their disempowered position. In both real and imagined terms, the sectarians possessed little ability to overturn the present power structure and assert their rightful place of leadership and authority.

The sectarian Dead Sea Scrolls offer insight into how the sectarians addressed these competing realities in a way that both confirmed their present overmatched position and affirmed their special status. Sectarian texts imagine an imminent end of days that would usher in a period in which all of its enemies—both foreigners and other Jews—would be vanquished in an end-time battle.[20] This portrait of a highly violent eschatological age is balanced by a remarkably nonviolent present time. No sectarian writings envision any present-time violent engagement with its perceived enemies. This approach stands in marked contrast to contemporary Jewish groups who responded very differently to their perceived oppressors. Both the Hasmoneans and the Zealots, for example, appealed to the "zeal of Phinehas" as part of their advocacy of immediate armed resistance against their enemies.[21]

While opposition to more powerful Jews and the Romans is pervasive throughout the sectarian writings, all hostile engagement is deferred until the end-time (see 1QS 9:21–23; 10:17–19; 1QH^a 14:20–21). Indeed, the very language

---

[19] On the sectarians' self-identity as the elect of God, see Alex P. Jassen, "Survival at the End of Days: Aspects of Soteriology in the Dead Sea Scrolls Pesharim," in *This World and the World to Come: Soteriology in Early Judaism* (ed. D. M. Gurtner; LSTS 74; London: T & T Clark, 2011), 193–210.

[20] This end-time military engagement is outlined in a group of interrelated war texts (1QM, 4Q471, 4Q491–496, 4Q285, 11Q14). For discussion of these texts, see especially Jean Duhaime, *The War Texts: 1QM and Related Manuscripts* (London: T & T Clark, 2004). On the eschatological war more specifically, see John J. Collins, *Apocalypticism in the Dead Sea Scrolls* (London: Routledge, 1997), 91–109.

[21] See 1 Macc 2:24–27; Josephus *B.J.* 4.155. See especially Martin Hengel, *The Zealots: Investigations into the Jewish Freedom Movement in the Period from Herod I until 70 A.D.* (Edinburgh: T & T Clark, 1989), 146–77. On the role of the "zeal of Phinehas" in sectarian ideology, see further Jassen, "War and Violence."

used in the *Rule of the Community* to defer violence—"I will return to no man the recompense of evil" (1QS 10:17)—is employed in the *War Scroll* to describe the point in time when God's fury is unleashed on the wicked:

> For into the hand of the oppressed you will deliver the [ene]mies of all the lands; into the hands of those who are prostrate in the dust, in order to bring down all mighty men of the peoples, to return the recompense of the wicked. (1QM 11:13–14; cf. 6:5–6; CD 7:9–10; 19:6–7)

The distinction between the lack of present-time hostile engagement and the expected eruption of eschatological violence is critical to framing the nature of the sectarians' relationship with their perceived enemies. As a powerless group, the sectarians were undoubtedly aware that they were no match for the Roman armies or even the more powerful Jews in Jerusalem. The sectarians articulated their opposition to the present world order in such a way that minimized the potential for present-time violent engagement, in which they recognized that they were overmatched. The violent eschatological vision serves in the present primarily as a rhetorical tool to empower the disempowered sectarian community. The sectarians crafted a "fantasy" of retributive violence in which the balance of power is reversed and their enemies are therefore brought to justice.[22]

In framing the sectarians' resistance to its enemies as rhetorical, I am positioning the Dead Sea Scrolls alongside other early Jewish and Christian literature that scholars have identified as advocating similar forms of imagined resistance. In recent years, scholarship on Jewish and Christian responses to the overwhelming power of empires has drawn heavily upon social-scientific analysis of how weaker members of a society respond when they are severely overmatched in physical strength.[23] Many texts reflect Jewish and Christian "fantasies" of future retributive

---

[22] I explore in greater detail this aspect of the community's violent worldview in Jassen, "Violence and the Dead Sea Scrolls" and "War and Violence." See similarly the article in this volume by Ehud Ben Zvi, p. 156.

[23] The most influential work in this regard is James C. Scott, *Domination and the Arts of Resistance: Hidden Transcripts* (New Haven: Yale University Press, 1990). See also idem, *Weapons of the Weak: Everyday Forms of Peasant Resistance* (New Haven: Yale University Press, 1985). Scott's work represents the theoretical underpinning of a wide body of scholarship on early Judaism and Christianity. Much of this has focused on the New Testament. See, e.g., Richard A. Horsley, *Jesus and Empire: The Kingdom of God and the New World Disorder* (Minneapolis: Fortress, 2003), and the many articles collected in three volumes edited by Horsley: *Paul and Empire: Religion and Power in Roman and Imperial Society* (Harrisburg: Trinity Press International, 1997); *Hidden Transcripts and the Arts of Resistance: Applying the Work of James C. Scott to Jesus and Paul* (SemeiaSt 48; Atlanta: Society of Biblical Literature, 2004); *In the Shadow of Empire: Reclaiming the Bible as a History of Faithful Resistance* (Louisville: Westminster John Knox, 2008) (with three contributions on the Hebrew Bible). On rabbinic literature, see Joshua Levinson, "The Athlete of Piety: Fatal Fictions in Rabbinic Literature," *Tarbiz* 68 (1999): 61–86 [Hebrew]; idem, "Tragedies Naturally Performed: Fatal Charades, Parodia Sacra, and the Death of Titus," in *Jewish Culture and Society Under the Christian Roman Empire* (ed. R. Kalmin and S. Schwartz; Leuven: Peeters, 2003), 349–82; Daniel Boyarin, *Dying for God: Martyrdom and the*

justice that will be meted out against the present-time oppressors—often by means of the same forms of domination previously employed by the oppressors. As in these texts, the internal discourse of imagined resistance in the Dead Sea Scrolls reverses the power of the Hasmoneans and Pharisees and the powerlessness of the sectarian community.

POWER AND (FALSE) PROPHECY IN SECOND TEMPLE JUDAISM

In spite of the sectarians' self-identity as the elect of God, sectarian writings preserve no explicit claims of prophetic identity for any of its leaders. The Teacher of Righteousness is commonly identified as having special access to God. Yet, he is never identified as a prophet. Indeed, the only contemporary individuals identified as prophets are the sectarian opponents.[24] This phenomenon can be explained in two ways. First, the sectarians recognized a shift in the way that humans accessed the divine word and accordingly crafted a new language that recognized the modified modes of prophetic and revelatory activity. At the same time, the Teacher of Righteousness and his followers had no doubt that they possessed unique access to God and that this relationship placed them in continuity with the classical prophets from ancient Israel.[25]

The second explanation pertains to the lingering suspicions regarding prophetic claims in the Second Temple period. Several late biblical and Second Temple

---

Making of Christianity and Judaism (Stanford: Stanford University Press, 1999), esp. 42–66; Beth A. Berkowitz, *Execution and Invention: Death Penalty Discourse in Early Rabbinic Judaism and Christian Cultures* (New York: Oxford University Press, 2006), esp. 153–79; Ra'anan S. Boustan, "Immolating Emperors: Spectacles of Imperial Suffering and the Making of a Jewish Minority Culture in Late Antiquity," in *Violence, Scripture, and Textual Practice*, 204–34. For Second Temple Judaism, see Kimberly B. Stratton, "Reinscribing Roman Violence in Fantasies of the End Times," in *Violence, Scripture, and Textual Practice*, 45–76; Richard A. Horsley, *Revolt of the Scribes: Resistance and Apocalyptic Origins* (Minneapolis: Fortress, 2010); Anathea E. Portier-Young, *Apocalypse against Empire: Theologies of Resistance in Early Judaism* (Grand Rapids: Eerdmans, 2011).

[24] On prophecy in the Dead Sea Scrolls, see James E. Bowley, "Prophets and Prophecy at Qumran," in *The Dead Sea Scrolls after Fifty Years: A Comprehensive Assessment* (ed. J. C. Vander-Kam and P. W. Flint; Leiden: Brill, 1998–1999), 2:344–78; George J. Brooke, "Prophecy and Prophets in the Dead Sea Scrolls: Looking Backwards and Forwards," in *Prophets, Prophecy and Prophetic Texts in Second Temple Judaism* (ed. M. H. Floyd and R. D. Haak; LHBOTS 427; New York/London: T & T Clark, 2006), 151–65; Alex P. Jassen, *Mediating the Divine: Prophecy and Revelation in the Dead Sea Scrolls and Second Temple Judaism* (STDJ 68; Leiden: Brill, 2007); Martti Nissinen, "Transmitting Divine Mysteries: The Prophetic Role of Wisdom Teachers in the Dead Sea Scrolls," in *Scripture in Transition: Essays on the Septuagint, Hebrew Bible, and Dead Sea Scrolls in Honour of Raija Sollamo* (ed. A. Voitila and J. Jokiranta; JSJSup 126; Leiden: Brill, 2008), 513–33; Kristin de Troyer, Armin Lange, and Lucas L. Schulte, eds., *Prophecy after the Prophets? The Contribution of the Dead Sea Scrolls to the Understanding of Biblical and Extra-Biblical Prophecy* (CBET 52; Leuven: Peeters, 2009).

[25] See Jassen, *Mediating the Divine*, 381–82 (cf. idem, "Prophets and Prophecy in the Qumran Community," *AJSR* 32 (2008): 299–334 [333–34]). See also Bowley, "Prophets," 2:372–73.

period texts paint a portrait of a society deeply suspicious of prophetic claims.[26] The sectarian community's concern for contemporary false prophets can be detected in three texts among the Dead Sea Scrolls. The *Temple Scroll* (11QT[a] 54:8–18) and the *Moses Apocryphon* (4Q375) both contain a set of laws based on Deuteronomic principles for identifying and prosecuting a false prophet. Similarly *4QList of False Prophets* (4Q339) contains a register of false prophets in Israel's history.[27] On the one hand, the concern in these texts for discerning between true and false prophecy suggests that prophetic activity was still very much alive in the Second Temple period.[28] These texts likewise indicate that the sectarians were sensitive to the widespread suspicions regarding contemporary prophetic claims. In this regard, the sectarians were likely hesitant to brand their own revelatory claims with this still suspicious terminology.[29] This same situation explains why the sectarians simultaneously ascribe prophetic claims to their opponents.

The emerging suspicions in the Second Temple period regarding prophecy are best illustrated by Zech 13:2–6:[30]

> (2) In that day, too—declares the Lord of Hosts—I will erase the very names of the idols from the land; they shall not be uttered any more. And I will also make the "prophets" and the unclean spirit vanish from the land. (3) If anyone "prophesies" thereafter, his own father and mother, who brought him into the world, will say to him, "You shall die, for you have lied in the name of the Lord"; and his own father and mother, who brought him into the world, will put him to death when he "prophesies." (4) In that day, every "prophet" will be ashamed of the "visions" [he had] when he "prophesied." In order to deceive, he will not wear a hairy mantle, (5) and he will declare, "I am not a 'prophet'; I am a tiller of the soil; you see, I was plied with the red stuff from my youth on." (6) And if he is asked, "What are those sores on your back?" he will reply, "From being beaten in the homes of my friends."

---

[26] On this issue, see more fully David L. Petersen, *Late Israelite Prophecy: Studies in Deutero-Prophetic Literature and in Chronicles* (Missoula: Scholars Press, 1977), 27–38 (esp. 37–38); Günter Stemberger, "Propheten und Prophetie in der Tradition des nachbiblischen Judentums," in *Prophetie und Charisma* (ed. W. H. Schmidt and E. Dassmann; Jahrbuch für Biblische Theologie 14; Neukirchen-Vluyn: Neukirchener, 1999), 145–74 (147–49); Armin Lange, "Reading the Decline of Prophecy," in *Reading the Present in the Qumran Library: The Perception of the Contemporary by Means of Scriptural Interpretations* (ed. K. de Troyer and A. Lange; SBLSymS 30; Atlanta: Society of Biblical Literature, 2005), 181–91 (181–84); Martti Nissinen, "The Dubious Image of Prophecy," in *Prophets, Prophecy and Prophetic Texts in Second Temple Judaism* (ed. M. H. Floyd and R. D. Haak; LHBOTS 427; New York / London: T & T Clark, 2006), 26–41.

[27] See my treatment of these passages in Jassen, *Mediating the Divine*, 299–306. *4QList of False Prophets* is discussed more fully below.

[28] As argued in Brooke, "Prophecy," 158–60; Jassen, *Mediating the Divine*, 299–306.

[29] See Jassen, "Prophets and Prophecy," 334 n. 117.

[30] On this passage, see especially (with earlier literature cited therein): Carol L. Meyers and Eric M. Meyers, *Zechariah 9–14* (AB 25C; New York: Doubleday, 1993), 399–404; Nissinen, "Dubious Image," 35–38; L. Stephen Cook, *On the Question of the "Cessation of Prophecy" in Ancient Judaism* (TSAJ 145; Tübingen: Mohr Siebeck, 2011), 58–63.

Zechariah 13:2 seems to target prophets who prophesy in the name of other gods, though it may also have in mind Yahwistic prophets.[31] The remainder of the invective, however, focuses exclusively on Yahwistic prophets. Verse three condemns the prophet who speaks falsely in the name of Yahweh, thereby invoking the Deuteronomic litmus test for true prophecy (Deut 18:18–22).[32] Moreover, this passage contains several allusions to "true" prophets from Israel's past. The "hairy mantle," for example, is likely an allusion to the prophetic mission of Elijah.[33] Zechariah 13:2–6 contrasts the true prophets of old with the illegitimate prophets of the present. In so doing, however, this passage simultaneously casts aspersions on all individuals claiming to be prophets.

As in other biblical presentations of illegitimate prophets, Zech 13:2–6 still refers to the prophets with the unqualified title "prophet" (נביא) even as it strongly condemns their message as illegitimate. Later Second Temple period texts, however, reframe these prophets as unequivocally "false." Thus, for example, the Septuagint translates נביא as ψευδοπροφήτης in all cases where the individuals are deemed to be false prophets, including Zech 13:2.[34] The accusation of false prophecy becomes a potent tool to delegitimize the very claim of these individuals to speak on behalf of God.[35]

This strategy is especially on display in Josephus's account of two charismatic prophets from the first century CE: the "Egyptian" (B.J. 2.259–63; Ant. 20.169–71; cf. Acts 21:38) and Theudas (Ant. 20:97–98; cf. Acts 5:36–38).[36] Josephus frames these two individuals as part of the same seditious millenarian tendencies that led to the disastrous revolt against Rome.[37] Josephus's condemnation of both as dangerous charlatans is achieved primarily through casting aspersions on their prophetic claims. For the Egyptian, Josephus denies any truth to his prophetic claims by introducing him simply as a "false prophet" (ψευδοπροφήτης; B.J. 2.261). As in the case of the Egyptian, Josephus traces the roots of the failed zealotry against Rome to a first century CE "false prophet" (B.J. 6.285; cf. 2.258). In all these cases, Josephus employs the designation "false prophet" alongside terms such as "imposter" (γόης) and "deceiver" (ἀπατεών) (e.g., B.J. 2.259; Ant. 20.167) to reject the very notion that

---

[31] See Meyers and Meyers, Zechariah 9–14, 371.

[32] Meyers and Meyers, Zechariah 9–14, 375.

[33] Nissinen, "Dubious Image," 36.

[34] On this transition, see James L. Crenshaw, Prophetic Conflict: Its Effect upon Israelite Religion (BZAW 124; Berlin: de Gruyter, 1971), 1–4; Jannes Reiling, "The Use of ΨΕΥΔΟΠΡΟΦΗΤΗΣ in the Septuagint, Philo, and Josephus," NovT 13 (1971): 147–56.

[35] See especially Reiling, "The Use of ΨΕΥΔΟΠΡΟΦΗΤΗΣ," 148.

[36] On these two and other so-called "sign prophets" in Josephus, see especially P. W. Barnett, "The Jewish Sign Prophets," in The Historical Jesus in Recent Research (ed. J. D. G. Dunn and S. McKnight; Winona Lake: Eisenbrauns, 2005), 444–62; Rebecca Gray, Prophetic Figures in Late Second Temple Jewish Palestine: The Evidence from Josephus (Oxford: Oxford University Press, 1993), 112–44.

[37] See Joseph Blenkinsopp, "Prophecy and Priesthood in Josephus," JJS 25 (1974): 239–62 (259–60); David E. Aune, Prophecy in Early Christianity and the Ancient Mediterranean World (Grand Rapids: Eerdmans, 1983), 127–29.

these individuals have any access to God.[38] A similar tactic seems to be employed in Acts 13:6 as part of a broader attempt to discredit Bar-Jesus, who is identified as a "magician" (μάγος) and "false prophet."[39]

Similar to the Septuagint's use of the term, Josephus's accusation of pseudo-prophecy can also represent a diversion from the scriptural description of an individual as simply a "prophet."[40] In *Ant.* 8.236, for example, Josephus introduces the "Old prophet from Bethel" (1 Kgs 13:11) as "a certain vile old man, a false prophet." Josephus's strategy for delegitimizing this prophetic figure is similarly found in *4QList of False Prophets*, where the same individual is listed among those "false prophets that arose against Israel" (4Q339 3).[41] Neither of these passages challenges the oracular capabilities of the prophet from Bethel. Rather, he is rebranded as the purveyor of misguided prophetic content.

The evidence of the Septuagint and Josephus indicates that by the end of the Second Temple period the charge of false prophecy had a wide currency. To be sure, Josephus and the Greek translators had significantly different motivations for branding specific individuals as false prophets. Yet, in both cases, these accusations have the effect of undercutting the revelatory reputation of the targeted individual and in so doing delegitimizing the content of the prophetic speech.

POWER AND (FALSE) PROPHECY IN THE DEAD SEA SCROLLS

As noted above, while the Dead Sea Scrolls sectarians shun explicit prophetic self-identity, they simultaneously display a keen interest in the prophetic claims of their opponents. This seemingly unexpected reversal must be positioned within the same dynamic between true and false prophecy in Second Temple Judaism. The sectarian concern with the prophetic claims of their opponents functions as a rhetorical strategy for delegitimizing the prestige and authority of their more powerful enemies in the eyes of the sectarian readers of these texts. In this section,

---

[38] See Louis H. Feldman, "Prophets and Prophecy in Josephus," in *Prophets, Prophecy and Prophetic Texts in Second Temple Judaism* (ed. M. H. Floyd and R. D. Haak; LHBOTS 427; New York/London: T & T Clark, 2006), 210–39 (230); Gray, *Prophetic Figures*, 143–44; Aune, *Prophecy*, 128–29. See also Burkett, "Sign Prophets," 448, 450, who proposes that the label "imposter" locates these false prophets alongside similar imposters from ancient Egypt's court magicians—in contrast to the true prophet of the Exodus, Moses.

[39] See Hans-Josef Klauck, *Magic and Paganism in Early Christianity: The World of the Acts of the Apostles* (Edinburgh: T & T Clark, 2000), 47–50; Rick Strelen, "Who Was Bar Jesus (Acts 13,6-12)?" *Bib* 85 (2004): 65–81 (66). As observed by Strelen, classical writers commonly associate the "magician" (μάγος) with the "imposter" (γόης). A more general concern for false prophets is found elsewhere in the New Testament. See especially Matt 7:15; 24:11; Mark 13:22; 2 Pet 2:1; 1 John 4:1, and treatment in Aune, *Prophecy*, 222–29.

[40] For the use of ψευδοπροφήτης in Josephus's scriptural rewriting, see *Ant.* 8.236, 242, 318, 402, 406, 409; 9.133-37; 10.66, 104, 111. These examples are treated more fully in Reiling, "The Use of ΨΕΥΔΟΠΡΟΦΗΤΗΣ," 155; Gray, *Prophetic Figures*, 129–30, 143.

[41] See further below.

I analyze several passages that employ this technique with Pharisaic and Hasmonean enemies as their target.

Delegitimizing Pharisaic Prophetic Claims

FALSE PROPHECY AND THE PHARISEES IN THE *THANKSGIVING HYMNS*: The first passage I
examine comes from the *Thanksgiving Hymns* (1QHᵃ 12:5–29).[42] This hymn employs
highly charged rhetorical language to outline the bitter struggle between the sectarians and their opponents. This particular hymn frames this conflict in terms of
competing claims of access to the divine.[43] Among the many recurring themes in
the hymn is the hymnist's distinct claim to have unfettered access to the divine.
This claim is underscored by the chiastic *inclusio* that frames the entire hymn (as
indicated by the underlining below). At the beginning of the hymn, the hymnist
declares:

> (5) *vacat* I give thanks to you, O Lord, for you have made my face shine by your
> covenant, and [ ] (6) [ ] I seek you, and as an enduring dawning, as [perfe]ct light,
> you have revealed yourself to me ... (8) Neither did they esteem me; even when
> you displayed your might through me.

Toward the end of the hymn, he once again asserts that:

> For (23) they esteem [me] not [thou]gh you display your might through me, and
> reveal yourself to me in your strength as a perfect light.

Without utilizing any explicit prophetic terminology, the hymnist asserts his identity as one who has unique access to the divine.[44]

In the intervening passages, however, it is the hymnist's enemies who are repeatedly identified with explicit prophetic terminology. The opponents are condemned for being led by "mediators of deceit" (מליצי רמיה) (ll. 6–7) and "mediators
of a lie" (מליצי כזב) (ll. 9–10).[45] The hymn continues by denouncing these same enemies as "seers of deceit (חזה רמיה) (l. 10) and "seers of error" (חזה תעות) (l. 20).[46]

---

[42] This hymnic unit is generally understood as part of a larger hymn that continues in
12:29–13:4 by describing the failings of humans. See Julie A. Hughes, *Scriptural Allusions and
Exegesis in the Hodayot* (STDJ 59; Leiden: Brill, 2006), 103–4. See parallel content in 4Q430 1 2–5;
4Q432 8 1

[43] For my earlier treatments of this hymn—focusing primarily on the sectarian revelatory claims therein—see Jassen, *Mediating the Divine*, 280–90; idem, "Prophets and Prophecy,"
311–18.

[44] See Jassen, "Prophets and Prophecy," 313–14, 317–18.

[45] On the prophetic sense of מליץ ("mediator"), see S. Holm-Nielsen, *Hodayot: Psalms from
Qumran* (ATDan 2; Aarhus: Universitetsforlaget, 1960), 161 n. 29; Hughes, *Scriptural Allusions*,
107; Nissinen, "Transmitting," 531.

[46] These passages use the common prophetic term חזה. On this term in the Hebrew Bible
and Second Temple texts, see discussion in Jassen, *Mediating the Divine*, 65–83.

Most significantly, the sectarian opponents are condemned for attempting to seek God with the aid of "lying prophets" (נביאי כזב) (l. 16).

The hymn employs a twofold approach to delegitimize the revelatory claims of the opponents. First, following the trend for Second Temple period texts discussed earlier, the very prophetic titles employed are combined with a range of adjectives that simultaneously deny any prophetic abilities for these individuals. Second, the would-be prophetic claims of the opponents are countered by the hymnist's claim to true revelation (see ll. 5–6, 8, 10, 22–23, 27–29), an assertion rhetorically strengthened by the *inclusio* that surrounds the entire hymn. The point of the hymn is clear: the prophetic claims of the enemies are unfounded and should not be trusted. In contrast, the hymnist is a recipient of true revelation.

In order to understand better the purpose of the delegitimization of the revelatory claims of the sectarians' enemies, we need to look more closely at the function of opponents' claims. Lines 9–11 lay bare the aspirations of the would-be prophetic opponents:

> But they are mediators of (10) a lie and visionaries of deceit. They have plotted wickedness against me, so as to exchange your law, which you spoke distinctively in my heart, for smooth things (חלקות) (11) directed to your people.

The hymn condemns the opponents for their misguided attempts to change the divine law. In keeping with the oppositional nature of the hymn, the hymnist locates the enemies' misguided application of the law alongside his affirmation to have received direct instruction from God on the correct understanding of the law.

The enemies are castigated for attempting to alter the law on behalf of the general public—to exchange the law for "smooth things" (חלקות). This accusation echoes the similar description in line seven of the enemies as "flattering (החליקו) themselves with words." The term חלקות ("smooth things") and the associated verb are generally regarded as a pun on the Pharisaic term *halakhot* (הלכות) and contain an implicit condemnation of the Pharisaic law and its exegetical basis. It thus stands behind the pejorative designation of the Pharisees as "Seekers after Smooth Things."[47] The use of the root חלק in both verbal and nominal form draws on scriptural usages that highlight misguided and deceitful teaching.[48] As applied to the Pharisees, it underscores the sectarian understanding of the Pharisees as "false interpreters of the Torah who derive incorrect legal rulings from their exegesis."[49]

The hymn associates the pursuit of "smooth things" with the misguided "spouters" (l. 6: מטיף), "visionaries" (l. 10: חזה), and "mediators" (ll. 7, 9: מליץ). The twofold use of חלק and מליץ echoes the similar twofold appearance of these expressions in poetic parallelism in column ten of the *Thanksgiving Hymns* (1QHª

---

[47] See bibliography above, n. 14.
[48] See VanderKam, "Those Who Look for Smooth Things," 476.
[49] Schiffman, "Pharisees and Sadducees," 341.

10:14–15, 31–32).[50] The constellation of these negative descriptions of the sectarians' enemies reinforces the portrait of the Pharisees as purveyors of false teachings who appeal to their position of authority in order to mislead the unsuspecting Jewish public. The hymn exposes this as nothing more than another form of false prophecy.

Lines 12–16 further frame the oppositional relationship between the sectarians and their enemies within the context of the appeal to divine sanction. The hymn balances the presentation of the hymnist's divine access by relating how the opponents also seek divine sanction for their actions. Thus, the hymn continues by relating a number of methods by which the sectarians' enemies attempt to gain divine approval for their interpretation of the Torah, all of which are categorically condemned by the hymnist. The primary strategy of the opponents is to consult God through the agency of lying prophets (l. 16):

> They are pretenders; they hatch the plots of Belial, (14) they seek you with a double heart, and are not found in your truth. A root producing poison and wormwood is in their scheming. (15) With a willful heart they look about and seek you in idols. They have set the stumbling block of their iniquity before themselves, and they come (16) to seek you through the words of lying prophets corrupted by error (נביאי כזב מפותי תעות). With mo[c]king lips and a strange tongue they speak to your people (17) so as to make a mockery of all their works by deceit.

This hymn paints a portrait of the sectarian opponents as illegitimate interpreters of the law who seek prophetic support for their attempts to mislead the broader public regarding the correct understanding and application of the law. In addition to the condemnation of these opponents as "seeking smooth things," several other keywords draw from other sectarian denouncements of the Pharisees. In so doing, the hymn reinforces the negative portrait of the secatarians' rival for the interpretation of the law.

"Lying" and "misleading" are common charges leveled against the Pharisees and their leaders. The *Damascus Document*, for example, describes the "Man of Mockery" (איש הלצון)—who is associated with the "Seekers After Smooth Things"— as "spouting on Israel false waters" (הטיף לישראל מימי כזב) and misleading Israel (ויתעם) (CD 1:14–15).[51] This individual is likely the same person as the "Man of Lie" (איש הכזב) and the "Spouter of Lies" (מטיף הכזב) known from other sectarian literature.[52] *Pesher Psalms* condemns the "Man of Lie" for misleading (התעה) the people with false teachings that divert attention away from the true "mediator of knowledge" (מליץ דעת) (4Q171 1–10 i 26–27). The "Spouter of Lies" similarly misleads "many" in *Pesher Habakkuk* (1QpHab 10:9). The emphasis in these passages on misguided leadership (תעה-*hiph'il*) echoes the portrait of the Pharisees in *Pesher Nahum* treated above.[53] It is therefore significant that one of the major themes of

---

[50] See Jassen, *Mediating the Divine*, 76–80.
[51] See VanderKam, "Pharisees," 233.
[52] VanderKam, "Pharisees," 234.
[53] Cf. Jassen, *Mediating the Divine*, 293–94. See also CD 5:20, discussed below.

the hymn in column 12 is the condemnation of the opponents for leading their followers astray (תעה-hiph'il/תעות: ll. 7, 16, 20). This portrait is enhanced by the hymn's use of "deceit" (מרמה/רמיה) as a *Leitwort* to characterize the opponents (ll. 10, 17, 21).

The payoff to this long onslaught of Pharisaic revelatory claims is clear. The Pharisaic self-identification as expert interpreters of the divine law is unequivocally illegitimate. More importantly, however, the Pharisaic attempts to draw on these prophetic claims in order to defend their erroneous interpretation of the law are equally illegitimate. Rather, the hymn reframes the Pharisaic claims as yet another example of their misguided leadership and false interpretation of the law. Again, the hymnist contrasts this portrait with his own claim that God "made my face shine by your covenant" (l. 5) and "spoke (the law) distinctly in my heart" (l. 10).

Moreover, the hymn couches a fantasy of retributive justice within the condemnation of the enemies. After outlining the misguided leadership of the Pharisees in lines 11–12, the hymnist imagines that God will recognize the enemies as among the lot of Belial and therefore reject them (ll. 12–13). The hymn later frames this rejection in terms of future divine judgment: "You shall cut off in ju[dgm]ent all deceitful men; seers of error shall no longer be found" (l. 20). This expectation was no doubt bolstered by scriptural images of retributive justice against "smooth speakers."[54] Thus, Ps 12:3–4 both condemns smooth speakers and eagerly anticipates the divine justice that will be meted out against them:

Men speak lies to one another; their speech is smooth (חלקות); they talk with duplicity.

May the Lord cut off all flattering (חלקות) lips, every tongue that speaks arrogance.

Similarly, Jer 23:12 uses the reduplicated form חלקלקות in outlining the anticipated downfall of the false prophets:

Assuredly, their path shall become like slippery ground (חלקלקות); they shall be thrust into darkness and there they shall fall; for I will bring disaster upon them, the year of their doom—declares the Lord.

The appropriation of these two visions of retributive justice would have been further reinforced by the use of חלקות and חלקלקות as keywords in Dan 11 to characterize both the detested Antiochus IV (vv. 21, 32) and other Jews who do not share Daniel's model of resistance (v. 34). As in Dan 11, the hymn anticipates the retributive justice awaiting Antiochus and the reversal of the power of the insincere Jews. The hymn continues by envisioning this future time when "those who are in harmony with you shall stand before you forever, and those who walk in the

---

[54] I am grateful to Dr. Shalom Holtz for kindly bringing these intertextual references to my attention.

way of your heart shall be secure for evermore" (ll. 21–22). In so doing, the hymn's fantasy of retributive violence is framed as a reversal of power: the currently empowered Pharisees will be judged and punished for their misguided leadership. At that time, the currently disempowered sectarians will be restored to their position of prestige and authority.

FALSE PROPHECY AND THE PHARISEES IN THE *DAMASCUS DOCUMENT:* The *Damascus Document* provides another example of the charge of false prophecy employed to delegitimize Pharisaic legal authority:

> And at the time of the desolation of the land, the movers of the boundary (מסיגי הגבול) arose and they led Israel astray (ויתעו) (21) and the land became desolate, for they (i.e., the movers of the boundary) spoke defiantly against commandments of God (sent) through Moses and also (1) through the ones anointed with the holy (spirit). And they prophesied falsehood (וינבאו שקר), so as to lead Israel away from (2) God. (CD 5:20–6:1)

This passage introduces a group identified only as the "movers of the boundary" who lead Israel astray during the time of the "desolation of the land." Scholars have long debated the historical framework presumed by this passage.[55] Several keywords and themes in this passage strongly suggest that CD 5:20–6:1, as in the *Thanksgiving Hymns,* intends to condemn the Pharisees for their misguided leadership and incorrect interpretation of the law. The expression "movers of the boundary" (מסיגי הגבול) appears elsewhere in the *Damascus Document* and sectarian literature.[56] Unfortunately, the fragmentary character of these passages precludes arriving at any definitive conclusions.

Closely related to this phrase, however, is the *Damascus Document*'s condemnation of those that move (ולסיע) the boundary (CD 1:16).[57] This passage should be situated in *Damascus Document*'s recurring motif of "moving the boundary." The "boundary" in these expressions refers to the law.[58] Presumably, this expression is employed in order to criticize the sectarian enemies for their faulty interpretation of the law. Through this mistaken approach to the law, they "move" the established boundaries of the law.

---

[55] I have treated many of these issues at length in Jassen, *Mediating the Divine,* 290–96.

[56] CD 19:15–16 ∥ 8:3 cites in full Hos 5:10, upon which the expression is dependent; 4Q266 (4QD^a) 1 a–b 4; 4Q280 (4QCurses) 3 2. The expression appears in complete isolation in 4Q471 1 2 and 4Q280 3 2. The similar phrase in *4QInstruction* (4Q416 2 iv 6; 4Q418 9 + 9a-c 7) and *4QInstruction-like Composition B* (424 3 9) seems unrelated to the expression in the *Damascus Document.* Both are likely dependent on a similar reading of Hosea. The analysis of the expression that follows draws on my treatment in Jassen, *Mediating the Divine,* 292–93.

[57] The parallel text in 4Q266 2 i 19 has ו[להסיע. The language of this phrase is taken from Deut 19:14 where the root סוג is employed, as in the other passages from the *Damascus Document.* Ginzberg questions whether the text in the *Damascus Document* should therefore be emended (*An Unknown Jewish Sect* [New York: Jewish Theological Seminary, 1976], 6). This seems unlikely in light of the Cave 4 parallel.

[58] See Naphtali Wieder, *The Judean Scrolls and Karaism* (London: East and West Library, 1962), 140–41; Chaim Rabin, *The Zadokite Documents* (Oxford: Clarendon, 1954), 4–5.

The passage in column one of the *Damascus Document* goes on to clarify the treacherous actions of those that move the boundary as: "They sought smooth things" (דרשו בחלקות) (CD 1:18). This characterization ensures that the intended historical referent in column one of the *Damascus Document* is the Pharisees, who are thus also the "movers of the boundary."[59] Based on this evidence, the "movers of the boundary" in CD 5:20 may similarly be identified with the Pharisees.[60] The identification of the "movers of the boundary" as the Pharisees is further corroborated by the application to them of the keyword "to lead astray" (תעה–*hiph'il*).[61]

CD 5:20–6:1 contains a constellation of interrelated accusations leveled against the "movers of the boundary." The charge that the "movers of the boundary" erroneously interpret the law is amplified by the accusation that they reject the commandments as transmitted through Moses and the Prophets (i.e., "the ones anointed with the holy [spirit])."[62] The reference to Moses and the Prophets is an allusion to the sectarian belief that the full meaning of the Torah has been progressively revealed, first to Moses and then to the ancient Prophets. Moreover, the sectarians regarded themselves as the next and last stage in the progressive revelation of law.[63] The Pharisees' rejection of the progressive revelation is therefore implicitly a rejection of the sectarians' present claim to possess the meaning of the Torah. Thus, the Pharisees are not condemned here for rejecting the Torah itself, but rather the sectarians' interpretation of the Torah as revealed throughout the generations. The Pharisees instead offer their incorrect interpretation. All of the charges leveled against the "movers of boundary" are consistent with other condemnations of the Pharisees in the sectarian scrolls.

The final accusation against the Pharisees in CD 5:20–6:2 is that "they prophesied falsehood." This charge is likely a continuation of the claim that the Pharisees falsely interpret the Torah. Yet, the *Damascus Document* provides no explanation as to why this condemnation is specifically framed as false prophecy. This accusation should likely be understood in the context of the earlier assertion that the "movers of the boundary" spurned the ancient lawgiving prophets. As noted above, the *Damascus Document* presents Moses and the Prophets here as the first two stages in the progressive revelation of law. The sectarians regard themselves as the most recent recipients of this progressive revelation and commensurate with the ancient prophets. The Pharisees are therefore condemned for rejecting the entire scope of revealed understanding of the Torah and instead offering their own false interpretation. From the perspective of the *Damascus Document*, however, the Pharisaic interpretation is illegitimate and therefore framed as the opposite of the true revelation to the sectarians. As in the *Thanksgiving Hymns*, the charge of false

---

[59] See VanderKam, "Smooth Things," 467.

[60] Schiffman, "Pharisees," 325.

[61] See Jassen, *Mediating the Divine*, 293–94.

[62] On the identification of "the ones anointed with the holy (spirit)" as ancient prophets, see Jassen, *Mediating the Divine*, 99–100.

[63] See Alex P. Jassen, "The Presentation of the Ancient Prophets as Lawgivers at Qumran," *JBL* 127 (2008): 307–37.

prophecy delegitimizes the teachings of the Pharisees and their claim to authority in Jewish society.

Delegitimizing Hasmonean Prophetic Claims

Several additional passages from the Dead Sea Scrolls reflect the degree to which the sectarians sought to delegitimize the prophetic claims of the Hasmonean priests/kings. Similar to the passages discussed above regarding the Pharisees, the indictment of Hasmonean prophetic claims as false provides a rhetorical tool for the sectarians to deny the legitimacy of the Hasmonean grip on power and to imagine a scenario in which the Hasmonean monopoly on royal and priestly power is reversed.

FALSE PROPHECY AND THE HASMONEANS IN 4QTESTIMONIA: The first text that is relevant to this discussion is 4QTestimonia (4Q175).[64] This manuscript combines four scriptural passages without any intervening exegetical elaboration:

1. Lines 1–8: Exod 20:22 according to the pre-Samaritan Pentateuch (= MT Deut 5:25–26 and 18:18–19)
2. Line 8–13: Num 24:15–17
3. Lines 13–20: Deut 33:8–11
4. Lines 21–30: *Apocryphon of Joshua* (4Q379) 22 ii 7–14

The combination of the first three passages has long been understood as affirming sectarian eschatological aspirations. Thus, the first passage from Exod 20:22 in the pre-Samaritan Pentateuch textual tradition anticipates the arrival of an eschatological prophet. Numbers 24:15–17 reflects an understanding of Balaam's prophecy as referring to the royal messiah, while Deut 33:8–11 is regarded as portending the priestly Messiah. Taken together, these passages confirm the scriptural basis for the sectarians' expectation of three eschatological protagonists.[65]

At first glance, the final passage seems ill fitted to this catena of eschatological prooftexts. The cited passage from the *Apocryphon of Joshua* contains an expansion of Joshua's curse against the rebuilder of Jericho (Jos 6:26):

> (21) When Joshua finished praying and offering psalms of praise, (22) he said, "Cursed be anyone who tries to rebuild this city! With his firstborn (23) he shall lay its foundation, and with this youngest he shall set up its gates!" (Jos 6:26). Be-

---

[64] The *editio princeps* appears in John M. Allegro with Arnold A. Anderson, *Qumran Cave 4/I (4Q158–4Q186)* (DJD 5; Oxford: Clarendon, 1968), 57–60. This text has been the subject of intense scholarly analysis. In addition to the bibliography provided in the following notes, see also the recent edition prepared by Frank Moore Cross in *The Dead Sea Scrolls: Hebrew, Aramaic, and Greek Texts with English Translations: Pesharim, Other Commentaries, and Related Documents* (ed. J. H. Charlesworth; PTSDSSP 6b; Tübingen: Mohr Siebeck; Louisville: Westminster John Knox, 2002), 312–19.

[65] See Géza G. Xeravits, *King, Priest, Prophet: Positive Eschatological Protagonists in the Qumran Library* (STDJ 47; Leiden: Brill, 2003), 57–58.

hold, one cursed man, one belonging to Belial, (24) is about to arise to be a fow[ler's n]et to his people and a source of destruction to all his neighbors. Then shall arise (25) [so]ns [after him,] the two of them [to b]e weapons of violence. They shall rebuild (26) [this city and s]et up for it a wall and towers, creating a stronghold of evil (27) [and a great wickedness] in Israel, a thing of horror in Ephraim and Judah. (28) [. . .] They shall [wo]rk blasphemy in the land, a great uncleanness among the children of (29) [Jacob. They shall pour out blo]od like water upon the bulwark of the daughter of Zion and within the city limits of (30) Jerusalem. (4Q175 21–30)

As many scholars have noted, the target of this expanded curse in the *4QTestimonia* is likely the Hasmonean king John Hyrcanus I (134–104 BCE), who undertook significant building projects at Jericho.[66] In its new location in *4QTestimonia*, the passage from the *Apocryphon of Joshua* condemns John Hyrcanus as a "man of Belial" whose building projects yield only violence and bloodshed.[67] Eshel has further argued that the death of Hyrcanus's two sons Antigonus and Aristobulus I (104/3 BCE) is regarded as the fulfillment of Joshua's curse on the builder of Jericho. This is based on the interpretation of "with his firstborn" (בבכורו) and "with his youngest" (ובצעירו) from Jos 6:26 as implying that these children will die on account of the actions of their father in rebuilding Jericho.[68]

Bertholet rightly notes that *4QTestimonia* never mentions the death of the two sons. Rather, lines 25–26 indicate that these sons worked together with their father to rebuild the city. She therefore renders the *bet* of בבכורו and בצעירו as simply "with" or "with the help of."[69] Following this interpretation, Jos 6:26 would have been understood as containing a general curse against the rebuilder of Jericho, followed by a declarative statement that this rebuilding was done with the aid of his sons. As further noted by Bertholet, however, even if the curse was not under-

---

[66] This suggestion is commonplace in scholarly literature on *4QTestimonia*. See especially Eshel, "The Succession of High Priests," 63–90; Katell Bertholet, "4QTestimonia as a Polemic against the Prophetic Claims of John Hyrcanus," in *Prophecy after the Prophets: The Contribution of the Dead Sea Scrolls to the Understanding of Biblical and Extra-Biblical Prophecy* (ed. K. de Troyer, A. Lange, and L. L. Schulte; CBET 52; Leuven: Peeters, 2009), 99–118. As noted by Eshel (pp. 69–70), scholars have offered a host of different explanations for the object of the curse in the *Apocryphon of Joshua*. The background for the composition of the *Apocryphon of Joshua*, however, must be distinguished from how the curse was understood in its use in *4QTestimonia* (so also Bertholet, pp. 102–3). For *4QTestimonia*, Eshel summarizes other suggestions for the Hasmonean identification of the man of Belial. Eshel's arguments in favor of identifying the man of Belial with John Hyrcanus, however, are much stronger.

[67] Note that Eshel, "The Succession of High Priests," 83–86, argues that the *Apocryphon of Joshua* is citing *4QTestimonia*. Bertholet, "4QTestimonia," 100–3, responds to each of Eshel's arguments and defends the more widespread view that *4QTestimonia* is citing the *Apocryphon of Joshua*.

[68] Hence NJPS on Jos 6:26: "At the cost of his firstborn . . . his youngest." This is clearly the understanding of Jos 6:26 in 1 Kgs 16:34.

[69] Bertholet, "4QTestimonia," 106–7. She is following an earlier suggestion by Carol Newsom, "The 'Psalms of Joshua' from Qumran Cave 4," *JJS* 39 (1988): 56–73 (60).

stood to refer to the death of Hyrcanus's sons, the other evidence pointing in the direction of identifying the "man of Belial" as John Hyrcanus is compelling.

This scathing invective against John Hyrcanus follows after three passages that affirm the anticipated arrival of a future prophet, king, and priest. As has been correctly observed by numerous readers of this text, 4QTestimonia polemically challenges John Hyrcanus's claim to all three of these offices.[70] Bertholet further suggests that 4QTestimonia is specifically directed at Hyrcanus's unification of all of these offices in one person. As the first three passages in 4QTestimonia affirm, these three offices should be held by three different people.[71]

The rejection of Hyrcanus's prophetic claims must be situated in broader traditions about Hyrcanus as a prophet. In several places, Josephus admiringly calls attention to Hyrcanus's prophetic capabilities (Ant. 13.282–83; 322–23). Most famously, Josephus concludes his account of Hyrcanus's reign with the following summation:

> He was esteemed by God worthy of three of the greatest privileges: the government of his nation, the dignity of the high priesthood, and prophecy; for God was with him, and enabled him to know futurities; and to foretell this in particular, that, as to his two eldest sons, he foretold that they would not long continue in the government of public affairs. (Ant. 13.299–300; cf. B.J. 1.68–69)

As noted by Rebecca Gray, Josephus's description of John Hyrcanus as a prophet seems to be drawing on a broader set of sources.[72] Indeed, the tradition of Hyrcanus's prophetic identity is known from later rabbinic literature (e.g., t.Soṭ. 13:5). It is very likely therefore that others besides Josephus acknowledged Hyrcanus's prophetic identity and similarly admired him for it. 4QTestimonia reflect an opposing stream in Second Temple Judaism that rejects the identification of Hyrcanus as a prophet alongside the rejection of Hasmonean royal and priestly claims.

The preceding description of the polemical nature of 4QTestimonia toward John Hyrcanus is entirely correct. In what follows, however, I suggest that there is an additional rhetorical layer to this text that positions it as yet another example of the sectarians' attempt to deny the legitimacy of Hasmonean power and prestige. 4QTestimonia does more than merely juxtapose the sectarians' eschatological expectations of a prophet, priest, and king with the negative portrayal of John

---

[70] See, e.g., John J. Collins, "'He Shall Not Judge by What His Eyes See': Messianic Authority in the Dead Sea Scrolls," DSD 2 (1994): 145–64 (150); Eshel, "The Succession of High Priests," 87; Armin Lange, "The False Prophets Who Arose against Our God (4Q339 1)," in Aramaica Qumranica: Proceedings of the Conference on the Aramaic Texts from Qumran at Aix-en-Provence (June 30–July 2, 2008) (ed. K. Berthelot and D. Stökl Ben Ezra; STDJ 94; Leiden: Brill, 2010), 205–24 (215–16).

[71] See Bertholet, "4QTestimonia," 104–5. On the more general criticism of the Hasmonean unification of priestly and royal powers, see Daniel R. Schwartz, "On Pharisaic Opposition to the Hasmonean Monarchy," in Studies in the Jewish Background of Christianity (WUNT 60; Tübingen: Mohr Siebeck, 1992), 44–56.

[72] Gray, Prophetic Figures, 22–23. See also Eshel, "The Succession of High Priests," 76–77.

Hyrcanus in the final passage. Rather, following a line of analysis initiated by Hanan Eshel, I suggest that the citation from the *Apocryphon of Joshua* subtly rejects Hyrcanus's claims to each of these titles and reinscribes him as nothing more than a false prophet. In so doing, *4QTestimonia* rejects the Hasmonean grip on priestly, royal, and prophetic power at the same time as it simultaneously affirms that the true bearers of these offices have yet to arrive.

Let us look first at the portrait of priestly authority in *4QTestimonia*. Line 25 identifies John Hyrcanus's sons as "weapons of violence." This expression draws from Gen 49:5, where this imagery is applied to Simeon and Levi on account of their attack on Shechem. Eshel has suggested that the conquest of Shechem was likely seen as analogous to the capture of Samaria by Hyrcanus's sons Antigonus and Aristobulus in 108 BCE (Josephus *B.J.* 1.64–66; *Ant.* 13.275–83). Shechem and Samaria are geographically close and, in both cases, the sons attacked and vanquished a city by themselves.[73] Several texts in the Second Temple period valorize the violence of Simeon and Levi.[74] Levi's actions in particular provide a potent template for priestly militancy. The model of an aggressive policy of militant expansion under priestly auspices would have provided significant support for the expansionist foreign policy of the priestly Hasmoneans.

4QTestimonia, however, reverses the broader Second Temple period understanding of Levi. The sectarians do not share in the valorization of Levi and its role in forging a militant priesthood. Rather, *4QTestimonia* draws upon the scriptural censure of Levi's violent actions to condemn both Hasmonean violence and their claim to represent the legitimate priestly heirs of Levi. *4QTestimonia* further rejects the notion that the priestly "weapons of violence" in line 25 represent the fulfillment of the citation from Deut 33:11 regarding Levi found earlier in lines 19–20: "Crush the loins of his adversaries, of those who hate him, so that they do not rise again."

4QTestimonia also contains a subtle rejection of Hyrcanus's claim to royal power. Line 24 denounces Hyrcanus for the "destruction to all his neighbors." John Hyrcanus was well known for his wars through which he greatly expanded the border of the Hasmonean kingdom and brought ruin to neighboring regions.[75] Among his many conquests was the neighboring region of Moab. As observed by Eshel, Hyrcanus's admirers no doubt saw his conquest of Moab as a fulfillment of Balaam's prediction found earlier in *4QTestimonia*: "A star rises from Jacob, A scepter comes forth from Israel; It smashes the borderlands of Moab, and the territory of Seth" (Num 24:17). The "star" and the "scepter" are widely understood in the

---

[73] Eshel, "The Succession of High Priests," 80.

[74] See, e.g., *Jub.* 30; *Aramaic Levi Document* 78–79. See further Christophe Batsch, *La guerre et les rites de guerre dans le judaisme du deuxieme Temple* (JSJSup 93; Leiden: Brill, 2005), 117–25; Joseph L. Angel, *Otherworldly and Eschatological Priesthood in the Dead Sea Scrolls* (STDJ 86; Leiden: Brill, 2010), 270–71.

[75] See, e.g., Josephus *B.J.* 1.62–63; *Ant.* 13.254–58; and Eshel, "The Succession of High Priests," 81.

Second Temple period to refer to a future royal (sometimes messianic) figure who will vanquish Israel's foes.[76]

Other allusions to Moab in 4QTestimonia, however, serve to reject the belief that Hyrcanus and his conquests are the fulfillment of Num 24:17. Eshel notes the similarities between the expression employed for Hyrcanus's expansionists wars in 4QTestimonia and Jer 48:39, which describes the dread experienced by Moab at its downfall and how Moab's destruction serves as an example for all its neighbors of God's destructive power:

4Q175 24: "Destruction (מחתה) to all his neighbors"

Jer 48:39: "How he is dismayed (חתה)! Wail! How Moab has turned his back in shame! Moab shall be a laughingstock. And destruction (מחתה) to all those near him."

The expression "destruction to all his neighbors" in 4QTestimonia serves two functions. It should be read in a straightforward way to affirm the reality of Hasmonean expansionist power and John Hyrcanus as the instrument of these conquests.[77] At the same time, the similarity to the expression in Jer 48:39 describing the dismay experienced by Moab and its neighbors following Moab's destruction fulfills two functions. First, it rejects the notion that the Hasmonean expansionist policies make the kingdom more powerful. Rather, Hyrcanus's empire will crumble just as Moab's. Second, by aligning Hyrcanus's and Moab's kingdoms, 4QTestimonia dispels any notion that Hyrcanus's actions represent the realization of Balaam's prophecy—notwithstanding the fact that Hyrcanus did in fact destroy Moab. The eschatological sense attached to Balaam's prophecy in 4QTestimonia reinforces the belief that Judea's neighbors—including Moab—will only be fully eradicated in the end-time war by the true royal messiah. Indeed, Moab appears in the War Scroll's list of Israel's arch-enemies that will be destroyed in the eschatological war (1QM 1:1–2).

Alongside the rejection of Hyrcanus's royal and priestly authority, the final passage in 4QTestimonia applies to John Hyrcanus several key expressions that serve to indict him as no better than a lying prophet. Line 24 describes the man of Belial as "a fow[ler's n]et (פ]ח י[קוש) to his people." The expression draws from Hos 9:7–8:

The days of punishment have come for your heavy guilt; the days of requital have come—Let Israel know it! The prophet was distraught, the inspired man driven

---

[76] See CD 7:19–21; 1QM 11:6–7; Ps. Sol. 17; Philo Praem. 95; cf. Tg. Onq., Ps.-J., Neof. on Num 24:17; y.Ta'an. 4:6 68d. See the discussion in John J. Collins, The Scepter and the Star: Messianism in Light of the Dead Sea Scrolls (2d ed.; Grand Rapids: Eerdmans, 2010), 71–73.

[77] See Bertholet, "4QTestimonia," 107–8.

mad by constant harassment. Ephraim watches for my God. As for the prophet, <u>fowlers' nets</u> are on all his paths, harassment in the house of his God.[78]

The passage in Hosea seems to describe the harassment of the true prophet against the background of prophetic conflict. The "fowlers' nets" are understood as a hostile impediment placed before the true prophet. *4QTestimonia* reorients the "fowlers' nets" to trap "his people." In drawing on this key expression, *4QTestimonia* likely intends to indict Hyrcanus for harassment of contemporary true prophets.[79] By reinscribing John Hyrcanus as the one who lays the net that ensnares prophets, *4QTestimonia* implicitly rejects Hyrcanus's prophetic identity and reorients him among all the false prophets. Moreover, the broader passage in Hos 9:7–8 is located in the future "days of punishment" when the guilty are expected to suffer for their misdeeds. The application of this passage to John Hyrcanus likely is framed by the sectarians' fantasy of eschatological retribution against its enemies. *4QTestimonia* reflects the wish that Hyrcanus will suffer that same fate for his iniquities as the condemned harasser in Hos 9:7–8.

Several other keywords in the final passages further associate John Hyrcanus with false prophets. The reference to "a thing of horror (ושערוריה) in Ephraim and Judah" (l. 27) is likely an allusion to Jer 5:30–31:

> An appalling, horrible thing (שערורה) has happened in the land: The prophets prophesy falsely, and the priests rule accordingly; And my people like it so. But what will you do at the end of it?

The twofold identification of Hyrcanus's action as "a thing of horror" and "blasphemy" (חנופה) (l. 28) echoes a similar twofold indictment of the false prophets of Jerusalem in Jer 23:14–15:

> But what I see in the prophets of Jerusalem is something horrifying (שערורה): Adultery and false dealing. They encourage evildoers, so that no one turns back from his wickedness. To me they are all like Sodom, and [all] its inhabitants like Gomorrah. Assuredly, thus said the Lord of Hosts concerning the prophets: I am going to make them eat wormwood and drink a bitter draft; for from the prophets of Jerusalem godlessness (חנפה) has gone forth to the whole land.

The employment of each of these keywords and their scriptural allusions make a clear rhetorical point: John Hyrcanus's prophetic claims are illegitimate. By reinscribing this same assessment for John Hyrcanus, *4QTestimonia* refashions his prophetic identity to include all the negative assessments of prophets while simultaneously anticipating the same reversal of power expected for ancient false prophets. Indeed, Jer 23:20 provides a template for the eschatological punishment of the false prophets:

---

[78] The expression also appears in Ps 91:3. See Eshel, "The Succession of High Priests," 80; Bertholet, "4QTestimonia," 108–9.

[79] Bertholet, "4QTestimonia," 109.

The anger of the Lord shall not turn back until it has fulfilled and completed his purposes. In the end of day you shall clearly perceive it.

By unmasking Hyrcanus's true identity as a false prophet, *4QTestimonia* delegitimizes his entire claim to power and authority, and by extension the Hasmonean grip on power. As such, *4QTestimonia* still awaits the future arrival of the true eschatological prophet, priest, and king who will vanquish the enemies of Israel in accordance with the predictions articulated in the earlier passages in *4QTestimonia*. Moreover, when these eschatological figures do arrive, it will herald the return of the sectarians to the very positions of power enjoyed by John Hyrcanus and the Hasmoneans.

FALSE PROPHECY AND THE HASMONEANS IN *4QLIST OF FALSE PROPHETS:* John Hyrcanus and his prophetic identity come into the crosshairs of the Dead Sea Scrolls sectarians once more in a fragmentary manuscript entitled *4QList of False Prophets* (4Q339) by its editors.[80] This text contains a list of eight individuals who are introduced as "[fal]se prophets who arose against Israel," נביאי ש[ק]רא די קמו בן ישראל[(4Q339 1).[81] The list of prophets begins with Balaam son of Beor and includes six other prophetic individuals known from the Hebrew Bible.[82] This particular list should be situated in the same setting as the reframing of false prophecy in the Second Temple period attested by the Septuagint and Josephus. Each of these individuals ap-

---

[80] See the *editio princeps* in Magen Broshi and Ada Yardeni, "4Q339. List of False Prophets ar," in *Qumran Cave 4.XIV: Parabiblical Texts, Part 2* (ed. M. Broshi et al.; DJD 19; Oxford: Clarendon, 1995), 77-79. This follows their earlier presentations of the text: "On *Netinim* and False Prophets," *Tarbiz* 62 (1992-1993): 45-54 (Hebrew); "On *Netinim* and False Prophets," in *Solving Riddles and Untying Knots: Biblical, Epigraphic, and Semitic Studies on Honor of Jonas C. Greenfield* (ed. Z. Zevit, S. Gitin, and M. Sokoloff; Winona Lake: Eisenbrauns, 1995), 33-37. For a recent discussion of this text with full bibliography, see Armin Lange, "False Prophets" (incorporating a response by Hanan Eshel and further discussion).

[81] The *editio princeps* has "arose in Israel." Aharon Shemesh, "A Note on 4Q339 'List of False Prophets,'" *RevQ* 20 (2000): 319-20, however, observes that Balaam, the first individual on the list, was not Israelite and thus could not arise "in Israel." Thus, he points to the adversative nature of ב קם, and suggests the translation "against Israel." See also Emile Puech's proposal that the final word on the line reflects ink traces that are best reconstructed as באלה[נ]ה, "against our God" (reported in Lange, "False Prophets," 206 n. 7).

[82] The "Old man from Bethel" (1 Kgs 13:11-31), Zedekiah son of Chenaanah (1 Kgs 22:1-28; 2 Chr 18:1-27), Ahab son of Koliath (Jer 29:21-24), Zedekiah son of Maaseiah (Jer 29:21-24), Shemaiah the Nehlemite (Jer 29:24-32), Hananiah son of Azur (Jer 28). Note that *4QTestimonia* and *4QList of False Prophets* present divergent approaches to Balaam's prophecy. While *4QList of False Prophets* brands Balaam a false prophet, *4QTestimonia* identifies Balaam as prophesying the future arrival of the Messiah. These texts reflect competing trends in ancient Judaism regarding Balaam's prophetic identity. See further discussion in Jay Braverman, "Balaam in Rabbinic and Early Christian Tradition," in *Joshua Finkel Festschrift* (ed. S. B. Hoenig and L.D. Stitskin; New York: Yeshiva University Press, 1974), 41-50; Florentino García Martínez, "Balaam in the Dead Sea Scrolls," in *The Prestige of the Pagan Prophet Balaam in Judaism, Early Christianity and Islam* (G. H. van Kooten and J. T. A. G. M. van Ruiten; TBN 10; Leiden: Brill, 2008), 71-82; Ronit Nikolsky, "Interpret Him as Much as You Want: Balaam in the Babylonian Talmud," in *The Prestige of the Pagan Prophet Balaam*, 213-30.

pears in their original scriptural contexts merely as prophets. *4QList of False Prophets*, however, casts aspersions on the contemptible nature of their prophetic message and accordingly brands each of them as a false prophet.[83] As noted above, the identification of the "Old man from Bethel" (1 Kgs 13:11) on this list of false prophets matches Josephus's reframing of this individual as "a certain vile old man, a false prophet."

The final line of this fragment preserves only three visible letters:]עון. The previous seven names on the list are all scriptural prophets who in hindsight are judged to be false prophets. Of the seven identifiable names, the "Old man from Bethel" (l. 3) and Shemaiah the Nehlemite (l. 7) are identified by their place name because that is the way they are introduced in their scriptural contexts (i.e., without a patronym). All the other names in the list are introduced with their patronym as in their scriptural contexts. Yet, no scriptural prophet is known whose patronym ends in עו-. Magen Broshi and Ada Yardeni, following an earlier suggestion made by Alexander Rofé and Elisha Qimron, proposed that a contemporary figure is in fact in view in the final line. They therefore reconstruct the final word as שמ[עון and the entire name as יוחנן בן שמ[עון—John Hyrcanus I.[84]

Why would somebody create a list such as this one and why would the Dead Sea Scrolls sectarians be interested in preserving it in their literary collection? In his initial discussion of this manuscript, Qimron proposes that the entire list was created with the final contemporary figure in mind.[85] By lumping together this contemporary figure with the paradigmatic false prophets from Israel's past, the list delegitimizes the would-be prophetic claims of this contemporary figure.[86]

This understanding of the function of the list makes good sense if this final figure is in fact John Hyrcanus. As noted above, Josephus portrays Hyrcanus as having prophetic capabilities and others likely shared his positive assessment of these traits. *4QList of False Prophets*, similar to *4QTestimonia*, reflects a stream within Judaism that rejects the glowing admiration of Hyrcanus's prophetic identity enshrined in Josephus's portrait. Many Jews during Hyrcanus's reign were either

---

[83] See Lange, "False Prophets," 212–13.

[84] See Alexander Rofé, "The 'List of False Prophets' from Qumran: Two Riddles and Their Solution," *Haaretz* April 13, 1994 (Hebrew); Elisha Qimron, "On the List of False Prophets from Qumran," *Tarbiz* 63 (1993–1994): 273–75 (275) (Hebrew); Broshi and Yardeni, "On *Netinim* and False Prophets," 36–37. Note that Broshi and Yardeni offer another possible reading in the *editio princeps* (based on another suggestion from Qimron): ונביאה די מן גב[עון, "[a prophet from Gib]eon" (Broshi and Yardeni, *Qumran Cave 4.XIV*, 79; see Elisha Qimron, "A Further Note on the List of False Prophets from Qumran," *Tarbiz* 63 [1993–1994]: 508 [Hebrew]). The assumption is that this offers further information about Hananiah son of Azur from line eight. While paleographically and conceptually plausible, this restoration appears incongruous with the rest of the list in which the individuals are only introduced with the place of residence and not the patronym if that is how they are known from their scriptural context. See Lange, "False Prophets," 206. Lange also notes that no other prophet is given two lines in the text.

[85] Qimron, "False Prophets," 275.

[86] See also Lange, "False Prophets," 212.

ambivalent toward his rule or antagonistic.[87] *4QList of False Prophets* likely emerges from one of these circles and takes direct aim at Hyrcanus's prophetic capabilities, which likely was considered by many as an important source of legitimacy for his reign. *4QList of False Prophets* does not include Hyrcanus in the seemingly rightful lineage of ancient Israelite kings, but rather as the heir to the lineage of ancient false prophets—indeed, the "pinnacle of false prophecy."[88]

4QList of False Prophets is most likely a product of the broader literary heritage of Second Temple Judaism and not composed by the Dead Sea Scrolls sectarians.[89] At the same time, the sectarians had a vested interest in preserving this text within their literary collection. *4QList of False Prophets* reinforces the sectarians' negative views of the Hasmoneans. More particularly, its reframing of John Hyrcanus as a false prophet underscores the sectarians' belief that both Hyrcanus's and the Hasmoneans' power in Judean society are illegitimate. The inclusion of Hyrcanus on this list also contributes to the sectarians' fantasy of retributive justice for their opponents. While each of the other false prophets on the list once enjoyed prestige and authority, they eventually suffer the consequences for their errant prophetic message. A similar fate is imagined for Hyrcanus and the Hasmonean rulers.

CONCLUSIONS

Faced with a present reality in which they recognized their marginalized and disempowered position, the Dead Sea Scrolls sectarians advocated for a nonviolent form of imagined resistance. I have outlined three ways in which the sectarians achieved these goals. First, they portray themselves as the persistent victim of violent oppression at the hand of their empowered enemies. This model goes beyond the actual historical circumstances that governed the relationship of the constellation of sectarian communities to their enemies. In crafting this dual narrative of victimhood and the empowered other, the sectarians heightened their self-perception as God's elect and underscored the aberrant nature of the present distribution of power.

In a related way, the second form of resistance involves the sectarians' attempt to chip away at their enemies' grip on power through rhetorical attacks on the legitimacy of the empowered groups. In this study, I have examined how the accusations of false prophecy were employed in order to delegitimize the power and prestige of the Hasmoneans and Pharisees. There is little evidence, however, that these rhetorical attacks were anything more than part of an internal discourse. The portraits of the Hasmonean and Pharisaic power represent a mix of historical reality and sectarian imagination fueled by the sectarians' narrative of victimhood.

---

[87] Much of this evidence is summarized in Lange, "False Prophets," 213–16.
[88] Lange, "False Prophets," 216.
[89] See discussion in Lange, "False Prophets," 209–10.

Third, the sectarains took refuge in their fantasy of eschatological retribution when the present imbalance of power would finally be reversed. Alongside the accusation of false prophecy, the sectarians imagined a future time when their enemies would experience the same fate as other false prophets. In this fantasy, the wicked—both foreigners and other Jews will suffer in ways commensurate with their contemporary oppression. The imagined future annihilation of its enemies allows the sectarians both to gain a measure of retribution for their current perceived suffering and envision their reversal from powerlessness to empowerment.

Index of Ancient Texts

Contributors

Ehud Ben Zvi is Professor, History and Classics, University of Alberta.

Joseph Blenkinsopp is John A. O'Brien Professor Emeritus of Biblical Studies.

Jeffrey L. Cooley is Assistant Professor of Hebrew Bible in the Theology Department of Boston College.

Göran Eidevall is Professor of Hebrew Bible at Uppsala University, Sweden.

Alex P. Jassen is Associate Professor of Hebrew and Judaic Studies in the Skirball Department of Hebrew and Judaic Studies at New York University.

Alan Lenzi is Associate Professer of Religious and Classical Studies, University of the Pacific (Stockton, CA).

Beate Pongratz-Leisten is Professor of Ancient Near Eastern Studies, Institute for the Study of the Ancient World, New York University.

Jonathan Stökl is Lecturer in Hebrew Bible / Old Testament at the Department of Theology and Religious Studies at King's College London.

C. A. Strine is Vice-Chancellor's Fellow at the Department of Biblical Studies, The University of Sheffield.